THE CHANGING POLITICS
OF GUN CONTROL

THE CHANGING POLITICS
OF GUN CONTROL

edited by
JOHN M. BRUCE
and CLYDE WILCOX

ROWMAN & LITTLEFIELD PUBLISHERS, INC.
Lanham • Boulder • New York • Oxford

ROWMAN & LITTLEFIELD PUBLISHERS, INC.

Published in the United States of America
by Rowman & Littlefield Publishers, Inc.
4720 Boston Way, Lanham, Maryland 20706

12 Hid's Copse Road
Cumnor Hill, Oxford X2 9JJ, England

British Library Cataloguing in Publication Information Available

Library of Congress Cataloging-in-Publication Data

The changing politics of gun control / edited by John M. Bruce and
    Clyde Wilcox.
        p.   cm.
    Includes bibliographical references (p.   –   ) and index.
    ISBN 0-8476-8614-0 (cloth : alk. paper). — ISBN 0-8476-8615-9
(paper : alk. paper)
        1. Gun control—United States.   2. Firearms ownership—Government
policy—United States.   3. Firearms—Law and legislation—United
States.   I. Bruce, John M., 1963–   . II. Wilcox, Clyde, 1953–   .
HV7436.C48   1998
363.3'3'0973—dc21   97-44519
                                                                               CIP

ISBN 0-8476-8614-0 (cloth : alk. paper)
ISBN 0-8476-8615-9 (paper : alk. paper)

Printed in the United States of America

∞ ™ The paper used in this publication meets the minimum requirements of
American National Standard for Information Sciences—Permanence of Paper
for Printed Library Materials, ANSI Z39.48–1984.

*In Memory
of
Sara Bruce*

Contents

Contents

Illustrations

Tables

Figures

Maps

Preface

When citizens from other countries visit the United States, one aspect of our culture that seems extremely foreign to them is gun laws. In 1996, the diplomatic corps in Washington looked on with a mixture of amusement and disdain as suburban Fairfax County debated whether to allow individuals to carry concealed guns into recreation centers and bars. Meanwhile, across the Potomac in Washington, children used guns, often more powerful than those carried by the police, to shoot one another over various slights, real or perceived.

Visitors may feel less safe in America because of the widespread private ownership of guns, but it is obvious that many Americans buy guns in order to feel more safe. When Fairfax County loosened its restrictions on licenses to carry concealed guns, well-educated, affluent suburbanites lined up to fill out the forms that would allow them to go armed about their business in Virginia. Many doubtless remembered the many western TV shows and movies in the 1960s in which the hero was forced to use his handgun to defend his family, his neighbors, or those who could not defend themselves. Indeed, these TV heroes could not put away their guns: Shane had to strap his on one more time and then ride off into the sunset. In almost every episode of many television shows of that era, the climax came when the hero reluctantly used his gun to kill someone who had evil intent.

Yet America's liberal gun laws are not solely explained by Hollywood's glamorous depiction of great gunslingers of the past. Many Americans believe that the Second Amendment guarantees an unlimited access to private guns. Others oppose gun control because of issues of basic civil liberties or because they are part of the vast rural hunting culture. Support for gun control, however, is based primarily on beliefs about the role of guns in violent crime. Most Americans vaguely support additional gun control, a few support it intensely, and

a different minority passionately opposes any controls on private ownership of guns.

For many years the politics of gun control has been stalemated with
a powerful, well-organized minority consistently defeating an ambivalent, disorganized majority. In recent years, however, there has been
some evidence that the politics of gun control may be changing. The
longtime alliance between the National Rifle Association (NRA) and
the police has disintegrated, and public perceptions of the NRA are
increasingly negative. The party positions on gun control are polarizing, creating the possibility of partisan issue voting on gun policy. This
has all taken place as the public has grown more fearful of a criminal
element that it perceives as being better armed than law enforcement.

This collection of essays explores the changing politics of gun control
over the past several decades. The contributors to this volume are all
scholars, not advocates, and although they surely all have positions on
the gun control issue, they have written about politics, not their own
policy preferences. We hope this collection will therefore serve to inform citizens and students about the way gun control policy is made
and debated, help them understand how politics in this area has recently changed, and enable them to better grasp some of the issues in
this confusing area of public policy.

In the spirit of full disclosure, it should be noted that we are both
from states with strong hunting cultures. We have both hunted, though
only the odd snake or rabbit was killed. We have both discharged a
variety of guns in target practice, but these guns were nearly all borrowed. Between us we own one gun, and it has spent considerable time
in the back of the closet. We both have relatives we love and respect
who are NRA members or are at least strong advocates of unrestricted
gun ownership (neither of us is a member of any pro- or antigun
group). We also have both lived for some time in a city where young
people use guns to settle scores and battle over turf, and we have both
known people who had a negative encounter with an armed individual. These elements combine to have some influence on our feelings
about guns in society. Neither of us would support a total ban on the
private possession of firearms, yet we each have a significant level of
discomfort with the arms race that we see on the streets of our respective communities.

We would like to thank a number of people who helped make this
book possible. Steve Wrinn at Rowman & Littlefield encouraged us and
offered sage advice. Robin Adler helped guide the process through
some of the rougher waters. Scott Horst took the project from manuscript to production, while Diane Hess enhanced the final product
through her work as copyeditor. Wesley Joe helped locate key data, as

did Heather Rush. Kevin B. Smith provided state information on the NRA's subscriptions. Meridith Wulff assisted in preparation of the manuscript. Victoria Biancolo provided Handgun Control's copy of state gun law summaries. Although the NRA was not a consistent source of information with respect to this project, their top-notch site on the World Wide Web was a resource consulted regularly.

John M. Bruce
Clyde Wilcox

1

Introduction

John M. Bruce and Clyde Wilcox

In March 1996, Thomas Hamilton entered a primary school in Dunblane, Scotland, and shot 31 young schoolchildren and their teacher. Sixteen children and the teacher died in the attack. In November, the Conservative party government responded by passing a law that banned the private ownership of all high-caliber handguns, and the new Labor party government strengthened the ban to include all handguns.

Although the United States did not experience a tragedy of the magnitude of Dunblane in 1996, there were countless smaller incidents of gun violence—children shot by children for their shoes, adolescents shot by adolescents in disputes over girlfriends or respect, bystanders killed as drug gangs battled for turf, and wives and children killed by disturbed husbands and fathers. In 1995, 11,019 Americans were murdered by handguns in acts not defined by the courts as self-defense. This figure dwarfs the number of British citizens killed in England, Wales, and Scotland by handguns—only 30. An additional 2,000 Americans were killed by other kinds of guns, and many others died in accidental shootings or used guns to commit suicide. The Republican-controlled U.S. House of Representatives responded by voting to repeal a law banning the sale of certain assault weapons. As the British debated banning all handguns, Virginians debated whether to allow concealed handguns in bars and recreation centers.

The difference between the British and U.S. response to gun violence is a product of a variety of factors. First, America has what many scholars have referred to as a "gun culture," an enduring love affair with firearms (see especially Spitzer 1995). This gun culture has several sources: the role of privately armed citizens in gaining independence

1

from Britain; the realities of the frontier, which demanded that settlers carry guns to protect them from animals and the Native Americans whose land they were invading; and the mythology of the Old West with gunfighters and bandits and lawmen. The gun culture is sustained by the popular culture: in the 1960s television was dominated by westerns in which all the protagonists carried firearms, in the 1970s detective shows proliferated in which the licensed private investigator was almost always forced to shoot the villain, in the 1980s crime dramas showed gritty urban police officers clearing the streets by discharging their weapons, and the 1990s has given us space operas with phasors and other variations on the ray gun.

With the popular culture providing positive images of guns, over the past four decades or so an average of about 50 percent of American households reported owning guns for sport and personal protection. In many southern and midwestern states, rural communities embrace hunting as recreation, and the percentage of adult men who engage in hunting in these areas is high. It is not uncommon for coal miners in the Appalachian Mountains to call a wildcat strike the first day of deer-hunting season, for example, because a majority of miners prefer to forgo a few days' pay in order to hunt. In urban areas, many citizens own firearms because they fear random crime and hope that a gun might help protect them from becoming the next victim. When long-time gun control proponent Carl Rowan shot and wounded an intruder on his Washington, D.C., property, it became clear that even those who believe that guns are dangerous sometimes buy them when they fear for their lives. When Fairfax County, Virginia, made it easier for residents to qualify for permits to carry concealed weapons, county officials were shocked at the long lines of registrants who presumably believed they might survive an assault by an armed criminal by drawing their gun quickly and shooting, much as the hero outguns the outlaw in so many western movies.

There is considerable debate about whether owning guns helps to deter or resist crime or whether guns in the home are more likely to be used against a family member in a dispute or in an accidental shooting. Indeed, nearly every "fact" that enters into debates over gun control is open to some dispute (see Kleck 1991 for a debunking of much conventional wisdom). But the widespread public use of guns in hunting, and the belief that they help prevent crime, help account for the difference in the British and U.S. responses. The Dunblane tragedy prompted most British citizens to imagine a world in which Thomas Hamilton could not own a gun. In the United States, when citizens learn of a gun tragedy in their community, many believe that they might possibly survive such an incident if they have a gun.

This suggests a second important difference between the U.S. reaction to gun violence and that in Britain and indeed throughout Europe. In Europe the problem of gun violence is widely defined as the guns themselves. Although obviously citizens can commit murder with an ingenious array of weapons, none has the capacity to kill as quickly and at such distances as firearms. In the United States, however, an array of definitions of the problem are in competition. Gun violence is the result of violent predators who need to be locked up or executed, says one group of policy entrepreneurs. Gun violence is the result of social problems that leave young urban citizens with little hope for the future, little education, and no jobs, says another. Those who claim that gun violence is primarily a problem of guns themselves represent only one set of competing policy activists.

A final reason for the different British and U.S. reactions to gun violence is the power of organized groups representing gun enthusiasts. The National Rifle Association, Gun Owners of America, and other groups help organize voters, campaign volunteers, and contributions in American elections and focus citizen communications to legislators when gun control legislation is under consideration by the U.S. Congress or state legislatures. The NRA and similar groups have substantial resource advantages over organizations that seek stricter gun control regulations, and they use these resources to help define the problem, to promote the belief that guns may protect their owners from violence, and to work against gun control in national, state, and local institutions.

The debate over gun control in America is organized by interest groups that favor stricter regulations and those that believe that all gun regulations violate the Second Amendment to the U.S. Constitution. The amendment, which states that "a well regulated Militia, being necessary to the security of a free State, the right of the people to keep and bear Arms, shall not be infringed," has not been interpreted by the U.S. Supreme Court as barring all regulations of guns or as allowing private ownership of all types of weapons. In recent years the NRA has moved away from Second Amendment claims in the courts to stress arguments based on federalism.

In general, proposals to regulate guns in America have fallen into several distinct categories. Some seek to regulate dangerous weapons such as cheap handguns like the Saturday night special and assault weapons. Others seek to regulate the types of individuals who may own or carry weapons, proposing, for example, waiting periods so that police can check for criminal records of prospective gun purchasers, or a ban on the private sales of firearms to minors. Some cities have attempted to reduce the number of weapons on the streets by buying guns from citizens. For decades, the politics of gun control has been static, but in recent years there has been some evidence that the underlying dynamic of gun control politics may be changing.

Continuity and Change in Gun Control Policymaking

The 1990s have been an active period in gun control policymaking in the United States. At the national level, Congress passed a ban on assault weapons, and the new Republican majority voted in the House but not the Senate to repeal that ban. Congress also passed the Brady Bill, which required states to perform background checks on individuals purchasing handguns and to impose a five-day waiting period if they are unable to perform instant background checks. The Supreme Court then struck down the requirement that states perform background checks, leaving intact the waiting period. At the state level, the NRA successfully pushed for passage of laws making it easier for individuals to carry concealed firearms and for states to honor concealed-weapons permits issued by other states. Local governments continued to enact gun control laws, but increasing numbers of states passed laws preempting local action and in a few cases even repealing local laws.

Despite the flurry of activity, the policy actions of the 1990s are not radically different from those in earlier decades, for neither the assault weapons ban nor the Brady Bill constitutes serious gun control by the national government. On the surface, not much has changed in the politics of gun control. For many years this policy arena has been characterized by stalemate between an organized, outspoken minority and an ambivalent majority. Gun control opponents are organized through groups such as the National Rifle Association, which has a large, well-funded political action committee and highly skilled lobbyists but whose greatest strength is its large, geographically dispersed, politically active membership. The NRA and similar groups represent a substantial percentage of those who ardently oppose gun laws, and these organizations have worked hard to shape the beliefs and political behaviors of their members. In contrast, small organizations such as Handgun Control, Inc., represent only a small minority of those who support stronger controls on firearms. The majority of citizens favors a variety of controls, but many Americans are torn between a belief in the abstract right to bear arms and the desperate hope that gun control will help reduce the violent crime that permeates American society. Whenever a highly publicized event of gun violence catches the public's eye, public concern spikes upward, and gun control supporters are sometimes able to use this increased salience to push through national and state legislation. Whenever there is a lengthy lull between these violent tragedies and the GOP controls key political institutions, gun control opponents are able to roll back earlier laws or codify gun-owner protections.

Yet beneath the surface, there is evidence of changing currents in gun control politics. Much of this change can be traced to an important power struggle within the NRA, which led to the election of a new and more radical leadership in 1977 in an event commonly referred to as the Cincinnati Revolt. Prior to the Cincinnati Revolt, the NRA leadership was firmly allied with law enforcement officials and provided important services to police across the country in various firearms training programs. After the hard-line faction took control of the organization, the NRA took increasingly more radical positions on issues such as Teflon-piercing bullets, plastic handguns, and assault weapons. This led to deepening conflict with police organizations and has transformed the interest-group coalition structure of the policy arena.

In the 1990s, the NRA was pulled further to the right by internal politics and by the mobilization of militia groups, whose membership grew in response to two highly publicized incidents. In June 1990, agents with the Bureau of Alcohol, Tobacco, and Firearms (BATF) arrested Randy Weaver and his son on weapons charges, then released them after Randy Weaver put up his cabin as bond. The BATF was primarily interested in using Weaver as an informant in an ongoing investigation of the Aryan Nation and the Order, with which Weaver had contacts. When Weaver repeatedly failed to show up for his court dates and informed the U.S. attorney that he would not cooperate with the court, the U.S. marshal negotiated with him for 18 months and then finally sent in the Special Operations Group to arrest Weaver. In the ensuing confrontation, one marshal was killed, Randy Weaver and Kevin Harris were wounded, and Vicki Weaver was accidentally killed. A federal jury in Idaho found Weaver and Harris not guilty of murdering the Marshal and found Weaver not guilty of the weapons charge but convicted him of failing to keep a court date. The government settled a lawsuit by Weaver for the death of his wife, paying him $3.1 million (Vizzard 1997).

In February 1993, BATF agents attempted to serve a search warrant on Mount Carmel, a highly armed and fortified compound of the Branch Davidians, a religious sect. The gun battle that ensued resulted in the death of 4 agents and 6 Branch Davidians and the wounding of 28 agents and 4 Davidians. A subsequent standoff lasted for nearly two months, and when the FBI Hostage Rescue Team injected tear gas into the compound, the inhabitants set multiple fires and many shot themselves and each other. More than 70 Davidians died, including many children. A U.S. district court jury convicted the survivors of weapons and manslaughter charges but acquitted them of murder and conspiracy (Vizzard 1997).

The NRA reacted angrily to both incidents and pressured Congress to hold multiple hearings on the Waco incident. The rhetoric of the organization changed, and it began attacking BATF and other law enforcement agents through its mailing campaign. Presumably such appeals helped bring some of the more radical elements of the gun culture into the NRA as members; in any event it created the perception in the eyes of the public and political elites that the NRA was a radical organization out of touch with mainstream American culture.

Gun control policy was once seen as a conflict between rural hunters of the NRA and northeastern liberals, but because of changes in the NRA it is increasingly seen as a battle between law enforcement officials and a radical pro-gun organization. The increase in urban violence with well-armed drug gangs and children carrying guns to school has also helped to redefine the issue. Increasingly, citizens see gun control as something that might protect them or their children, not as something that might prevent them from protecting themselves, and they see the NRA as a radical organization with too much influence on policymakers.

The transformation of the gun control issue is also evident in the relationship of the NRA and elected officials. Although at one point a coalition of rural and southern Democrats and most Republicans opposed gun control, congressional Democrats are increasingly united in their support of gun control regulations, in part because many southern and western Democrats who once supported the NRA were defeated in 1994 but also in part because party leaders believe that gun control can become an important wedge issue in dismantling the GOP coalition. Although House Republicans continue to embrace the NRA, passing a repeal of the assault weapons ban in March 1996, GOP leaders who play on the national stage are increasingly distancing themselves from the group.

When Ronald Reagan, a lifetime NRA member whose administration was not friendly to gun control, announced in March 1991 in characteristically direct language his support for the Brady Bill, he provided political cover for many politicians. In 1983, for example, Reagan had addressed the NRA, praising the organization and its leaders and decrying gun control. Reagan's speech, delivered while wearing a bulletproof vest to an audience that had been carefully disarmed by the Secret Service, echoed the standard NRA line that the organization's members are law-abiding citizens who do not use guns for violence (Sugarmann 1992). In 1991, Reagan not only endorsed a bill that was anathema to the NRA but also visited President Bush and urged him to withdraw his opposition to the bill.

In the 1990s, the NRA has increasingly embraced the rhetoric and symbols of antigovernment organizations and militia groups. Fundraising letters by the organization proclaimed in bold letters that the "Final War" had begun and accused the BATF of using "stormtrooper" tactics and being "jack-booted thugs." In response to these letters, George Bush tore up his NRA membership card; Colorado senator Ben Nighthorse Campbell and General Norman Schwartzkopf resigned their membership; and Michigan representative John Dingell, who had also earlier referred to the BATF as "thugs," resigned his seat on the NRA board of directors. Schwartzkopf called the NRA "radical, they appeal to a fringe element of gun owners." (Anderson 1996, 15–16). GOP candidate Patrick Buchanan endorsed a Clinton proposal that the NRA donate the revenues from its fund-raiser to the widows of federal agents slain in the course of duty. When Bob Dole ran for president in 1996, he softened and eventually reversed his support for a repeal of the assault weapons ban, and the repeal of the ban on assault weapons died because Dole refused to bring it to the Senate floor. The depth of elite reaction to the NRA was remarkable.

Do these changes presage change in gun control policy? Before we can answer this question, we must first analyze the gun control policy arena. In the next section, we consider alternative conceptions of the gun control issue that might help us understand the politics surrounding it.

The Politics of Gun Control Policymaking

In his insightful book *The Politics of Gun Control*, Robert J. Spitzer suggests that we can best conceive of gun control policymaking as an example of social regulation—similar in many ways to regulations on prostitution, drugs, abortion, and sexual behavior (Spitzer 1995). Such policies, also referred to by some as "morality policies," generally involve an effort by one group to modify existing moral values or behaviors through the force of law (Tatalovich and Daynes 1988). Gormley (1986) notes that moral issues are not generally technically complex, are highly salient to the public, and evoke substantial citizen participation. Others note that the presence of competing moral visions makes social regulation policy especially difficult for contending parties to compromise on (Lowi 1988; Mooney and Lee 1995). These characteristics of moral and social issues help provide some regularities in moral issue policymaking, discussed later on.

Is gun control an example of social regulation, similar perhaps to issues such as abortion? There are some important similarities between gun control and abortion politics, and also some subtle differences. First, both abortion and gun control are "easy" issues in that they require little technical information to form opinions, but a number of factors make gun control the "less easy" issue. Most of the debate about abortion concerns whether and when women may obtain abortions, but at least some of the debate over gun control is about which measures to adapt and their efficacy in reducing crime and accidental deaths. Both abortion and gun control involve clashes between well-organized interest groups, but although these groups have achieved relative parity in the abortion debate, the pro-gun organizations retain considerable financial and membership advantages over groups seeking additional regulations on firearms. Activists on both sides of the abortion and gun control issues have intense preferences with the conservative side more highly motivated, but the motivational advantage to the pro-gun forces is substantially greater than that enjoyed by the pro-life groups. Both abortion and gun control involve a clash of values, but gun control supporters are often motivated by a policy goal to reduce crime instead of a deeply held value such as the sanctity of life, privacy, or individual liberty. Finally, although both abortion and gun control are moderately salient to voters, ranking behind such issues as the economy, education, and the environment, gun control appears to be less central to the average citizen than abortion.

Although gun control differs in many subtle ways from other issues of social regulation, it is helpful to conceive of gun control policymaking as an example of social regulation. Clearly the political battles over gun control are intense and involve competing sets of organized interests that seek to build larger, more permanent coalitions—factors characteristic of moral regulation. In *The Politics of Sin* Kenneth Meier argues that morality politics at the state level is characterized by political actors with their own personal positions and preferences, citizen input in policymaking, and heated policy debate between opposing issue and partisan coalitions; as in redistributive policymaking, these characteristics all appear to be true of battles over gun control. Spitzer suggests that social regulatory policy is characterized by several distinct relationships:

1. Public opinion that is difficult to rally yet essential to action.
2. Intense, polarizing single-issue groups.
3. Parties that use the issue to attract voters.

4. Substantial state and local autonomy, and even policy creation.
5. Federal policymaking dominated by Congress, which rarely innovates.
6. Presidential involvement that is mostly symbolic.
7. Federal agencies with little authority, whose fate is determined by politics.
8. Courts that occasionally intervene to redefine the issue.

As we will see in the chapters that follow, gun control politics fits this model quite well. Although a majority of Americans support increased regulations on firearms, they also support an abstract right to bear arms, and gun control is rarely a top priority for them. Yet recent national gun control legislation has usually been aided by spikes in public concern brought about by incidents of gun violence. The gun control policy arena is clearly characterized by active and well-organized single-issue groups, and the intensity of these groups is perhaps best seen in a bumper sticker distributed by pro-gun groups in the 1980s: "You'll take my gun from me when you pry it from my cold dead fingers."

It is also clear that the political parties have used the gun control issue to attract and hold voters. The GOP mobilized gun enthusiasts in 1994 behind a quiet promise to repeal the ban on assault rifles (which passed the House of Representatives but was never debated in the Senate), and GOP presidential candidate Patrick Buchanan appealed to NRA activists when he repeatedly used phrases such as "lock and load" on the stump. The Democrats signaled their increasing unity behind gun control efforts by inviting Sarah Brady, head of Handgun Control, Inc., and her husband, James Brady, who was wounded in the attack on Ronald Reagan in 1981, to speak at their presidential nominating convention.

The substantial autonomy of state and local governments in gun control legislation is evident in the countless ordinances in cities across the country and the many bills enacted in state legislatures each year. Indeed, the NRA and other pro-gun groups have learned that they fare best in state legislatures and so have pushed hard in recent years for states to prevent local governments from enacting gun control measures. The rapid spread of laws that allow citizens to carry concealed weapons and put the burden on state governments to show that a citizen should not be allowed to do so is an example of state initiatives, and the NRA is currently focusing efforts on passing state laws that would force authorities to honor permits issued in neighboring states.

Major gun control legislation has come from Congress, which has routinely ignored requests by presidents for tougher laws. NRA power in Congress is substantial, and new gun control legislation has been rare. Presidents have often failed to achieve their goals in gun control legislation, although the continued efforts of Lyndon Johnson were doubtless vital to the passage of the Gun Control Act of 1968, and Bill Clinton's lobbying played an important role in the passage of the assault weapons ban in 1994.

The role of federal agencies in gun control policy is the subject of great debate. The NRA routinely portrays the Bureau of Alcohol, Tobacco, and Firearms as an overzealous organization filled with agents whose primary purpose is to disarm America. Clearly the agency's fate has on occasion hung in the balance, as when the Reagan administration sought initially to end the agency and then proposed to divide its powers among other bureaus. Finally, the courts have yet to redefine the gun control issue, although the Supreme Court did strike down the Brady Bill in 1997, primarily because it posed a burden on state law enforcement officials.

Overall, then, it appears that gun control politics fits nicely into the framework of social regulatory or morality politics that many scholars have developed over time. The social regulatory model would suggest that little is likely to change in gun control politics in the near future, since the policy arena is dominated by a status quo–oriented Congress and characterized by opposing interest groups and a generally unmobilized public. Yet occasionally, social regulatory policies change in substantial and even fundamental ways. The United States ended slavery in the nineteenth century and passed and then rescinded a ban on alcohol early in the twentieth century. More recently there has been substantial change in policies regulating the role of women in society, politics, and the workplace and of policies relating to gays and lesbians (Wilcox 1996). In 1997, the once-powerful tobacco lobby suddenly collapsed, and tobacco companies negotiated for protection from lawsuits by offering to allow regulation.

Some of these changes were gradual, others far more sudden. Recently, political scientists have begun to examine those circumstances in which rapid policy change unfolds. John Kingdon (1995) argued that circumstances sometimes create "windows of opportunity" for policy change. Baumgartner and Jones (1993) described American policymaking as alternating between periods of incremental change and periods of rapid change. Thus American policymaking is best characterized as "punctuated equilibrium" rather than stalemate: just as many biologists now believe that evolution unfolds in short bursts of rapid change, so policy change occurs rapidly whenever a window of opportunity arises and conditions are ripe.

What, precisely, are the conditions that might lead to rapid policy change? Kingdon suggests that windows of opportunity open when three streams converge—a problem stream, a policy stream, and a political stream. The convergence of these streams does not guarantee that policy will change but merely creates an opportunity for skilled policy entrepreneurs to effect their policy goals. In Chapter 5, Marcia Godwin and Jean Schroedel discuss the opening of such a window of opportunity in California, which led to passage of a ban on assault weapons at the end of the 1980s, and the events that led to the closing of this window. At the state level such windows open and shut in a seemingly chaotic manner as gun violence increases the salience of gun control to voters and to interest groups and others who promote specific policy proposals and as politicians achieve and lose control of the policy agenda. At the national level, such a window opened in the early 1990s with a Democratic Congress and a president who favored gun control, signing the Brady Bill into law. The new GOP Congress seems more likely to repeal gun control laws than to pass additional ones. The election of a Republican president allied with the NRA might actually create a window of opportunity to repeal previous legislation.

Yet Baumgartner and Jones are writing about something more substantial than a window of opportunity to pass specific legislation; their focus is on the events that destabilize policy monopolies. For many years, the two sides of the gun control dispute have achieved a basic stalemate; gun control activists have won some relatively minor regulations, and gun control opponents have occasionally repealed these laws. What would be needed for this stable system to unravel?

Policy systems become unstable primarily as issue definitions change, thereby permitting the mobilization of new participants in the policy arena. For many issues including guns, there are multiple possible definitions of potential policy problems, and groups often contend to define an issue. This is evident in the abortion debate in the very names adopted by the two movements: pro-life activists want to define the issue as one of fetal life, and the pro-choice side seeks to frame the issue as one of personal liberty. In the area of gun control, issue definition is also the subject of a political struggle. Consider, for example, the problem of crime. When an adolescent shoots another over a pair of Nike shoes, is this a problem of young predators who need strong punishment, of a society that has failed its youth, or of too easy access to guns? The NRA's slogan that "guns don't kill people, criminals do" is an effort to insist on one definition of the crime problem.

Baumgartner and Jones (1993) write of a "policy image" that is a mixture of empirical evidence and emotive appeals. These appeals vary in their tone, which these scholars view as a critical component to rapid policy change: "Tone is critical to issue development because rapid changes in the tone of a policy image held by key social actors (such as the mass media) often presage changes in patterns of mobilization" (26). In short, a different tone in media coverage or interest-group appeals may make it possible for groups and policy entrepreneurs to press their case upon institutions.

There is little doubt that the tone of media coverage of the NRA has changed since the late 1970s. A group that was once seen as a civic-minded collection of hunters is now viewed as a radical organization that resists reasonable regulations. Indeed, in the 1990s the NRA has been increasingly seen as allied with militia groups and armed survivalists in conflict with agencies of law enforcement. In the wake of the Oklahoma City bombing in 1995, this was not a politically viable image for the organization. Indeed, after years of internal feuding and faced with financial crises and declining membership (Davidson 1993), in May 1997 the NRA board finally ousted hard-line vice president Neil Knox and replaced him with actor Charlton Heston. Wayne LaPierre, who won reelection in a hotly disputed contest, said that these elections represented a struggle between those who favored mainstream strategies and those who adopted the "fringe" ideologies of the radical antigovernment militias (Claiborne 1997).

Yet thus far, there is little evidence that the issue of gun control is being redefined in such a way as to expand the scope of the conflict, bringing in new actors such as public health authorities or parents' organizations to the side of gun control or civil liberties organizations to the cause of gun-owner rights. Instead, the gun control issue appears to be slowly undergoing what Carmines and Stimson (1989) have called "issue evolution." Although Ted Jelen argues in Chapter 12 that there has been little evidence for increasing partisan differences in gun ownership or gun control attitudes in the general public, Samuel Patterson and Keith Eakins suggest in Chapter 3 that congressional voting on gun control issues has become increasingly partisan. Republicans were more supportive than Democrats of the Gun Control Act of 1968, then more supportive than Democrats of the Firearms Owners' Protection Act of 1986 (also known as McClure-Volkmer), which essentially repealed the 1968 bill. By the 1990s, Republicans were far more likely than Democrats to oppose the ban on assault weapons and the Brady Bill, and in 1996 the split in House voting on a measure to repeal the assault weapons ban was quite partisan; Republicans favored the repeal by 183–42, and Democrats opposed it by 130–56.[1]

The widening party division on gun control in Congress may well lead to a widening partisan gap in public support for gun control. Greg Adams (1997) argues that abortion became a partisan issue in the mid-1980s because national political elites increasingly took different positions on abortion, and the public soon picked up on these cues. He argues that "as elites become more unified within their respective parties . . . , each party's message grows increasingly distinct and more potent. Eventually, those who do not conform to both their issue and preferences find that they must reevaluate one or the other, and an issue evolution becomes a possibility." (721). There is evidence that party leaders have persuaded some voters on abortion but that a surprising number of Americans may have switched their partisanship because of the issue—first with pro-life Democrats becoming Republicans and more recently with pro-choice Republicans switching to the Democratic party.

The issue evolution on abortion has posed a difficult problem for the GOP, which has begun a painful internal debate on its recent stance in favor of a constitutional amendment to ban abortion. Should gun control undergo a similar evolution, this likely would also be bad news for the Republicans. Substantial majorities of Americans favor additional gun control, and it is possible that the gun control issue could accelerate the defection of suburban Republican women if the issue were to become a partisan one. In the current political climate, the GOP does not want to become, in the public mind, the party of the NRA.

How likely is it that the politics of gun control will undergo a rapid transformation? In the next section we consider the issues involved in predicting the future of gun control politics.

The Future of Gun Control Politics

Predicting the political future is always risky business, as the Las Vegas oddsmakers who set the line at 1,000–1 against George McGovern's winning the 1972 Democratic nomination learned. Although science fiction writers once imagined that future social scientists would develop powerfully predictive equations, in practice most political scientists have been startled by the rapidity of the demise of the Soviet Union, the end to apartheid in South Africa, and even the end to the dominance of the tobacco lobby in Washington (Wilcox 1997). Several factors suggest that the next millennium will begin with a continued stalemate on gun control politics; other factors suggest the possibility of more rapid change. Rapid change might take the form of repeal of existing gun control laws and an increased arming of the population, but we focus in this section on what we view as a more likely change toward increased gun regulations.

One factor that suggests future stability is the personnel currently heading key political institutions. At the national level, the most important factor is the GOP control of Congress, which survived in 1996 despite a coordinated push by the Democratic party, labor unions, and environmental groups. Although national party leaders may want some distance from the NRA, congressional leaders are quite aware of the resources the group has poured into its election campaigns and are more likely to repeal existing laws than pass additional ones. Indeed, the most likely short-term legislative change would be a new Republican president signing a repeal of Brady or the assault weapons ban, much as Ronald Reagan signed legislation gutting the Gun Control Act of 1968. The Supreme Court is currently dominated by a right-center bloc, which has consistently opposed national regulations that interfere with state prerogatives, but seems unlikely to overturn long-established precedent and discover a constitutional right to firearms in the Second Amendment. The current president, Bill Clinton, favors gun control, but he cannot enact new legislation without Congress. He can, however, direct the bureaucracy in its enforcement of laws and use his role as a nationally elected figure to rally public support.

At the state level, the NRA has enjoyed a string of successes on such issues as the right to carry concealed firearms, reciprocity agreements to honor carry permits issued by other states, and preemption of local firearm statutes. The NRA has the resources—especially a large, active membership and the infrastructure to mobilize that membership—to influence many state legislatures at once, but the gun control coalition does not. Thus it seems unlikely that the states will pass substantial new gun control initiatives soon, and indeed the string of legislative victories for the gun lobbies may well continue in state capitols across the country.

Although the key actors who dominate national and state institutions are generally not favorable to additional gun control and indeed might support rolling back existing regulations, electoral fortunes can quickly change. In 1990 George Bush seemed a sure bet for reelection and the Democrats seemed poised to control Congress for the foreseeable future, and although the GOP majority in Congress seems secure at the time of this writing, the Democratic party might recapture Congress in the near future. Yet Democratic majorities did not pass substantial gun control legislation during the decades they controlled Congress. It would take more than a shift in partisan control to effect rapid change in gun control politics.

Three factors seem critical to long-term policy change in gun control. First, if the party positions on gun control continue to diverge, mass publics may pick up party cues on the issue. Some strong partisans may adjust their policy preferences on gun control, and those who feel strongly about gun control may adjust their partisanship. If the GOP becomes the party of the Christian Right, the gun lobby, and tobacco, it will probably experience some significant defections among suburbanites who support Republican economic policies but favor gun control, choice on abortion, and regulations on tobacco. The dance of party positions on issues is an inherently chaotic process, but the possibility surely exists for the Republicans to eventually pull back from the embrace of the NRA under such circumstances, leaving the Democrats the party of gun control and the Republicans the party of "moderate" gun control. Such an alignment might lead to more rapid policy change.

Second, the role of other groups in the policy arena is key. If influential groups seek to define gun access as a safety issue, the issue may become redefined and policy change could occur. The rapid passage of gun-free schools legislation suggests that safety concerns can lead to rapid policy enactment. Public health groups, parent-teacher associations, and business groups all have a stake in less gun violence, and if these groups stake a position on gun control, the issue could be transformed.

Finally, the activity of the NRA is critical to the future of gun control. The NRA retains significant resources—a large, geographically dispersed, and loyal membership; the ability to quickly communicate with members; infrastructure in the form of state NRA chapters and gun clubs; skilled lobbyists; and a large political action committee. Yet the image of the NRA has been seriously tarnished, and many prominent conservatives have denounced the organization. If the NRA remains in conflict with police groups and continues to attack the BATF and other organizations with rhetoric borrowed from militia groups, it is likely to incite a countermobilization that will neutralize and possibly even reverse its electoral strength. If the group begins to position itself as a more moderate organization, however, it seems likely that gun control politics will continue at a stalemate.

Is it possible for the NRA to reposition itself? There is at least some evidence that the organization is trying. In recent months the NRA has supported police groups in lobbying for a few isolated anti-crime provisions that were not directly related to guns. Moreover, the election of Charlton Heston over Neil Knox marked a move away from the radical rhetoric of the militias toward a more presentable front. Whether the man who once played Moses can help lead the NRA out of its difficulties or part the troubled waters that surround the organization remains to be seen.

If the NRA remains committed to confrontation and continues to embrace the language of militia groups, it is likely that more moderate organizations of gun owners will proliferate. Already a number of such organizations exist, but their membership remains small. Should such organizations flourish and embrace moderate gun control policies, the dynamics of gun control will surely change.

The Plan of the Book

In the chapters that follow, a number of scholars explore recent trends in gun control politics. We begin by examining policymaking by national institutions. Wendy Martinek, Kenneth Meier, and Lael Keiser focus on executive policymaking in the embattled Bureau of Alcohol, Tobacco, and Firearms. Samuel Patterson and Keith Eakins consider the actions of Congress in recent times, and Karen O'Connor and Graham Barron review the activities of the U.S. Supreme Court.

Because much of the action in gun control policymaking is at the state level, Chapters 5–8 focus on states. Three case studies investigate gun policymaking in single states. Marcia L. Godwin and Jean Reith Schroedel describe the short-lived window of opportunity that enabled gun control advocates in California to ban the sale of certain assault weapons. James Gimpel and Robin Wolpert discuss a referendum in Maryland in 1988 in which the NRA sought to repeal a state law banning the sale of certain handguns. Harry Wilson and Mark Rozell explore the politics of Virginia's recent law making it easier for citizens to carry concealed handguns. Finally, John Bruce and Clyde Wilcox examine gun laws across the states, seeking to explain the differences between those states with very liberal laws and those enacting very conservative laws.

Chapters 9–12 explore citizen input in the policy process. Ronald Shaiko and Marc A. Wallace focus on the grassroots power of the NRA, and Diana Lambert writes of the growing strength of groups like Handgun Control, Inc. David Harding focuses on public support and opposition to gun control laws, and Ted Jelen discusses how gun control attitudes and gun ownership influence citizens' voting decisions.

Notes

1. One independent in the House, who caucuses with the Democrats, also opposed the repeal.

2

Jackboots or Lace Panties?
The Bureau of Alcohol, Tobacco,
and Firearms

Wendy L. Martinek, Kenneth J. Meier, and Lael R. Keiser

The Bureau of Alcohol, Tobacco, and Firearms, commonly known as the ATF or BATF, is the agency charged with administering federal alcohol, tobacco, and firearms laws as well as federal laws relating to commercial arson and explosives. Regardless of whether one believes these items should be regulated, booze, smokes, and guns are three things most Americans feel strongly about. Given its role in regulating these industries, the ATF has often been embroiled in controversy. The bureau's role in the regulation of alcohol, its original bread-and-butter issue, has dropped to virtual insignificance, and its work in the area of tobacco has been and continues to be largely ignored. This leaves the regulation of firearms, perhaps the most controversial issue, front and center in terms of ATF activity. Opponents of gun control see the ATF as arbitrary and abusive. Proponents discern a weak agency hamstrung further by tepid laws and powerful opponents. Few agencies generate such contradictory perceptions. In this chapter we seek to go beyond public perceptions and assess the role of the ATF in gun control policy.

Administrative History

The earliest precursor of ATF regulations was Treasury Secretary Alexander Hamilton's 1791 tax on spirits. Abolished 11 years later but only after triggering the 1794 Whiskey Rebellion, the tax was reinstated to raise revenue for federal forces in the Civil War. At that time, three detectives, ancestral ATF agents, so to speak, were hired to combat tax evasion. The enactment of Prohibition with the Eighteenth Amendment resulted in the creation of the Prohibition Unit, the earliest twentieth-century incarnation of the ATF, within the Bureau of Internal Revenue of the Treasury Department. This unit, subsequently renamed the Bureau of Prohibition, established the mythic past of the ATF. Its most famous member was undoubtedly Eliot Ness. Ness and his group of hand-picked agents, known as "the Untouchables," spearheaded an antibootlegger effort intended to deprive Al Capone and other mob bosses of a main source of income, the illegal production and distribution of liquor.[1] With the end of Prohibition, the name was changed to the Alcohol Tax Unit, and it was again lodged in the IRS. The agency was transformed into the Alcohol and Tobacco Division in the early 1950s accompanying the expansion of its jurisdiction to include tobacco, and yet again to the Alcohol, Tobacco, and Firearms Division when given additional jurisdiction over firearms with the Gun Control Act of 1968. The original jurisdiction over firearms had come with the 1934 National Firearms Act, designed to restrict automatic weapons (the weapons of choice of organized crime), and the 1938 Federal Firearms Act, intended to restrict the interstate sale and transportation of firearms.[2]

The most recent name change, from the Alcohol, Tobacco and Firearms Division to the Bureau of Alcohol, Tobacco and Firearms, occurred July 1, 1972. Treasury Department Order Number 221 separated the ATF from the Internal Revenue Service and elevated it to full bureau status within the Treasury Department as part of the Nixon administration's war on crime. The separation of the ATF from the Internal Revenue Service was helpful to the IRS in that the publicity given ATF agents involved in criminal enforcement, inevitably referred to as IRS agents, was antithetical to voluntary compliance with federal tax regulations, which was then being promoted (Larson 1994, 136). And from the perspective of ATF agents, divorce from the IRS meant no longer being in the employ of the nation's tax collector, a situation that had not been relished by the ATF. Former ATF director Rex Davis observed, "When our law-enforcement officers were asked who they were, they would say Treasury agents" (Larson 1994, 135).

Organization of the ATF

The ATF has headquarters in Washington, D.C., with regional offices for regulatory, or compliance, operations and field division offices for law enforcement activities. Currently, there are 5 regional offices (Midwest, North Atlantic, Southeast, Southwest, Western) and 24 field division offices. The director reports to the Treasury Department's assistant secretary for enforcement, as does the U.S. Customs Service and the U.S. Secret Service. Figure 2.1 depicts the current organizational structure of the bureau. What has remained constant since its elevation to bureau status has been the existence of top-level positions specifically charged with overseeing the fundamental responsibilities of the bureau: regulatory enforcement and criminal enforcement.

Another manifestation of continuity is the low turnover in the top bureaucratic positions. There have been only four directors of the ATF during its existence as a full-fledged bureau. Rex D. Davis was an assistant regional commissioner and then the director of the Alcohol, Tobacco, and Firearms Division of the Internal Revenue Service (Larson 1994, 135). Davis had worked his way up from his first position as a

FIGURE 2.1
ATF Organizational Chart, January 1996

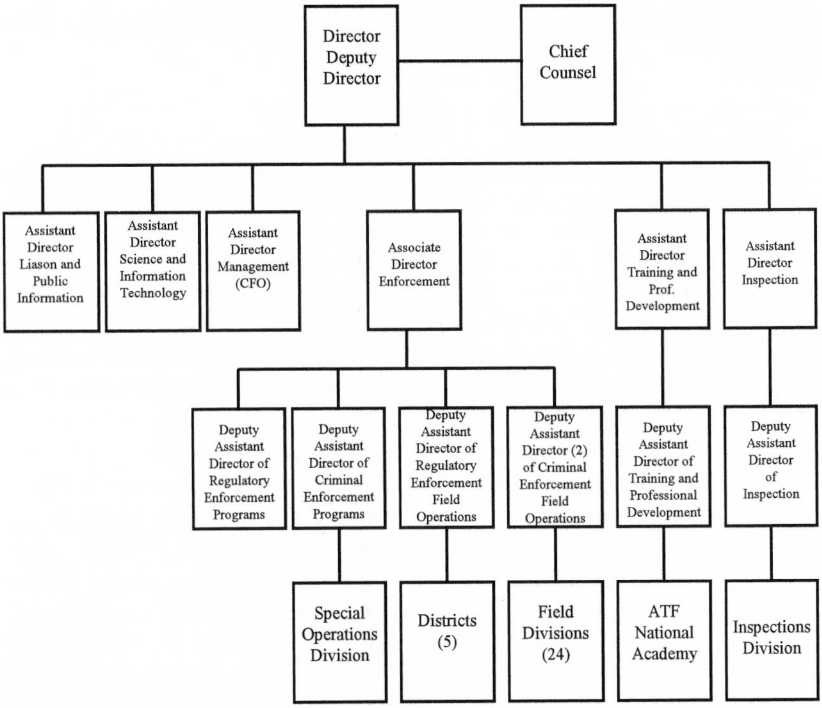

Source: GAO 1996b, 17.
Note: The Chief Counsel is the legal advisor to the ATF but is overseen by Chief Counsel, Dept. of the Treasury.

field agent (Davidson 1993, 50). Upon the ATF's elevation to a bureau, Davis assumed the post of director, where he remained until his retirement in July 1978. Glenn R. Dickerson then assumed the position of director, resigning to take a position as deputy commissioner for international affairs in the U.S. Customs Service in 1982 during an attempt by the Reagan administration to dismantle the agency (Thornton 1982b). The third person to hold this job was Stephen E. Higgins, who began his career in the agency as an inspector and held various posts before becoming deputy director in 1979. Higgins had been characterized as "a quick study" and a "very accomplished motivator" by then Assistant to the Director for Congressional and Media Affairs, James Pasco (Hershey 1985, II:5). The image of a golden boy was rapidly tarnished, however, by the events that occurred at the Branch Davidian compound near Waco, Texas, in 1993. As a result of those events, or more accurately, as a result of the handling of the situation in the months following the raid, Higgins was removed from his post. Former Secret Service director John W. Magaw replaced Higgins. A former high school teacher and Ohio state trooper, Magaw joined the Secret Service in 1967. He had served as the head of protection for the president and first lady prior to becoming director of the Secret Service in 1992.

The Changing Priorities of the ATF

Little, if any, public controversy has attached to the ATF's involvement in regulatory or law enforcement activities having to do with tobacco. Much of this work is routine collection of taxes from the major cigarette manufacturers. The ATF was specifically given law enforcement responsibility for interstate contraband cigarette trafficking by Treasury Department Order Number 120–1, December 1978; but the number of these cases is small.

Alcohol regulation originally dominated the bureau's agenda but clearly no longer does so. The primary vehicle used by the ATF to regulate the alcohol industry is the 1935 Federal Alcohol Administration Act. This legislation was intended to inhibit the involvement of organized crime in the alcohol industry and dissuade legitimate liquor manufacturers and distributors from engaging in nefarious practices. An example of one such practice involved retailers being required to deal exclusively with a particular wholesaler or face having supplies cut off altogether. Another scheme forced retailers to purchase products in plentiful supply in order to have access to those that were not so plentiful (Sugarawa 1982). "Revenooers," a moniker for ATF agents derived from the name of their former parent agency (the IRS), were actively involved in policing the illegal liquor trade, breaking up stills, and tracking moonshiners, especially in the back country of the Southeast. Over 20,000 federal alcohol arrests were made annually from the end of prohibition to the beginning of World War II (Meier 1994, 159). In 1973, 2,589 stills were reported seized; that number dropped precipitously to 28 in 1980, less than a decade later.[3]

Two factors reduced the efforts of law enforcement regarding alcohol cases. First, the federal government failed to increase its alcohol taxes. As a result, the tax portion of the price of alcohol dropped. With inflation, the economic incentive to manufacture alcohol then diminished. Second, bootleggers found a commodity that was easier to produce and more profitable to sell, marijuana (Meier 1994, 160). By the 1990s, the ATF rarely referred more than ten alcohol cases a year for prosecution; the bureau's alcohol functions had become almost totally regulatory. One example of the bureau's remaining responsibilities is ensuring that the alcohol content listed on the labels of wine and other spirits matches the actual content of the bottles. Brewed alcoholic beverages, however, are not within the jurisdiction of the ATF.[4] Part of the funds earmarked for alcohol regulation are used to purchase alcohol at randomly selected retailers. The items purchased are then sent to bureau labs for analysis.

With the decline in alcohol cases, firearms became the major law enforcement priority of the agency. Table 2.1 presents data on the change in ATF activities from 1973 to 1995. Earlier data are difficult to acquire because the Bureau of Alcohol, Tobacco, and Firearms was not a separate agency within the Department of the Treasury, and thus the federal government did not list its expenditures separately before 1973.[5] Although these data began to be gathered well after the start of the ATF's shift in priorities, they clearly demonstrate the trend. The firearms portion of the total budget increased from 43.2 percent in 1973 to 67.8 percent in 1995. Within the law enforcement category, firearm expenditures increased from 61.3 percent to 80.5 percent. With the addition of regulatory duties under the Gun Control Act of 1968 and the Brady Bill, the proportion of the regulation budget devoted to firearms also increased from 8 percent in 1973 to 39 percent in 1995. The change in priorities, particularly in law enforcement, is best illustrated by the last set of figures in Table 2.1. In 1960, 95.6 percent of agency arrests were for alcohol violations; in 1995, 95.1 percent of the arrests were for firearms violations.

The mission statement of the agency clearly emphasizes its law enforcement responsibilities: "The mission of the Bureau of Alcohol, Tobacco and Firearms (ATF) is: to reduce the criminal use of firearms and

TABLE 2.1
The Changing Priorities of the Bureau of Alcohol, Tobacco and
Firearms (in percentages)

	1960	*1973*	*1995*
Total Expenditures			
Alcohol	--	52.2	16.6
Firearms	--	43.2	67.8
Other[a]	--	4.6	15.6
Law Enforcement Expenditures			
Alcohol	--	32.2	0.4
Firearms	--	61.3	80.5
Other[a]	--	6.5	19.1
Regulation / Compliance			
Alcohol	--	91.2	53.4
Firearms	--	8.0	39.0
Other[a]	--	0.8	7.6
Arrests			
Alcohol	95.6	46.2	0.2
Firearms	4.4	47.7	95.1
Other[a]	NA	6.0	4.7

Sources: Calculated from United States (1996). 1960 data taken from the *Annual Report of the Administrator of the United States Courts.* Washington, DC: Office of the Administrator of the Courts.
[a]Includes explosives, tobacco.

to assist other Federal, State, local and foreign law enforcement agencies in reducing crime and violence by effective enforcement of the Federal firearms laws" (BATF 1996). The pattern in Table 2.1 reflects the persistence of the law enforcement mission. In fiscal year 1995, ATF devoted 69.4 percent of its budget to law enforcement. To say that the ATF is a law enforcement agency solely concerned with firearms is only a modest exaggeration.

Few aspects of an agency are as important as its mission (Wilson 1989). Law enforcement agencies see themselves as paramilitary organizations set apart from traditional government bureaucracies. Such agencies generally lack policy analysis capabilities and see their function as vigorously enforcing the law. Because they deal with suspects rather than citizens, they are quite likely to see the situation as dire and needing even stronger action. Couple this mission with the myth of the Untouchables, and much of the ATF's behavior can be explained.

Bureaucratic Strength and the ATF

Although bureaucracies can be major players in the policy process, their authority is derived from legislative and executive actors. If these political actors withdraw their support, the agency usually lacks authority to directly influence policy. The ATF has had its fair share of attacks from Congress and the executive. Members of Congress and various presidents have even tried to eliminate the ATF altogether. The ATF is more open to such attacks than other agencies because it has no statutory independence. Unlike other agencies, such as the Occupational Safety and Health Administration, the Bureau of Alcohol, Tobacco, and Firearms was not created through statute. Rather, it was created via a Treasury Department order. Consequently, the bureau can be abolished without adopting new legislation.

Despite the dependence of public agencies on executive and legislative actors for survival, they are not necessarily passive actors pushed along at the whim of other subsystem members. They shape as well as respond to pressures from other political actors (Rourke 1984). Bureaucracies can manipulate the environment in the subsystem to gain more support. Through promoting and advertising the importance of their function, facilitating the organization of clientele who support their goals, and providing information to other subsystem actors, public bureaucracies can increase the support they receive from the environment and the influence they have on policy. However, not all public bureaucracies are created equal. They vary in their ability to increase their support from the environment and their capacity to influence policy

and thus vary in their bureaucratic strength. Dimensions of bureaucratic strength include fiscal resources, expertise, professionalism, legislative authority, political salience, and discretion.

Fiscal Resources

One indicator of a powerful bureaucracy is the ability to extract resources from its environment (Rourke 1984; Meier 1993). When we
compare budgets of different agencies, however, we see that many of
the factors that influence budgets are outside their control. As a result,
perhaps the best comparisons for the ATF are to those agencies that
perform the same function, agencies Downs (1967) would call competitors.

Table 2.2 shows the budgets of the six major law enforcement agencies of the federal government in 1970 and 1995. As the growth rates
demonstrate, these were good times for law enforcement agencies.
Crime was a major issue, and politicians sought electoral gain with
larger and larger programs. Within the law enforcement agencies, the
relative weakness of the ATF is apparent. Although its budget grew a
whopping 692 percent in 25 years, it clearly was the least favored of
the law enforcement agencies. By 1995, in fact, the ATF had become
the smallest of the six federal law enforcement agencies.

An interesting pattern not revealed by Table 2.2 is the relative sup-

TABLE 2.2
The Decline in Budget Support for the ATF

Federal Law Enforcement Budgets ($millions)

Agency	1970	1995	Growth Rate
ATF	49.9	395.0	692%
FBI	252.9	2,428.0	860%
DEA	27.9	930.0	3,233%
Secret Service	32.8	492.0	1,400%
Immigration	105.7	1,057.0	900%
Customs	128.5	1,913.0	1389%

Source: Calculated from United States (1996).

port for the ATF under different presidents. Intuitively, given the tie of the National Rifle Association to conservatives and the support of gun control advocates for liberal Democrats, one might expect that the agency would fare best under Democratic administrations. Table 2.3 shows that nothing could be farther from the truth. Budget gains under Republican presidents were 2.5 times the size of gains under Democratic presidents. Even Ronald Reagan was no exception. Although the 21 percent gain in his first term reflects his unsuccessful attempt to abolish the agency and is an all-time low for a Republican president, the ATF grew by 53.4 percent during his second term. The traditional Republican support for law enforcement appears to outweigh the Republicans' aversion to gun control.

Expertise

The ability of a bureaucracy to influence its policy environment is partly a function of its knowledge and specialization relative to the

TABLE 2.3
ATF Budget Growth by Presidential Term

President	Percent Growth
Kennedy/Johnson	18.8
Johnson	41.1
Nixon	62.1
Nixon/Ford	58.4
Carter	7.6
Reagan, first term	21.1
Reagan, second term	53.4
Bush	50.0
Clinton	- 2.1[a]
Republican Average	49.0
Democratic Average	19.0

Source: Calculated from United States (1996).
[a]Two years.

other actors in the subsystem. Specialization permits an agency to develop independent sources of knowledge so that it need not rely on the industry (or others) for its information. When a bureaucracy has the capability to provide other subsystem actors with expert knowledge, it has power over other subsystem actors and can directly influence their policy decisions. Other subsystem actors will be more likely to defer to the advice of bureaucrats when the bureaucracy has a reputation for expert information (Meier 1993; Rourke 1984). Although law enforcement agencies rarely become knowledge powerhouses like the research agencies, they can and do develop expertise.

Judging the ATF on this dimension is a mixed bag because whereas it evidences some technical expertise, it operates with major liabilities. A study by the General Accounting Office (GAO) found that the training provided by the ATF to its agents on the use of deadly force is consistent with the types of training FBI and DEA agents undergo (GAO 1996b). Articles published in *Police Chief*, the primary publication of the International Association of Chiefs of Police, have often portrayed the bureau as a knowledgeable, desirable partner in law enforcement.[6] In fact, Daniel Hartnett, then associate director of law enforcement of the ATF, authored a technical article in the April 1990 issue of the *Police Chief* detailing the bureau's advances in the analysis of physical evidence. The ATF also received kudos for tracing the gun used by would-be Reagan assassin John W. Hinckley Jr. in under 16 minutes (King 1988).

The constraints the bureau faces with regard to expertise, however, are not to be taken lightly. The ATF still lacks the necessary personnel to perform its functions in a timely manner. For example, the bureau's 250 gun control agents have responsibility for 280,000 gun dealers (Spitzer 1995, 164). The insufficient number of inspectors is exacerbated by the requirement that the agency process license applications within 45 days (Thomas 1992). The laxness of the licensing process has yielded some eye-opening incidents. The Violence Policy Center, a D.C. research group, issued a 1992 study that described two examples of this laxness (Thomas 1992). In the first example, a federally licensed dealer in Los Angeles sold 1,500 guns, of which only 4 were actually registered in California. In the second example, a dealer in Detroit was involved in hundreds of firearms sales but failed to record any of them as was required by law. California alone has 21,000 federally licensed dealers; Texas has 17,000 (Thomas 1993). In 1992, the *Washington Post* quoted ATF spokesman Jack Killorin as saying, "The volume of licensees has outstripped our ability to keep up" (Thomas 1992, B3). Simply put, the agency has more work to do than it is equipped to do.

Perhaps the most formidable obstacle to augmenting the ATF's expertise has been the repeated attacks on its character. Politicians and anti–gun control interest groups have gone to great lengths to sully the reputation of the ATF as an expert and professional agency. A particularly interesting episode, with more ups and downs than a roller coaster, almost resulted in the elimination of the bureau except for a last-minute change of heart by the NRA. Prior to Reagan's assuming office, the Heritage Foundation, a conservative Washington, D.C., think tank, prepared a report concluding that consolidation of the ATF with existing agencies could result in major budget savings (Behr 1981). This report formed the basis of an administration proposal to consolidate the ATF with other federal agencies. The intention was to transfer the responsibility for the enforcement of firearms and explosives laws to the Secret Service and the enforcement of alcohol and tobacco laws to the Customs Service. Certainly the ATF was not the sole target of budget cuts; 30 to 40 agencies, boards, and commissions were slated for extinction (Dewar 1981). However, Reagan was clearly no ally of the bureau. He had made campaign promises to eliminate it and was himself an NRA member (Larson 1994, 140). In fact, the NRA actively campaigned for Reagan, spending $171,000 on his behalf (Keller 1982).

The National Rifle Association was initially ecstatic over the administration's proposed dismantlement of the ATF. As part of its efforts to popularize this proposal in Congress, the NRA produced a film entitled *It Can Happen Here*, purporting to document the many abuses of the Alcohol, Tobacco, and Firearms Bureau. The film highlighted stories of individuals who claimed to have been unfairly targeted and subsequently ruined by the bureau and quoted Representative John Dingell (D-MI) as describing ATF agents as "a jack-booted group of fascists who are . . . a shame and a disgrace to our country" (Farley 1981, A1). The bureau was given a temporary stay of execution through the intervention of Treasury Secretary Donald Regan (Spitzer 1995, 166; Gailey 1981) but lost over $13 million of its $159 million 1982 budget (Gailey 1981). Within the ATF, there seemed to be no question that the perils the bureau faced were directly and almost completely attributable to the NRA. Unidentified employees were variously quoted as saying, "They're [the NRA] wiping us out" and "The N.R.A. has finally won" (Gailey 1981, A1). Director Glenn R. Dickerson was quite explicit in his assessment of the NRA's role when he said the bureau was being "destroyed by cuts that are in a large measure due to the N.R.A. campaign against us" (Gailey 1981, A1).

By spring 1982, the bureau's reprieve seemed to be coming to an end, and its future was uncertain as the administration and members of Congress renewed efforts to disband it. An about-face on the part of the NRA, however, radically altered the political landscape surrounding this issue. Rather than celebrating the imminent demise of the bureau it had despised from its inception, the NRA began lobbying for its salvation. The NRA's change of heart stemmed not from a newly found respect for the ATF but from fear of what a highly respected Secret Service might do if it gained jurisdiction over federal firearms regulation and law enforcement, as it was slated to do under the dismantlement plans. An anonymous Senate source was quoted in the *Washington Post* as saying, "The NRA suddenly realized they weren't going to have BATF to kick around anymore. The Secret Service is more respected and well known, and not as vulnerable to attack by the NRA. They realized they had outsmarted themselves" (Thornton 1982a, A21). NRA director of public affairs John D. Aquilino Jr. acknowledged the advantages as far as his organization was concerned in having the ATF, especially if weakened with staff and budget reductions, continue to administer firearms laws. "One of the few saving features [of BATF] is the fact that its management has been so lax that the efficiency with which they enforce a bad law [i.e. the 1968 Gun Control Act] has been quantum leaps below what it could be" (Keller 1982, 730). Rather than have enforcement in the hands of an agency with more prestige and resources (namely, the Secret Service), the NRA's preference was to "turn BATF into the Karen Ann Quinlan of law enforcement" (Thornton 1982a, A21) and keep it, rather than the Secret Service, the responsible organization. One reason the NRA may have reassessed its position with regard to the abolition of the ATF was the lack of strong opposition to the move by gun control advocates (Keller 1982; Spitzer 1995, 166; Sugarmann 1992, 125–126). As an example, an NRA spokesman made the following assertion: "Anything Teddy Kennedy backs, I think the honest citizens of this country should take a fast leap to the other side" (Davidson 1993, 52–53).

In its quest to resuscitate the Bureau of Alcohol, Tobacco, and Firearms, the NRA joined an effort already under way by members of the liquor industry. The Washington counsel for the Wine and Spirits Wholesalers of America harked back to the gangster-related past of the alcohol industry. "We're dealing with a product that has a history, to our regret, a dark history, before and during the prohibition" (Sugarawa 1982, A9). The president of the National Association of Beverage Importers noted that an industry lobbying in favor of the bureau that regulates it was not so unusual when one considered that "not too many other industries have been the subject of two constitutional amendments" (Sugarawa 1982, A9). Beyond these motivations, officials of the Treasury Department suggested that the opposition to the ATF's dismantlement by these and similar organizations stemmed from their fear that the discretion accruing to larger companies without the regulation of the ATF would seriously disadvantage the smaller companies represented by such associations (Sugarawa 1982). A Wall Street attorney representing two large wineries also gave more profit-driven rationales in his testimony before a Senate appropriations sub-committee. He asserted that abolishing the ATF would have negative ramifications for both domestic and foreign markets. Domestic consumption would drop as a result of inferior products flooding the market, and U.S. exports would decline dramatically as other countries questioned the product integrity of American exports (U.S. Senate 1982). As an aside, the tobacco industry, although seemingly satisfied with the way things were under the ATF, reportedly was not unduly worried regardless of the final disposition of the issue (Keller 1982).

The dismantlement plan finally died but left the ATF temporarily hobbled by personnel and budget reductions. Moreover, although the opponents of the agency supported its continued existence, they did not necessarily temper their criticism. Representative John Dingell (D-MI) had been particularly colorful in his denunciation of the ATF, referring to the members of the bureau as fascists and thugs and characterizing the whole agency as evil. Even in withdrawing his support for the dissolution of the agency, Representative Dingell's censure of the ATF was harsh: "If you were to fire all of the BATF and move its functions to the Secret Service, that might correct the matter. If you move the people from BATF to Secret Service the practical effect would be to contaminate the Secret Service with the kind of undemocratic, un-American approach to law enforcement that we have so long seen in BATF" (U.S. Senate 1982, 123).

Professionalism

An important dimension of expertise, albeit hard to assess, is professionalism. Using the professional or unprofessional behavior of a single individual or small group of individuals within an organization as indicative of the conduct of the organization as a whole is problematic. Nevertheless, some incidents can at least inform our assessments of professionalism. An event known as the Good Ol' Boys Roundup is pertinent in this case.

This event, held annually near the Ocoee River in eastern Tennessee, began in 1980 and was organized some years by former ATF agent Gene Rightmyer. What purportedly began as an innocent family-type gathering apparently developed into an event that critics might be more inclined to call the Good Ol' *White* Boys Roundup. Among the unappealing activities cited in the media were the sale of T-shirts with racially derogatory slogans and the posting of "nigger hunting licenses." Accounts conflict over whether Rightmyer, who worked in the Alabama and Tennessee office of the ATF prior to retiring in 1994, participated in or condoned the racial incidents. In a deposition taken from a black ATF agent involved in a class action lawsuit against the bureau for discrimination, the agent testified that Rightmyer told two black colleagues, "You were born trash, you will live trash and you will die trash" (Abramowitz 1995, A4). Another black agent, however, testified that Rightmyer apologized to him for the use of racial epithets by others attending the event. Current ATF director John W. Magaw reportedly learned of the allegedly racist nature of the gathering via the Internet and subsequently ordered an investigation. Testifying before the Senate Judiciary Committee in 1995, Magaw said, "Apparently knowledge of the roundup has been widespread within ATF. The racial and discriminatory allegations being made are most serious, and if true will be dealt with and should have been dealt with years ago" (Abramowitz 1995, A4).

ATF agents were a distinct minority among attendees. According to Magaw, of the approximately 300 law enforcement officers who attended the event in spring 1995, 6 active and 10 to 15 retired members were from the bureau (Vobejda and Cooper 1995). Despite this fact, members of militias, who feel they are unfairly targeted by the ATF, were instrumental in making the racial character of the event public. The Gadsden Minutemen, an Alabama-based militia, launched Operation Achilles Heel specifically to discredit the ATF, according to the group's spokesman (Abramowitz and Mintz 1995). Militia member Jeff Randall attended the 1995 roundup in the guise of a police officer and filmed the event with a 35mm camera to document its racially discriminatory nature. Randall publicized his observations locally and says he was then contacted by an anonymous individual who produced a 1990 videotape of the roundup that included footage of a "nigger checkpoint" sign posted on the grounds.[7] Subsequently, that individual was identified as former Fort Lauderdale, Florida, police officer Richard Hayward.

If incidents such as the Good Ol' Boys Roundup are widespread, they indicate an agency totally lacking in professionalism. Even if the participation was as limited as Magaw suggests, it represents behavior that should not be tolerated by any government agency. Because law enforcement agencies place a greater burden on their employees during off-duty hours than a civilian agency would, the extent of participation raises serious questions about the ATF's ability to enforce the law equitably.

Legislative Authority

In addition to expertise and professionalism, an agency's ability to influence policy depends on its legislative authority. All agencies involved in regulation must have legislative authority to operate, but all grants of legislative authority are not equal (see Sabatier 1977, 421–431). The more specific the expressed goals, the less discretion is available to the bureaucracy. Legislation concerning gun control is very specific about what types of weapons the agency can regulate and what types of activities Congress will allow.

Under current law, the ATF's firearms regulatory responsibilities center on the processing and review of firearms license applications to determine applicants' qualifications under the 1968 Gun Control Act (as amended by the Firearms Owners' Protection Act of 1986) and the conduct of periodic compliance inspections of licensees (GAO 1996a, 3). Firearms dealers must obtain a federal license, but an individual not engaged in the business of wholesale or retail firearms sales or repairs is not considered a dealer and is not required to obtain a license.

> The term "engaged in the business," as applied to a dealer in firearms, is defined . . . in part, as a person who devotes time, attention, and labor to dealing in firearms as a regular course of trade or business with the principal objective of livelihood and profit through the repetitive purchase and resale of firearms. The definition further provides that such term shall not include a person who makes occasional sales, exchanges, or purchases of firearms for the enhancement of a personal collection or for a hobby, or who sells all or part of his personal collection of firearms. (GAO 1996a, 4)

In practice, it is impossible to prevent individuals from fulfilling the letter but not the spirit of the law. And there are certain benefits to becoming a dealer in name only. A federal license "enables you to acquire at wholesale prices thousands of varieties of weapons and have them shipped right to your home" (Larson 1994, 124). With the issuance of a license, the ATF retains the authority to conduct an unexpected inspection once a year. Whether such an inspection takes place is dependent on the workload and availability of inspectors. It is important to note that the frequency of inspection is set by law rather than left to the discretion of the ATF.

Dealers are required to have buyers complete Form 4473 to consummate any sale. On this form, the buyer is required to provide his name, address, date of birth, and place of birth and certify that he is not prohibited by law from owning a firearm. The buyer's signature, indicating that he is not prohibited from owning a firearm, is the full extent of the certification. Upon completion, the form is retained by the dealer for 20 years or until the dealer goes out of business, whichever comes first. In effect, the dealer is considered the custodian of the records on behalf of the Bureau of Alcohol, Tobacco, and Firearms. If and when the dealer goes out of business, these records are turned over to the bureau. Because there is a backlog in the microfilming of records, a substantial number of records are stored in hard copy in the bureau's Out-of-Business Records Section. ATF staff may be required to sort through boxes of records stored in the warehouse to locate needed information. The bureau estimated that $3.5 million would be needed to eliminate the backlog for fiscal years 1992 through 1996, but its request for the funds was denied.

The fact that dealers, and not the ATF, retain the purchaser paperwork indicates an absence of discretion. Gun control opponents in Congress and the NRA have worked hard to ensure the ATF does not have the tools (or in the case of dealer records, the raw material) to create a comprehensive database. The ATF is legally prohibited from centralizing such records. This prohibition is stipulated in the federal budget as follows: "No funds appropriated herein shall be available for salaries or administrative expenses in connection with consolidating or centralizing, within the Department of the Treasury, the records, or any portion thereof, of acquisition and disposition of firearms maintained by Federal firearms licensees" (United States 1996, 803). The events leading up to this prohibition began in March 1978 when President Carter announced new rules promulgated by the ATF to aid in the enforcement of the 1968 Gun Control Act. The proposed regulations required each firearm to carry a unique serial number; the report of any theft or loss to the bureau within 24 hours by all gun manufacturers, importers, and dealers; and the submission of quarterly reports of all sales. Public response to the rules was swift and overwhelmingly negative. The most egregious of the rules, according to the NRA and other opponents of gun control, were the seemingly innocuous quarterly sales reports. These reports were not to include the names and addresses of gun purchasers but nonetheless were seen as laying the groundwork for the compilation of a gun registry. The bureau defended the quarterly reports and their intended computerization as valuable tools to be used exclusively to aid in the identification of firearms used in crimes. Bureau defenses fell on largely deaf ears as volumes of mail poured in, running 18 to 1 against the implementation of the new rules ("Gun Friends" 1978). And the letters were stridently anti-ATF, not just antirules. For example, one letter was addressed to Gestapo Headquarters (Babcock 1978).

The bureau maintained that it already had the authority to implement the regulations without receiving permission from Congress. Opponents, however, decried the rules as usurping congressional authority. Ultimately, those against the computerization of the firearms records prevailed when the estimated $4.2 million needed for implementation was cut from the ATF's budget by Congress. Subsequent budget appropriations for the ATF have included the explicit prohibition noted previously against the use of any funds for such a program.

Late in 1989, the ATF did implement its own automated system designed to assist in tracing, but it is very limited in accordance with congressional prohibitions. The congressional prohibition against computerized centralization is a political statement about the ATF's image with lawmakers and undercuts the bureau's efforts to enforce the firearms laws. In sum, the legislative authority of the ATF is highly restricted by Congress.

Political Salience

Bureaucracies are directly affected by the salience (perceived importance by the public) of their policy issues. Salience determines the willingness of political elites to intervene in the process (Gormley 1986). Political elites reap higher rewards for intervention when an issue becomes salient than when a policy generates little interest among interest groups or the general public. With salient issues, political elites closely watch the activity of the bureaucracy. The bureaucracy will, therefore, have less discretion to affect policy.

The issue of gun control is highly salient to interest groups and the general public. One measure of salience is the coverage accorded an issue or agency in the media. Figure 2.2 illustrates the incidence of articles appearing in the *Washington Post* from 1972 through April 1996. Unfortunately for the ATF, salience generally means negative publicity. The ill-fated raid and siege at Waco occurred in 1993, and the incident continued to receive extensive coverage in 1994 and 1995, as investigations of exactly what occurred and the trials of 11 surviving Branch Davidians for murder and conspiracy took place. The second concentration of media coverage by the *Washington Post* occurred in 1977 and generally dealt with the formulation of new wine regulations by the ATF. In 1981–1982, the Reagan administration attempted to dissolve the bureau. Members of Congress, especially allies of gun control opponents, followed the president's lead and exploited the high visibility

FIGURE 2.2
Coverage of the ATF

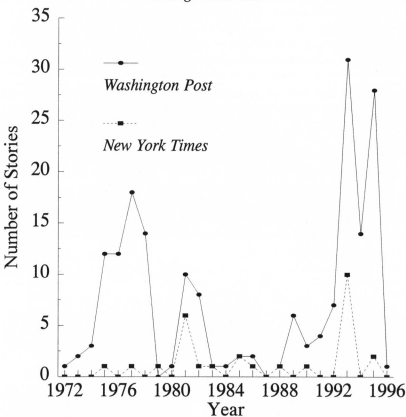

Source: Compiled by authors.

accorded the planned disbanding. Salience, rather than an advantage for the ATF, has been a liability.

Autonomy and Discretion

Agency power is considered a function of both resources and autonomy in the use of those resources. The ATF's resources have not grown as fast as those of other regulatory agencies. Since law enforcement agencies all perform similar functions, certain budget items should reveal some indicators of relative autonomy. Table 2.4 shows two such indicators.

The federal budget makes a specific authorization for personnel and specifies how much can be spent in overtime pay. For law enforcement

TABLE 2.4
Measures of Autonomy and Discretion, 1995

Agency	Overtime Percent	Budget Dollar/Employee
ATF	0.6	94,468
FBI	11.1	99,164
DEA	17.8	141,932
Secret Service	23.3	106,836
Immigration	37.4	87,557
Customs	5.4	117,450

Source: Calculated from United States (1995).

agencies, the ability to use overtime is crucial, since it allows them to pursue promising cases that were not anticipated, particularly those that require a great deal of resources. Although an agency always has the option of seeking a supplemental appropriation after the fact, prior authorization of overtime grants the agency additional discretion. On this measure, the ATF is clearly the weakest of the six federal law enforcement agencies; less than 1 percent of its personnel costs is allocated for overtime.

Since law enforcement agencies are personnel intensive, that is, their major expense is salaries, the ratio of expenditures to employees reveals the extent of discretionary funds. Again, the ATF does poorly in this comparison, rating fifth out of six agencies, leading only the Immigration and Naturalization Service. Both indicators suggest that the ATF has less autonomy in its use of resources than other federal law enforcement agencies. Coupled with its lower level of resources and highly restrictive laws, this lack of financial autonomy suggests a fairly weak agency.

Interest Groups and the ATF

Because public bureaucracies need congressional and presidential support, the strength of interest groups opposing and supporting the agency has a profound impact on its power to influence public policy. Interest groups use their power to convince elected officials to intervene in the bureaucracy's activity and directly pressure it to act in ways favorable to their interests. The strength of interest groups depends on their size (membership), resources, cohesion, prestige, and intensity of commitment. Due to its responsibilities, the ATF must deal with interest groups representing the gun industry, advocates against gun control (specifically the National Rifle Association), advocates for gun control, and the alcohol industry.

Larger interest groups are perceived as more powerful because a great many members confer legitimacy on the claims of the group (Stigler 1971). Great size is, however, not sufficient. For an interest group to influence the policy environment successfully, it also needs resources. Groups that have more resources can use them to mobilize members and influence elected officials through campaign contributions. In addition to size and resources, an interest group's strength is affected by its cohesion and the intensity of its members' support. Interest groups cannot present a unified, and therefore effective, front to policy officials if strong disagreements exist within the group over goals. The more cohesion within the membership, the more likely an interest group will have power to affect a bureaucracy's policy environment. As is the case with increased cohesion, an interest group's power is increased when its members intensely believe in the group's goals, in which case they are more likely to commit their personal resources toward the achievement of the goal and to base their electoral choices on the basis of candidate performance on issues of concern to the group.

Because the enforcement of gun control regulations is the primary responsibility of the agency, interest groups concerned with the issue of gun control dominate the ATF's environment. More appropriately, the NRA dominates the ATF's environment. In contrast to the NRA, gun control advocate groups are much smaller in size and resources. Perhaps the most well known gun control group is Handgun Control, Inc. (HCI). It dominates the gun control movement to the point that it is equated in the public mind with the movement itself (Sugarmann 1992, 253). Although gun control advocates are gaining members and financial resources, they still lag significantly behind their chief opponent, the NRA. HCI membership in 1985 stood at 120,000 with a budget of $3 million (Davidson 1993, 176). In contrast, by 1994 its membership had risen to 400,000 members and its budget to $7 million. Compare these figures to the NRA with more than 3 million members in 1993. Furthermore, the NRA had the resources to spend $1.6 million to aid the passage of the Firearms Owner Protection Act in

1986 (Spitzer 1995, 150)[8] and over $7 million to defeat the 1988 presidential bid of Dukakis (Davidson 1993, 142). The organization also spends liberally to aid candidates it likes, as evidenced by the $1.5 million it spent on Bush's 1988 presidential campaign (Stone 1993, 1336). Of perhaps greater importance to the members of Congress, the NRA spent $8.4 million on congressional races for the 1983 to 1992 period (Stone 1993, 1336). "But some lawmakers say more intimidating still is the human clout the rifle association can muster against a wayward lawmaker. Members who vote against the lobby can return home to find their town meetings and phone lines dominated by irate gun rights advocates" (Idelson 1993, 1023).

If the ATF has a natural constituency as a law enforcement agency, it would be the civilian law enforcement organizations. Two of the most notable law enforcement organizations are the Fraternal Order of Police and the International Association of Police Chiefs. Police organizations have generally been supportive of the bureau.[9] During the attempted dismantlement of the agency in the early 1980s, numerous police and fire departments submitted laudatory letters in support of the ATF. One letter from the director and chief of the Dayton Fire Department characterized the assistance provided by the ATF as "invaluable" and its role in the Department's success as "integral" (U.S. Senate 1982). However, prior to passage of the Firearms Owners' Protection Act (McClure-Volkmer) in 1986, which in effect served as a wake-up call, police organizations were not effective lobbyists. Since the NRA was typically supportive of law-and-order candidates, under most circumstances, it would seem, police organizations and the NRA should not be at odds. However, the NRA had opposed the prohibition on armor-piercing bullets (also called cop-killer bullets) and strongly favored McClure-Volkmer, two positions antipathetic to the police organizations. Particularly galling to some law enforcement leaders was the NRA's depiction of support for McClure-Volkmer as representative of law enforcement's views (Davidson 1993, 98).[10] Although law enforcement leaders attempted to dissuade senators from voting in favor of McClure—Volkmer by having uniformed police officers line the corridors outside the Senate chamber on the day of the vote, they were unsuccessful. Eventually, McClure-Volkmer passed, albeit without the provisions that would have allowed the interstate sale of handguns and the sale of new machine guns. In the words of Baltimore police chief Neil Behan, "It was at that point that we realized we had to organize in some fashion, to be able to present ourselves as a large organized group to the legislators—to offset the tremendous lobbying capability of the NRA" (Davidson 1993, 98–99).

Despite recent law enforcement support for the ATF, it appears to get less such support than the other law enforcement agencies. Local police forces are far more likely to have contact with the FBI and their labs and databases or the Drug Enforcement Agency (DEA) (through joint operations). Police are also more likely to identify with the elite federal agencies, the FBI and the Secret Service, than the ATF. Thus the ATF has sporadic support from law enforcement agencies and must deal with continued and focused opposition from the NRA. In total, this is not an environment conducive to gaining policy autonomy.

Is the ATF an Arbitrary Agency?

Critics of the ATF assert in no uncertain terms that the bureau is a "rogue agency" that arbitrarily and with no consideration for basic civil rights harasses and persecutes innocent, law-abiding citizens. The emphasis is on law-abiding. For example, an advertisement taken out by the NRA in 1986 asserted that congressional testimony by the ATF showed that 75 percent of cases filed by the ATF were against law-abiding citizens. The *Washington Post*, however, reported that in reality, 74 percent of those recommended for prosecution had previous criminal records (Cohen 1995). The "ATF official" quoted in the ad was Vernon D. Acree, who never was an ATF official. The closest Acree ever got to being an ATF official was in his capacity as an IRS official overseeing the agency. Acree has been quoted as saying, "I never worked for ATF. I'm a little concerned, frankly that the NRA may have taken it a bit out of context" (Kurtz 1986, A1). More recent statistics compiled by the ATF show that for fiscal years 1990 through 1995, 46 percent of the suspects arrested on the basis of firearms investigations had previous felony convictions (GAO 1996b, 6–7). Two episodes in recent history are particular favorites of agency opponents as examples of ATF abuses: Ruby Ridge and Waco.

Ruby Ridge and Waco

Randy Weaver, his wife, son, and three daughters lived in a cabin in the woods on Ruby Ridge in rural northern Idaho. In October 1989, Weaver sold two shotguns that had been shortened below the legal minimum length to an ATF informant. Based on information obtained via the informant, ATF agents felt that Weaver matched the profile of a major firearms supplier (Lardner 1995). Weaver failed to appear for a court hearing on the issue and was indicted. In August 1992, U.S. marshals were reconnoitering the Weaver homestead in preparation for arresting him when they came upon a friend of Weaver's, Weaver's son, and his dog. An exchange of shots left Weaver's son and one of the marshals dead. The deaths brought in the FBI; and before Weaver surrendered, his wife was also dead. Note that ATF agents were not involved either in the initial confrontation or in the shooting of Randy Weaver's wife. The FBI, not the ATF, was the primary law enforcement agency involved.

The ATF was more immediately involved in the events at Waco, Texas, in 1993 but not a participant in the final raid on the Branch Davidians that ended with the death of approximately 80 cult members. David Koresh and his followers had been stockpiling weapons at their compound near Waco, Texas, for over a year. These weapons included at least 45 assault rifles, grenades, and a grenade launcher. Concern over the weapons violations was exacerbated by charges that sexual abuse of children was taking place in the compound. ATF undercover agents infiltrated the cult and set a raid date of March 1. The initial raid depended on the element of surprise, which had been compromised. As a result, instead of a smooth operation resulting in the arrest of Koresh, 4 ATF agents were killed and 16 wounded. The FBI then took over and was responsible for the final assault on the compound on April 19, 1993.

ATF procedures require a written plan detailing the actions planned before any operation, such as the raid on the Branch Davidian compound, takes place. The written plan for the Waco operation, however, was completed hurriedly in the week just prior to the March 1 raid. Subsequent to the raid, various authorities began to request a copy of the raid plan. The support coordinator, incident commander, and tactical coordinator of the raid agreed among themselves that the plan as it stood was incomplete. They altered and distributed it without any indication that it was a revised version of the original plan. The Treasury Department report on its investigation of the events at Waco concluded, "The alterations indicate not an attempt to create a plan that existed in the minds of the tactical planners and raid commanders on February 28. Rather, they suggest a self-serving effort to clarify the assumptions on which the planners had relied and enhance the reader's sense of their professionalism" (Department of the Treasury 1993, 208). Subsequently, the incident commander and the tactical coordinator, Phillip J. Chojnacki and Charles Sarabyn, respectively, were placed on administrative leave.

Initially ATF director Stephen Higgins was unaware that the element of surprise, so crucial to the success of the operation, had been compromised and that Koresh had become aware of the imminent raid. However, Associate Director–Law Enforcement Daniel Hartnett, Deputy Associate Director–Law Enforcement Edward D. Conroy, and Chief of

Intelligence David Troy all were aware early on that the element of surprise had been lost. They made repeated public statements to the contrary and as a result lost their posts. Director Stephen Higgins was also found culpable. The Treasury Department's report concluded, "Higgins must accept responsibility for continuing to take public positions on the issue when repeated questions from the media and information readily available to him should have made it clear that he was on shaky ground. Higgins never adequately questioned his subordinates to determine the facts until early April" (Department of the Treasury 1993, 205). Higgins submitted a letter announcing his retirement effective October 30, but two days after he submitted the letter, Treasury Secretary Lloyd Bentsen removed Higgins from his post, replacing him with former Secret Service director John W. Magaw.

The evidence of Ruby Ridge and Waco do not provide a basis for concluding that the ATF is an arbitrary or capricious agency. ATF was not involved in Ruby Ridge; and although it was responsible for the inept first raid in Waco, it was not responsible for the final resolution. What transpired in the aftermath of the raid in Texas, the misleading and unprofessional behavior of those involved, however, is certainly troubling.

GAO Assessment

The GAO's report on the ATF's use of force (GAO 1996b) provides less subjective data on which to base an assessment of the agency's behavior. For the period of fiscal year 1990 through fiscal year 1995, the ATF averaged just under 12,800 investigations per year. The incidence of reported intentional shootings at suspects during this period averaged 6.5 per year, and the incidence of alleged excessive force involving bureau agents, slightly over 4 per year. The GAO's review of ATF records concluded "that all intentional shootings were justified[;] . . . most allegations of excessive use of force were unsubstantiated; and [the agency] sanctioned agents it determined had engaged in misconduct" (GAO 1996b, 4). In comparing the ATF's policies regarding the use of deadly force to those of the FBI and DEA, the GAO found them comparable. Of course, uniformity should have been expected at the time the GAO report was being completed due to the decision by the Departments of Treasury and Justice to adopt uniform policies for their agencies in fall 1995. But more interesting, the ATF's policy prior to the uniformity decision had also been quite consistent with those of its sister agencies (GAO 1996b, 5). The portrait provided by the GAO report on the whole is of an agency very much like counterpart agencies.

Other Indicators of Arbitrary Activities

The data examined by the GAO in assessing ATF actions that violate civil rights can be supplemented by data provided by the federal criminal justice system. Courts, in theory, protect citizens from arbitrary treatment at the hands of law enforcement agencies. Prosecutors should be more likely to decline to prosecute a case when officers have violated civil rights. Judges should be more likely to dismiss such cases were they to be prosecuted. When such cases actually do go to trial, the government should be more likely to lose. And should there be a conviction, the probability of an appeal should be higher.

Unfortunately, the database for federal criminal cases does not distinguish cases by arresting agency but rather by the law that was violated. As a result, we cannot compare the ATF to each of the other law enforcement agencies (the most appropriate comparison) but can only compare it to all five other agencies together and, because of the nature of drug crimes, the Drug Enforcement Agency. The latter comparison is especially useful because DEA has long had a reputation for being capricious and arbitrary in enforcement (Meier 1994; Lindesmith 1965).

Table 2.5 presents federal criminal data for 1988–1993 for all crimes, crimes involving fraud (and therefore subject to more discretion), drug crimes, and firearms crimes. Although prosecutors declined to prosecute nearly 31 percent of the ATF's cases, that figure is much lower than the overall average (albeit slightly higher than the DEA's). ATF cases are not distinguishable by their conviction rate (86.2%), which is slightly higher than the total rate and the DEA's rate. Similarly, the percentage of cases dismissed by the judge (13.5%) is not high, relatively speaking.

Although a slightly higher percentage of defendants insist on a trial on firearms violations, the acquittal percent is below the government average (but slightly higher than the DEA's). A substantial portion of firearm convictions generate appeals, but still the ATF's percentage is below that of the DEA.

The pattern of data presented in Table 2.5 shows that the ATF is not unusual for a federal law enforcement agency in terms of what happens to its cases. Whereas we cannot conclude that federal law enforcement agencies are or are not generally capricious and arbitrary (that would necessitate some comparison figures), there are no data to suggest the ATF is more abusive of citizens than other federal law enforcement agencies.

Conclusion

The contrasting images of the ATF are resolved by a more detailed look at the agency. In reality, the ATF is not a powerful bureaucracy. It is

TABLE 2.5
The Arbitrary Agency? Case Data for Selected Federal Offenses,
1988–1993

Type of Violation

	All	*Fraud*	*Drugs*	*Firearms*
Total Suspects Arrested	643,206	170,519	198,891	38,565
Prosecutions	365,928	85,177	148,900	24,815
Percent Declined to Prosecute	43.1%	50.1%	24.4%	30.8%
Terminations	358,522	69,393	124,553	19,403
Convictions	292,578	60,119	102,139	16,725
Percent Convicted	81.6%	86.4%	82.0%	86.2%
Dismissals	55,189	7,647	16,818	2,627
Percent Dismissed	15.4%	11.0%	13.5%	13.5%
Trials	43,009	5,284	18,057	3,139
Percent of Cases That Go to Trial	12.0%	7.6%	14.9%	16.2%
Trial Convictions	33,674	4,063	15,445	2,559
Acquittal Percent	21.7%	24.1%	14.4%	18.5%
Cases Appealed	54,695	7,110	29,424	4,343
Percent Appealed	18.7%	11.8%	28.8%	26.0%

Source: Calculated from *Annual Report of the Administrator of the U.S. Courts,* Washington, DC: Office of the Administrator of the Courts.

limited by legislation that details a specific and limited jurisdiction and is restricted in the procedures it can use to trace firearms. Compared to other law enforcement agencies, it has few resources and even less autonomy. The ATF is the weak sister of federal law enforcement agencies. It is an agency dominated by its environment. The ATF is often blamed for events it had no or little involvement in, and the ATF's actions reflect exactly what Congress and the president want—an agency on a short leash.

In terms of arbitrary behavior, perhaps the most important issue, we found little evidence to distinguish the ATF from the other federal law enforcement agencies. It is clearly no worse than its federal cohorts. What is clear, however, is that the NRA gains a distinct advantage if it can facilitate the perception of the ATF as a lawless group of jack-booted thugs. Protecting the civil rights of Americans is extremely important, but the credibility of the NRA on this issue can be considered no better than on other issues where the facts can be verified.

Notes

1. The Bureau of Prohibition's actual performance fell far short of the legendary Untouchables' reputation. The agency was corrupt, patronage-ridden, capricious, and generally ineffective (see Meier 1994, 141–145).

2. The impetus behind passage of the National Firearms Act was the growing intolerance of organized crime–related violence. Certainly its chances of passage were enhanced by the assassination attempt against President Roosevelt. The legislation banned the sale of machine guns and provided for the registration, licensing, and taxation of fully automatic firearms, short-barreled rifles, and shotguns. The Federal Firearms Act required gun manufacturers, dealers, and importers of firearms and pistol and revolver ammunition to have federal licenses. Two loopholes in the act, the modest cost of a dealer's license and the permissibility of dealers receiving firearms in interstate commerce, created incentives for private parties to obtain dealer licenses.

3. The trend from 1973 through 1980 is as follows: 1973, 2,589; 1974, 1,813; 1975, 899; 1976, 477; 1977, 336; 1978, 201; 1979, 30; 1980, 28.

4. Brewers are not regulated by the ATF largely due to persuasive lobbying on the part of brewers during the formulation and passage of the Federal Alcohol Administration Act.

5. One can get some data on total expenditures for alcohol and tobacco, since this is listed as a line item within the Internal Revenue Service budget.

6. An excellent example is an article appearing in the March 1991 issue of the *Police Chief* that favorably described the involvement of the ATF in a local enforcement program known as COP (Career Offender Project).

7. The irony of the militia movement's criticizing the ATF for racist behavior and attitudes should not be lost on the reader.

8. The Firearms Owners' Protection Act, also known as the McClure-Volkmer Act, was the first significant piece of federal legislation regarding gun control since the 1968 Gun Control Act. McClure-Volkmer resulted in major revisions to the 1968 law. It prohibited the establishment of a comprehensive

firearms registration system and prohibited the ATF from conducting any more than one unannounced inspection per year.

9. Interestingly, however, the NRA established the Law Enforcement for the Preservation of the Second Amendment organization headed by Leroy Pyle, an NRA board member, as an anti–gun regulation police group. There also exists a set of ostensibly independent organizations, headed by Gerald Arenberg and his associates, that take anti–gun regulation stances. These include the National Association of Chiefs of Police, the American Federation of Police, the American Law Enforcement Officers Association, Inc., and the Venerable Order of the Knights of Michael the Archangel, Inc. "They [any organization purporting to represent police] all look the same on television. As a result, Arenberg's organizations have begun to gain a higher profile on Capitol Hill, testifying before Congress and promising to represent the view of the 'cop on the beat' " (Sugarmann 1992, 196).

10. The International Union of Police Associations was the sole major police organization to support passage of McClure-Volkmer (Kurtz 1986).

3

Congress and Gun Control

Samuel C. Patterson and Keith R. Eakins

The Republicans won a stunning victory in the 1994 congressional elections, capturing control of both congressional houses for the first time in four decades. The new Republican Congress, and especially its ambitious conservative majority in the House of Representatives, eagerly pursued the legislative aims of its policy manifesto, the Contract with America. Though it was not part of the manifesto, many Republicans yearned to undo the Clinton administration's approach to crime, particularly to divert the trend toward increasing federal regulation of firearms. Twenty-nine of the 34 House Democratic incumbents who were defeated in the election had voted for the 1994 crime bill that prohibited the manufacture or importation of 19 specific semiautomatic weapons. This "assault weapons ban" legislation had been strongly opposed by the NRA, the 2.6 million-member organization fervently dedicated to preventing the passage of federal gun control laws.

House and Senate Republican leaders promised their rank-and-file members that an assault-weapons-ban repeal would be offered in 1995, but this was postponed in the aftermath of the April 1995 bombing of the federal building in Oklahoma City. Nevertheless, the House GOP leadership determined to schedule consideration of repeal in March 1996 despite some dissension in the Republican caucus among those who believed a vote would "send the wrong message," suggesting that Republican members were in the NRA's pocket. On March 22, House Rules Committee chairman Gerald Solomon (R-NY) offered the House a "closed" rule providing for consideration of the proposed Gun Crime Enforcement and Second Amendment Restoration Act. The closed rule required an "up or down" vote on the repeal proposal, prohibiting amendments and strictly limiting the time for debate.

In short order, as House vernacular prescribes, "a recorded vote was ordered," and "the vote was taken by electronic device." The repeal bill passed by a vote of 239 to 173. For representatives who had served in the previous Congress (the 103rd), the vote was nearly redundant; all members who voted for the assault weapons ban in 1994 voted against the 1996 repeal except for Sanford Bishop (D-GA), who had voted against the Brady Bill but reluctantly for the assault weapons ban. Three Republicans and one Democrat who had opposed the 1994 assault weapons ban nevertheless voted against the repeal (Peter Torkildsen, R-MA; Jim Ramstad, R-MI; Dick Zimmer, R-NJ; and Peter De-Fazio, D-OR). Accordingly, almost all the difference in the vote margins between 1994 and 1996 owed to the fact that 66 of the 74 freshman Republicans voted for repeal and another, George Radanovich (R-CA), was paired for repeal. Although the 1994 assault weapons ban passed the House by a very partisan vote, the 1996 repeal vote was even more partisan: 70 percent of the Democrats voted against repeal, and 81 percent of the Republicans voted in favor of repeal.

The anti–gun control adherents in the House, some of them Democrats, got what they needed most, an opportunity to go on record for their pro-gun constituents; the freshmen members, in particular, had the chance to justify the election campaign support they had received from the NRA (only 1 of the 60 new members who received NRA funding in 1995 voted against repeal). But the repeal vote was, after all, largely symbolic and political. It was apparent that the Senate would not consider the repeal issue. Senate Majority Leader Robert Dole (R-KS) indicated that he did not plan to schedule the repeal for Senate consideration and that he did not think it could pass the Senate. That, for the time being, was the end of the fight to repeal the ban on assault weapons. But that struggle epitomizes the story of gun control issues in Congress's hands since the 1960s.

Controlling Guns by Law

The problem of guns and crime in America has evolved so that it has become difficult for Congress to make effective policy decisions free from emotionalism, misconceptions, partisan myopia, undue lobbying pressure, or shortsighted political motives. Whereas national public opinion is generally quite favorable to regulation of firearms, many articulate and vocal Americans fervently oppose any gun controls on the "foot in the door" theory—that allowing minimal regulation would open the door to massive government prohibition of gun ownership. The principal single-interest groups, the NRA and Handgun Control, Inc. (HCI), face off uncompromisingly, preponderantly devoted to preventing or supporting federal gun control legislation. The gun control issue is inextricably intertwined in wider consideration of policies to fight crime, encouraging confusion of gun control and crime control. And firearms regulation has now become highly partisan, precipitating volatile disagreements between congressional Republicans and Democrats.

Moreover, debate over gun control issues is frequently very contentious and the decibel count is often high (Nisbet 1990, esp. 11–86). Congressional deliberation is said to be "fierce," "polarized," and "emotionally-charged." Members' remarks in debate are noted for their "virulence," members are said to be fervently "passionate," and members are charged with being "vitriolic." Gun control debate carries a very sharp edge. The 1996 repeal debate in the House replayed the emotionalism of the issue. Representative Patrick Kennedy (D-RI), a freshman Democrat and Senator Ted Kennedy's (D-MA) son, said:

> Families like mine all across this country know all too well what damage weapons can do, and you want to arm our people even more. You want to add more magazines to the assault weapons so they can spray and kill even more people.
>
> Shame on you. . . . This is nothing but a sham, to come on this floor and say you are going to have an open and fair debate about assault weapons. My God, all I have to say to you is, play with the devil, die with the devil.

Rules Committee chairman Gerald Solomon (R-NY) took umbrage, responding that "my wife lives alone 5 days a week in a rural area in upstate New York, [and] has a right to defend herself when I am not there, and don't you ever forget it" (*Congressional Record*, March 22, 1996, H2675). Away from the microphone, Solomon said to Kennedy, "Let's just step outside" (Greenblatt 1996, 803).

The brief debate on the assault weapons ban repeal replayed the standard arguments about gun control that characterize congressional debate. Some members echoed the familiar argument about the meaning of the Second Amendment to the U.S. Constitution—the "right to bear arms" (see Cottrol 1994). Bill Emerson (R-MO) said he had "anxiously awaited this opportunity to restore the second amendment rights of all Americans, which were unjustifiably stripped away by one of the worst laws this country has ever seen" (*Congressional Record*, March 22, 1996, H2678). Others argued over whether the assault weapons ban had been or would be effective in controlling guns or reducing crime. Bob Wise (D-WV) exemplified the pro-repeal argument that the legislation is ineffective; he asked, rhetorically, "How many prosecutions have there been since 1994, since this was passed? One" (*Congressional Record*, March 22, 1996, H2676). But members such as Benjamin Cardin (D-MD) contended that the law "is a reasonable effort to have less . . . assault weapons in the state, [and] it has saved lives and will continue to save lives" (*Congressional Record*, March 22, 1996, H2677).

Partisan disputations peppered the debate. Some Democrats complained that the repeal had been brought to the floor without committee deliberation, hearings, or report; Charles Schumer (D-NY) lamented that the rule for consideration of the repeal had been "brought to the floor faster than an Uzi's bullet" (*Congressional Record*, May 22, 1996, H2673). Republicans argued that the gun control issue had been debated fully, and the repeal merited only brief debate and an "up or down" vote. Some Democrats claimed, a few stridently, that the Republican leaders were pandering to the NRA for campaign money; Nydia Valazquez (D-NY) said Republican members "should be ashamed of yourselves, letting the NRA pistol whip you again" (*Congressional Record*, March 22, 1996, H2678). Still others made the familiar pro-gun argument that "guns don't kill people, people kill people" and that the law ought to be focused on criminals rather than on guns. Indeed, the repeal proposal included language strengthening penalties against those committing crimes using guns. The strongest argument on this score was rendered by Mac Collins (R-GA), who spoke of a criminal who shot and killed a Georgia police officer: "We got rid of that scum, we executed him. . . . Let us get rid of the scum, not law abiding citizens" (*Congressional Record*, March 22, 1996, H2693).

Gun control has not always been such an emotionally charged political issue. Many laws regulate firearms in this country; the vast majority are state and local laws (see Kleck 1991, 323–358). The most famous of these, New York's Sullivan Act, was passed by the New York legislature in 1911. Federal laws on the subject have been few and far between. Beginning in the 1920s, on the wings of urbanization, spectacular crime waves, and wider possession of guns, demands grew for modest federal legislation to help states and cities enforce their firearms regulations. For instance, in 1927, Congress passed legislation prohibiting sending handguns in the mail. But major federal legislation was seldom seriously considered and rarely enacted. And new gun control legislation has tended to result from a shock to the peace and order of the community in the form of a major escalation of criminal violence.

The first major congressional legislation was the National Firearms Act of 1934, which levied a heavy federal tax on the manufacture and distribution of gangster weapons—machine guns, sawed-off shotguns, and silencers. Passage of this legislation was prompted by an alarming rise in urban crime—punctuated by the 1929 St. Valentine's Day massacre in Chicago, when five mobsters machine-gunned to death a group of seven rival gang members—and, more immediately, by the attempt in 1933 to assassinate President Franklin D. Roosevelt in Miami. Then in 1938, Congress passed the Federal Firearms Act, prohibiting shipment of firearms across state lines by manufacturers or dealers lacking a federal license and in other ways restricting the interstate shipment of guns (see Korwin 1995). "The first serious discussion of a more extensive federal role in firearms regulation came in the early years of the New Deal," but the legislation of the 1930s was largely "a symbolic denunciation of firearms in the hands of criminals, coupled with an inexpensive and ineffective regulatory scheme that did not inconvenience the American firearms industry or its customers" (Zimring 1975, 137, 143).

The Gun Control Act of 1968

After three decades of relative quiet on the gun control front, a new wave of demand for a stronger federal role swelled in the 1960s. This demand was fueled by the assassination of President John F. Kennedy in Dallas on November 22, 1963; the urban riots beginning in 1964; and the murders of Martin Luther King in Memphis on April 4 and Robert F. Kennedy in San Francisco on June 6, 1968. The House of Representatives passed an omnibus crime bill containing gun control provisions the day after Robert Kennedy was assassinated, and a few weeks later, with the tide in favor of stricter federal firearms regulations, Congress enacted the Gun Control Act of 1968.

The 1968 legislation had a tortuous history. It was championed, beginning in the early 1960s, by Senator Thomas J. Dodd (D-CT), a member of the Judiciary Committee and chairman of its Subcommittee on Juvenile Delinquency. In 1963, Dodd introduced legislation to tighten restrictions on the sale of handguns through the mail. He added "long guns"—rifles and shotguns—to his bill after President Kennedy was murdered with a military-style, mail-order rifle. Dodd's bill, along with others, was referred to the Commerce Committee, chaired by Senator Warren G. Magnuson (D-WA). Both the Commerce Committee and the Subcommittee on Juvenile Delinquency held hearings on these gun control bills beginning in December 1963 and running through the end of April 1964. Although NRA leaders had taken a hand in drafting

Dodd's bill, they did not inform their members of this fact. NRA publications stimulated substantial anti–gun control mail addressed to members of Congress. Moreover, Senator Magnuson opposed the legislation. The Commerce Committee refused to report the bill to the Senate floor.

In March 1965, President Lyndon B. Johnson sent his first crime control message to Congress, proposing strict gun control legislation. Senator Dodd introduced the administration bill in the Senate, and in contrast to the earlier bills, it was referred to the Judiciary Committee on the rationale that it dealt with the Second Amendment right to bear arms. Senator Dodd's Juvenile Delinquency Subcommittee and the House Committee on Ways and Means held extensive hearings on the legislation, but under heavy pressure from the NRA, the American Legion, and gun importers, manufacturers, and dealers to defer consideration, they reported no bill. In March 1966 the Senate Juvenile Delinquency Subcommittee approved a watered-down version of the administration's gun control bill and sent it to the full Judiciary Committee, where it languished for seven months and then was rejected.

With the continuing support of President Johnson, Dodd again introduced the administration's gun control proposal in 1967 and his subcommittee again held hearings, but the full Commerce Committee refused to act on the bill. However, new developments were evidenced in the House of Representatives. House Judiciary Committee chairman Emanuel Celler (D-NY) introduced the administration's gun control bill; subcommittee hearings were held, and the subcommittee reported the bill favorably to the full committee. Despite strong urgings by President Johnson and House Speaker John W. McCormack (D-MA) that the bill be reported to the House floor, the committee refused to act on it. These delays and inactions contributed to growing pressures to enact gun control legislation, but pro–gun control forces were poorly organized and the NRA's efforts against the administration's proposals were relentless.

President Johnson and his administration intensified their fight for anticrime and gun control legislation. In his 1968 State of the Union message, the president urged Congress to pass a gun control law that would prevent "mail order murder." In June 1968, President Johnson sent Congress a special message in which he ardently proposed "first, the national registration of every gun in America," and "second, . . . that every individual in this country be required to obtain a license before he is entrusted with a gun" (see *Congressional Quarterly Weekly Report*, June 28, 1968, 1634). The president's overall crime legislation, the Safe Streets and Crime Control Bill, was debated at length in both the Senate and the House of Representatives during 1968, when the proposal was subjected to a number of weakening amendments. This legislation was ultimately adopted by both houses of Congress and signed by President Johnson, although the president lamented the bill's weak anticrime provisions, including its gun control section.

The tide of support for stronger federal gun control laws became more or less irresistible after the murders of Senator Robert F. Kennedy and Rev. Martin Luther King Jr. President Johnson sent Congress proposed legislation requiring registration of all firearms and prohibiting mail-order sales of rifles and shotguns. A number of senators and representatives who previously had opposed strict legislation switched to support of a strong bill. Pro–gun control advocates, marshaled by the bipartisan Emergency Committee for Gun Control, had finally organized themselves to counteract the well-funded efforts of the NRA to frustrate federal gun regulation. The House Judiciary Committee promptly reported a bill to extend the restrictions on handgun sales to long guns and restrict the sale and transportation of guns and ammunition. After a three-week delay the bill was cleared by the Rules Committee. The House passed the bill on July 24, 1968, after four days of debate and a bipartisan vote of 305–118. In the course of its deliberation, the House voted on 45 amendments to the bill, accepting 18 and rejecting 27—including amendments to require registration of all firearms and the licensing of all gun owners.

The Senate Judiciary Committee approved a gun control bill with provisions similar to those of the House bill; the Commerce Committee waived its right to partake in consideration of the bill. After five days of debate, action on 17 amendments, and 11 roll-call votes, the full Senate on September 18 adopted the bill by a bipartisan vote of 70–17. In the House-Senate conference to iron out differences in the two houses' versions of the legislation, the Senate's stronger provisions for ammunition controls prevailed over the House version; Senate conferees accepted language from the House bill regarding interstate shipment of weapons. Congress cleared the final bill on October 9–10, the Senate by voice vote and the House by the unexpectedly close vote of 160–129 with a third of the members not voting.

The new gun control law contained three major provisions (Wright, Rossi, and Daly 1983, 246–247; Zimring 1975). First, it prohibited the traffic in firearms and ammunition between states, evening out controls on gun traffic between the more restrictive and the less restrictive states. Second, it denied access to firearms to specifically defined groups—convicted felons, fugitives from justice, drug addicts, the mentally ill, and minors. Third, it banned the importation of surplus military firearms into the United States and prohibited the importation of guns and ammunition not certified by the secretary of the Treasury as legitimate souvenirs or for sporting purposes. The legislation restricted interstate shipments of guns and ammunition to those manufacturers, importers, dealers, or collectors who were properly licensed by the U.S. government. The provisions of the new law proved difficult to enforce, and Congress did not provide sufficient funding to the Treasury Department's Division of Alcohol, Tobacco, and Firearms (after 1972, reorganized as the separate Bureau of Alcohol, Tobacco, and Firearms—BATF) for effective enforcement.

The Gun Control Act of 1968 was the most substantial congressional regulation of firearms in 30 years. It was also one of the most contentious and controversial bills considered by Congress in the post–World War II era (Spitzer 1995, 146). In signing the legislation, President Johnson said, "Today we begin to disarm the criminal and the careless and the insane . . . but this bill . . . still falls short because we just could not get the Congress to carry out the requests . . . for the national registration of all guns and the licensing of those who carry those guns" (*Congressional Quarterly Weekly Report*, November 1, 1968, 3066). The legislation was adopted with some reluctance by Congress, spurred by the shocks of rising crime and the brutal assassinations of popular leaders. The legislative process generated a great deal of conflict despite the fact that the provisions of the ultimate legislation were modest. One scholar has said that "the Gun Control Act was the most sweeping federal gun regulation up to that time [but] its scope was very modest [and] its impact was minimal" (Spitzer 1995, 147).

The Firearms Owners' Protection Act of 1986

The ink was barely dry on President Johnson's signature on the Gun Control Act of 1968 when efforts were initiated to undermine its minimal regulation of firearms. Two congressional archenemies of federal gun control, Representative Harold Volkmer (D-MO) and Senator James McClure (R-ID), had for years sought ways to revise and weaken the 1968 act. After 20 years of effort, opportunity knocked in the mid-1980s. Congress adopted the so-called McClure-Volkmer amendments, in the form of the Firearms Owners' Protection Act of 1986.

Anti–gun control advocates had several times sought to repeal or eviscerate the Gun Control Act of 1968, but in the 1970s their attempts were frustrated by virtue of Senator Ted Kennedy's (D-MA) chairmanship of the Senate Judiciary Committee. Kennedy's pivotal committee role—using the tactics of filibustering and the "disappearing quorum"—successfully prevented action to repeal the 1968 law. In the House of Representatives, a similarly protective role was played by

Representative Peter Rodino (D-NJ), who chaired the House Judiciary Committee after 1973 and who "routinely strangled the NRA's bills" (Davidson 1993, 55). When Volkmer entered the House in 1977 he vowed repeal of the 1968 law. The Republican successes in the 1980 election, which placed Ronald Reagan in the White House, gave the Republicans a Senate majority, and renewed strength in the growing membership and determination of the NRA precipitated greater repeal efforts.

The McClure-Volkmer Bill proposed repealing the 1968 law's prohibitions on sales of certain firearms to persons from another state; allowing certain convicted felons to own guns (if their crimes involved only business practices); legalizing ammunition purchases by mail and relaxing the ammunition record keeping required of dealers; prohibiting the government from banning the importation of sporting weapons; exempting gun dealers from recording firearms sales under certain circumstances; and constraining the power of the Bureau of Alcohol, Tobacco, and Firearms to inspect dealers' records of firearms sales. On the key issue, that of a ban on the interstate sale of firearms, both sides of the gun control fight agreed to a compromise that would repeal the ban for all weapons except for small handguns—the so-called Saturday night specials.

The McClure-Volkmer Bill languished for many months in committee, and when it finally was reported by the Senate Judiciary Committee in 1984, no action was taken by the Senate. But the NRA anointed it a "bill of rights for America's gun owners," and pressures for adoption of the bill escalated (Davidson 1993, 58). Senator McClure reintroduced the bill in the 99th Congress—on January 3, 1985. Rather than again sending the bill through the process of Senate committee deliberation, Majority Leader Robert Dole (R-KS) ordered it immediately listed on the Senate calendar for floor debate and action.

A few weeks later, Dole called for a Senate vote on the proposed legislation. After much tugging and pulling between gun control advocates and opponents, and after the McClure-Volkmer proposal had won 52 Senate cosponsors, the Senate voted on July 9 to pass the legislation relaxing some of the provisions of the 1968 law and making easier both gun ownership and the transportation of guns across state lines. The amendments adopted, together called the Firearms Owners' Protection Act of 1986, passed the Senate by a vote of 79–15. On the House side, the Democrats remained the majority party, and Representative Rodino remained chairman of the Judiciary Committee. Staunchly opposed to weakening the 1968 law, Rodino sought vigorously to marshal the gun control supporters in the House. But the momentum on the gun control issue had now shifted toward the position

of the NRA and other anti–gun control groups. Supporters of the Mc-
Clure-Volkmer Bill in the House successfully discharged the bill from
the Judiciary Committee, and after some intricate parliamentary ma-
neuvers and five roll-call votes on amendments and motions, the
House passed the bill on April 10 by a wide margin, 292–130.

The Reagan administration played only a minor role in congressional deliberation about gun control issues, although part of the by-
play during the legislative process involved NRA efforts to neutralize
Attorney General Edwin Meese's reservations about the McClure-Volkmer Bill (Davidson 1993, 67–69). The passage of the 1986 legislation
represented "the zenith of the NRA's influence on Capitol Hill"
(Spitzer 1995, 150; also Leddy 1987). The organization campaigned vigorously in Washington, D.C., and at its grass roots for Senate action,
the success of the discharge strategy in the House, and ultimate House
approval. As a leading student of interest group influences on Congress has pointed out, "The success of the NRA and its allies . . . dem-
onstrates clearly how a passionate and well-organized minority
interest can prevail over an unorganized and dispassionate majority
interest" (Wright 1996, 189). The NRA's grassroots lobbying and its
contributions to the congressional campaigns of pro-gun candidates
significantly influenced the voting of members of Congress on the Mc-
Clure-Volkmer bill (Langbein and Lotwis 1990).

The lawmaking process entailed various other changes in the basic
law, the Gun Control Act of 1968, during the 1980s (see Jacobs, Foster,
and Siegel, 1995, 18–20). The worrisome increase in the threat of firearm use against police officers activated law enforcement groups' (the
Fraternal Order of Police, the National Sheriff's Association, the National Troopers Coalition, and the International Association of Chiefs
of Police) concerns about gun control. Moreover, the organizational
strengthening of the leading pro–gun control group, Handgun Control, Inc., sharpened lobbying efforts to regulate firearms. In 1985 Congress enacted amendments to the 1968 Gun Control Act (called the
Law Enforcement Officers Protection Act) to prohibit the manufacture
and importation of "cop-killer" bullets capable of penetrating the bulletproof vests frequently worn by law enforcement officers. This legislation for the first time pitted the nation's police officers and the NRA
against one another. Further legislative efforts evolved from growing
concern about the danger of airplane hijacking, provoking Congress to
pass the Undetectable Firearms Act of 1988. This legislation prohibits
the manufacture of so-called plastic guns, which cannot be detected by
airport security equipment. But a major shock to the American political
system, the attempted assassination of President Ronald Reagan, precipitated the most dramatic gun control law of the 1990s.

The Brady Bill

On March 30, 1981, only a few weeks after his inauguration as president of the United States, Ronald Reagan stepped outside the Washington Hilton Hotel in the nation's capital, accompanied by members of his staff and Secret Service agents. A man with a handgun—John W. Hinckley Jr.—approached the entourage, firing at the president. Indeed, most assassinations or attempted assassinations of major political figures in the United States have been carried out with handguns (Clarke 1982, 269). President Reagan and three others were wounded. One of the wounded was the presidential press secretary, James S. Brady, who was permanently disabled by his injuries. "Without John Hinckley," one writer argues, "there would be no Brady bill" (Kopel 1995, 57). Moreover, Brady became a symbol of the evils of unfettered handgun ownership, and his wife, Sarah Brady, became the head of Handgun Control, Inc., the leading group seeking congressional support for laws regulating firearms.

The Gun Control Act of 1968 banned the sale of handguns to felons and fugitives from justice, but it was not difficult for criminals to acquire firearms by lying about their criminal record. Law enforcement groups and Handgun Control, Inc., argued that the law needed to require background checks on purchasers of guns, which would necessitate a waiting period. The Bradys determined to see such a change in gun regulation. The Brady Bill was introduced in Congress in February 1987, but its prospects suffered from opposition by President Reagan and subsequently by President George Bush and House Speaker Tom Foley (D-WA).

Following considerable behind-the-scenes maneuvering after the Brady Bill cleared the House Judiciary Committee and strong-arm tactics by the NRA in lobbying against the bill, a substitute was offered by NRA-backed Representative Bill McCollum (D-FL) that would have required the attorney general to develop an instant check system whereby dealers could access a Justice Department computer database for information about prospective gun purchasers. When a vote was finally recorded in September 1988, the McCollum substitute won by a lopsided House vote of 228 to 182 (see Davidson 1993, 193–199). The Brady Bill had failed its first congressional test.

But the struggle for minimal gun control legislation intensified. Handgun Control, Inc., won the support of the bar, the medical association, trade unions, law enforcement officers, and many public officials for handgun control. President Bill Clinton, elected in 1992, announced his firm support for the Brady Bill. Public opinion polls showed strong support for a waiting period and background check for gun purchasers. The leverage of the NRA had weakened; its adamant opposition to even the most minimal gun regulation, in the face of growing problems of crime and drug-related violence, came to seem extreme. Lobbying in support of gun control became more focused and more effective. It also became more visible as James Brady himself began to lobby personally for handgun control. He told senators, "Many members of Congress don't want to stand up for the Brady bill because of all the aggravation they'd get from the gun lobby," but "their aggravation is minimal compared to the aggravation I face every day. . . . I want action on the Brady bill" (Biskupic 1989, 3314).

In 1991, the Bush administration sought the enactment of sweeping anticrime legislation. The proposals were swept up in the infighting between the Bush White House and the congressional Democratic party majority, and no legislation was enacted. The bill was, however, notable for the fact that both House and Senate versions incorporated provisions for a waiting period for purchasing handguns. The struggle continued throughout 1992 with intense party conflict especially reflected in cloture votes in the Senate on anticrime legislation. When efforts to pass a crime bill were exhausted, Senate Majority Leader George J. Mitchell (D-ME) and pro–gun control advocate Howard M. Metzenbaum (D-OH) sought Senate approval of the Brady Bill apart from the provisions of the failed anticrime effort. Anti–gun control Republicans, led by Larry E. Craig (R-ID), squelched the effort to regulate handguns.

With President Bill Clinton in the White House, the climate for gun control brightened. When Clinton addressed Congress on economic issues shortly after his inauguration, he digressed in order to endorse handgun legislation. "If you pass the Brady bill, I'll sure sign it," the president said (Idelson 1993, 1021). The threat of a presidential veto, very real during the Reagan and Bush administrations and requiring a two-thirds congressional vote to override, was now not a factor in the gun control deliberations. After seven years of congressional consideration and revision, the Brady Bill provided a waiting period of five days for gun purchases. This waiting period would be in effect only until the Justice Department had put into place a nationwide instant-check system to determine if purchasers had a criminal record. No matter what the status of the instant-check system, the waiting period would be abolished in five years. Although it was difficult to argue that the Brady Bill would, if passed, have a major impact on gun ownership, it had become an important symbolic issue (see, for instance, Sugarmann 1992, 259–263).

Both symbolic and substantive issues provoked a vigorous, partisan debate in the House of Representatives. The House considered several floor amendments and adopted the five-year sunset provision. But other weakening amendments were rejected, including one by Bill Mc-Collum (R-FL) preempting state waiting periods as soon as the instant-check system functioned. On November 10, 1993, the House passed the bill by a vote of 238–189. Nearly three-fourths of the House Democrats voted for the Brady Bill; about seven-tenths of the Republicans opposed it. On the Senate side, the Brady Bill's advocates competed for floor consideration with a very controversial crime bill and a sweeping proposed ban on so-called assault weapons. In mid-November, an agreement had been reached among Senate leaders—Majority Leader George J. Mitchell (D-ME), Minority Leader Bob Dole (R-KS), and Judiciary Committee Chairman Joseph R. Biden Jr. (D-DE)—on a compromise version of the bill. But floor debate was very tense, and two cloture motions failed on November 19.

It was feared that the bill was dead. But President Clinton pressed for passage, and some Republicans who had voted against ending debate had a change of heart, unwilling to take the blame for killing the bill. The compromise bill finally passed the Senate by a vote of 63–36 with Republicans split and most Democrats voting yea. After a raucous conference between members of the two houses, the provisions of the House bill were largely agreed to, and the conference report was finally agreed to on November 24 by a lopsided vote in the House and a voice vote in the Senate. President Clinton signed the bill on November 30. The Brady Bill, now the Brady Handgun Violence Prevention Act of 1993, was the first major piece of gun control legislation in a quarter of a century.

The Struggle to Ban Assault Weapons

Stockton, California, rarely makes the national news. But a drifter named Patrick E. Purdy with a long criminal record and suffering from drug and alcohol abuse came back to Stockton just after Christmas in 1988. Shortly before lunch on January 17, 1989, he went onto the schoolyard of Cleveland Elementary School, where he had attended kindergarten through second grade, and opened fire on children and teachers with an AK-47 assault rifle. He killed 5 students and wounded 29 other students and a teacher; then, he killed himself (Davidson 1993, 3–19). This and other incidents involving "assault weapons"—semiautomatic, magazine-loaded rifles, shotguns, or handguns—precipitated growing public and government concern (Kopel 1995, 159–232). A spate of bills was introduced in Congress to prohibit the importation, manufacture, sale, and ownership of assault weapons. In March 1989 the Bush administration ordered a ban on importing 40 different foreign-made assault weapons, including the offensive AK-47, suspending some 110,000 applications to the BATF for assault weapons ownership. This represented a reversal of position for President Bush, a longtime NRA member and opponent of gun control legislation; evidently he had been urged by administration drug czar William J. Bennett. The import ban was expanded and made permanent in July.

At the same time, congressional efforts were under way to enact controls on assault weapons, both imported and of domestic manufacture. In the Senate, Howard Metzenbaum (D-OH) and Dennis DeConcini (D-AZ) introduced somewhat different versions of the assault ban legislation. DeConcini's bill, also supported by Metzenbaum, won Judiciary Committee approval by the narrow margin of 7 to 6 largely because Senator Patrick J. Leahy (D-VT) switched from opposition to support for the ban and Senator Arlen Specter (R-PA) abstained. As the pending crime bill headed toward the Senate floor, Senator Dianne Feinstein (D-CA) proposed different language for the assault ban, providing a middle ground between the Metzenbaum and DeConcini proposals. The three senators agreed on a joint proposal to prohibit the manufacture or importation of 19 specific semiautomatic weapons including the Uzi, the TEC-9, and the Street Sweeper and their copycats and to ban magazines holding more than ten rounds of ammunition. The Feinstein compromise exempted 650 sporting and hunting weapons and existing semiautomatic weapons. It won Senate approval in November 1993 as part of the crime bill. First, the Senate voted by the slim margin of 49–51 to reject a motion to kill the Feinstein amendment; then the ban was approved by the more comfortable margin of 56–43.

In August 1993, President Clinton announced the central features of the administration's anticrime measures, including a ban on assault weapons. On the House side, an assault weapons ban had been defeated by 70 votes in 1991, the day after George J. Hennard killed 22 people, wounded 23 others, and then killed himself with an assault rifle in Killeen, Texas. In 1993, House consideration of the anticrime bill advocated by President Clinton involved lengthy deliberation and negotiation. The 115 new House members elected in 1992 were not yet on record on gun control issues, and their positions were uncertain. By then the gun control issue had aroused very emotional debate and vigorous lobbying activity, especially on the part of the NRA.

The House Judiciary Committee did not report a bill providing an assault weapons ban until April 1994, grudgingly agreed to by committee chairman Jack Brooks (D-TX), a staunch foe of gun control who bowed to White House pressure but hoped the ban would lose on the House floor or in conference with the Senate. The House Democratic leaders were divided with Speaker Foley opposed to the weapons ban and Majority Leader Richard Gephardt (D-MO) in favor of it. The mood was tense in the House when the assault weapons ban was considered in May. President Clinton vigorously sought House members' support for the ban. Thanks to the switched vote of Representative Andrew Jacobs Jr. (D-IN), the measure passed the House by the narrow margin of 216–214 (Idelson 1994). Most House Democrats (70%) voted for the ban; most Republicans (78%) voted against it. In August both the House and Senate approved the conference report for the omnibus crime bill that embraced the assault-weapons-ban provisions. Approval came only after a remarkable procedural setback on the House floor and vociferous but unsuccessful Republican efforts to make last-minute changes in the conference report (Spitzer 1995, 152–157). President Clinton signed the Violent Crime Control Act, including the assault weapons ban, on September 13, 1994.

The assault weapons issue had an exhausting legislative history. The vehemence of conflict over gun control has been abetted by the high salience of this issue in American politics. In the two decades before 1988, "no bill to expand gun control came to a vote on the floor of either house of Congress," but "from 1988 to 1994, twenty-seven floor votes on gun bills were taken (on assault weapons, banning handgun sales to minors, and the Brady bill)" (Spitzer 1995, 170). In the five years prior to the enactment of the assault weapons legislation, both House and Senate had voted on the assault weapons ban six times. These votes reflected the highly conflictual politics surrounding the gun control issue, the vigorous pro- and anti–gun control lobbying involved, the unusual procedural maneuvering undertaken, and the partisanship evoked by the issue.

Salience and Conflict

Until the 1960s, firearms legislation was considered largely a matter for the states and municipalities. The federal government, and the publics to whom its representatives responded, paid virtually no attention to issues of gun control. But beginning with the wrenching public reaction to the assassination of John F. Kennedy in 1963, subsequent highly publicized gun violence, and the massive growth in the manufacture, distribution, and ownership of firearms, gun control evolved as a highly salient issue in American politics. The congressional reverberations of higher national salience for gun control issues were often hesitant, minimal, and grudging. Moreover, from the 1960s to the 1990s, federal regulation of firearms became highly conflictual and ultimately polarized along political party lines.

The Clash of Interests

The contours of the political landscape of gun control have changed over the past several decades. Until after World War II, the NRA paid little attention to the congressional arena and very few gun control laws were proposed (Leddy 1987, 196–200). In the early 1960s, some NRA leaders actually supported legislation sponsored by Senator Thomas J. Dodd (D-CT) that would have prohibited the mail-order sale of pistols and revolvers. But by 1965, the NRA was positioned in stout opposition to federal regulation, urging its 700,000-plus members to write members of Congress in strong opposition to President Lyndon B. Johnson's firm crime and gun control proposal. By the end of the 1960s, NRA opposition to any federal regulation of guns reached a peak. In its house organ the NRA editorialists tarred gun control advocates as "fanatics" and "extremists determined to destroy what we know and treasure as the American way of life" (from the *American Rifleman*; quoted in the *Congressional Quarterly Weekly Report* 26 April 12, 1968, 814). Thereafter, the NRA relentlessly opposed any federal regulation of firearms.

For a number of years there were no organized, powerful pressure groups to counterbalance the considerable political clout of the NRA in the legislative arena. The NRA grew in membership and budget and expanded its lobbying activities. In the late 1960s efforts were made to counter the NRA's lobbying power, but the efforts of police organizations, city officials, and the American Bar Association to support gun controls largely took the form of endorsements, not organized lobbying efforts. Coalitional attempts, such as the formation of the Council for a Responsible Firearms Policy and its Emergency Committee for Gun Control, sought to mobilize pro–gun control groups. Through petition drives and advertising, the gun control advocates and groups waged a battle for adoption of the Gun Control Act of 1968.

These pro–gun control political activities spotlighted regulatory efforts and stimulated very vigorous, energetic lobbying efforts by the NRA, which had grown to a membership of more than 900,000. The Gun Control Act became law, but anti–gun control efforts were redoubled, and the pro–gun control forces were still not sufficiently well organized for long-term pressure politics. However, by the mid-1980s Handgun Control, Inc., and law enforcement groups emerged as credible lobbyists through their experience in attempting to forestall passage of the Firearms Owners' Protection Act of 1986, the NRA-favored legislation weakening the 1968 law. In addition, public concern over crime has served as a check to the NRA's lobbying power. The NRA is still by far the most formidable player in gun control politics, but the group's political power—both in myth and reality—has waned in the past decade.

During the gun control legislation battles of the 1960s, the NRA, although it had no registered lobbyists, was the most powerful gun rights organization. It still enjoys this distinction, although it has undergone significant change. Its membership has risen from 900,000 in 1968 to about 2.6 million today. This substantial increase has provided the group with a wider base of grassroots support as well as a more ample budget. In 1967 the group spent only $131,000 on legislative activities, but by 1992 NRA expenditures on political activities had increased to $28.9 million (see Stone 1993, 1335). The NRA also has its own political action committee (PAC), the Political Victory Fund (PVF), set up in 1976 in order to provide campaign funds to candidates and incumbents favoring NRA positions. The key to the NRA's effectiveness has not changed over the years. It is the group's ability to keep its large membership informed about gun control legislation and induce it to bring considerable and immediate pressure on Congress through phone calls, letters, face-to-face meetings, and other forms of communication.

Several factors help account for the political strength of the NRA. First, the group has been around for a long time and has considerable political experience and expertise. Traditionally, the group has had close ties with powerful leaders in government and the gun industry, and it has used these advantages well to strengthen the organization financially and politically. NRA board members and executives have included political professionals such as Pentagon officials and congressional leaders. Second, the NRA often motivates its members by fostering an emotionally charged us-against-them atmosphere and characterizing pending gun control legislation as crises leading to the government ban of gun ownership. The information it sends its members, although often deceptive and inaccurate, is also polemical and alarmist and therefore effective at inducing immediate action. Third and probably most important, the NRA membership is composed of a core group of individuals who share a strong, vital culture in their passion for firearms. These individuals are intensely devoted to gun rights and are highly motivated for political action when they perceive a need to defend and protect their cause. In addition, in contrast to gun control supporters who may consider a number of different issues when casting a legislative vote, NRA members' advocacy rests solely on congressional candidates' position on gun control. Its forte is single-issue politics. The group has been credited with the defeat of a few former legislators who faced tough reelection bids as well as numerous migraine headaches for those unfortunate legislators who became its targets. Risk-averse legislators, especially those in southern and western congressional districts, are well aware of the extreme devotion NRA members have for their cause and may support NRA positions in order to avoid the hassle from gun devotees in their district.

However, some of the NRA's tactics that served them relatively well in the past are now sapping their political strength. Traditionally, the group has taken extremely rigid positions on legislation, bitterly opposing even very modest restrictions on guns and ammunition. The group's zero-tolerance approach to gun control is based in part on its belief, not fully unjustified, that there are gun control advocates who would not stop pushing for additional measures until guns were completely banned. Yet this tough stance has caused problems for the NRA's public image. The most notable example is the group's initial opposition in the mid-1980s to the ban of what gun control advocates shrewdly termed "cop-killer bullets"—ammunition that could pierce a police officer's protective armor. This and the NRA's more recent unyielding position against the Brady Bill and the assault weapons ban have fueled the public's perception of the NRA as extremist. This public perception has led to the dilution of the NRA's power on the congressional battleground.

Pro–gun control groups first sprang up to support firearms legislation after the political assassinations in the 1960s. However, these groups did not achieve much power and prominence relative to the NRA until Sarah Brady joined Handgun Control, Inc. (HCI) in the mid-1980s. In 1981, HCI's membership numbered approximately 100,000. It currently has a membership of over 400,000 and an annual budget exceeding $7 million (Spitzer 1995, 115–116). Though HCI still has only a fraction of the resources possessed by the NRA, it proved itself a force to be reckoned with through its successful fight to enact the Brady Bill. The group's success can be attributed partially to its tactics, which it modeled after its formidable adversary, the NRA. Like the NRA, HCI has worked to foster a strong grassroots membership, but the organization also embraces the NRA strategy of using inflammatory and dubious rhetoric to frame the issue and discredit the opposition.

The NRA and the police traditionally had maintained a fairly warm relationship. Thousands of police were NRA members, and the group conducted some training programs for local police. A struggle in the mid-1980s over legislation banning armor-piercing bullets badly strained relations between the NRA, which had initially opposed the bill, and law enforcement. And when police groups became actively involved in opposing the NRA-sponsored legislation weakening the Gun Control Act of 1968 and when they witnessed the NRA's aggressive lobbying, relations between the two groups markedly deteriorated. By 1993, the NRA and major police organizations were at each others' throats, exchanging bitter charges and vitriolic newspaper and magazine advertisements (e.g., see Davidson 1993, 102).

An equally significant change was the entrance of law enforcement groups in the gun control lobbying arena. Prior to their involvement in the struggle over the Firearms Owners' Protection Act, law enforcement groups had mainly confined their legislative efforts to occasionally testifying in congressional hearings and endorsing bills. These groups, such as police chiefs, black law enforcement executives, and police unions were heterogeneous and frequently disagreed with each other on issues. However, faced with the prospect of the repeal of the 1968 Gun Control Act and the attendant potential harm it could cause to law enforcement, police groups suddenly became unified and organized in opposing the NRA bill. Although they were inexperienced and late in their lobbying efforts against the 1986 bill, law enforcement emerged as an energized and credible lobbyist in gun control politics.

It is not easy to overstate the crucial role of the president of the United States in providing decisive leadership for or against federal regulation of guns. One need only recall the role of President Lyndon B. Johnson in the passage of the Gun Control Act of 1968. He fervently lobbied Congress on behalf of effective controls on firearms, saying, "in the name of sanity . . . and in the name of safety and in the name of an aroused nation . . . give America the gun control law it needs." He also argued that "we must eliminate the dangers of mail-order murder" (*CQ Weekly,* June 14, 1968, p. 1464). During the administrations of Presidents Ronald Reagan and George Bush, the politics of gun control legislation was attenuated. President Bush was himself an NRA member and did not advocate new gun control legislation. In contrast, President Bill Clinton vigorously advocated the Brady Bill and the assault weapons ban, and both he and key cabinet members lobbied heavily for these proposals. And when the new legislation appeared jeopardized by NRA opposition, President Clinton appealed directly to voters to write their representatives in support of gun control legislation.

Public opinion polls reveal that Americans consistently and overwhelmingly have supported stronger gun control measures, though not outright abolition of all guns. As recently as October 1996, 61 percent of the respondents in the CNN-*USA Today* Gallup poll said they thought that "laws covering the sale of firearms should be made more strict." Yet historically, gun control legislation has been difficult to pass unless public sentiment is fervid in reaction to a perceived crisis. The Gun Control Act of 1968 passed only because of public outrage over a rash of political assassinations. And the Brady Bill and the assault weapons ban passed only when the frustration and anger over rampant violent crime became the public's number-one concern. When such fervor was not present, gun rights proponents were relatively successful. They scaled back gun control laws in the Firearms Owners' Protection Act of 1986 and for the next six years blocked passage of the Brady Bill. However, this pattern could be changing to the detriment of gun rights advocates. Public opinion recently has been souring against the NRA, indicated by polls showing growing public dissatisfaction with its mostly negative influence. In addition, public worry about the growing rate and violence of crime does not appear to be diminishing. The rapid increase of violent juvenile crime, the proliferation of weapons found in schools, and the persistent media coverage of violent crimes are serving to create a deepening, lasting public concern about crime. If gun control advocates can continue to frame the gun control debate in terms of linking gun control with crime reduction, gun rights advocates may be facing a bleak future.

Who Votes for Gun Control?

Congressional voting on gun control legislation reveals three interesting patterns of cleavage. One of these is *regional*. Members of Congress from the South have a marked propensity to oppose federal gun controls; eastern members show consistent support for federal regulation of firearms. Another pattern of cleavage is *urban-rural*, involving differences between representatives and senators from urban constituencies on the one hand and rural members on the other. Finally, *party polarization* is evident in votes on federal gun control proposals, pitting Democrats against Republicans, especially in the 1990s.

Congressional decisionmaking on gun control issues hews very strongly to regional origins. This regional cleavage is most notable between the South and West and the rest of the country; southern representatives and senators are particularly inclined to disfavor federal firearms regulation. After all, private ownership of weapons is especially prevalent in the South and the West. Well over half of southerners regularly report to pollsters that they have guns in their homes (compared to well under a third of easterners), and South–non-South differences in gun ownership run in the range of 12 to 22 percentage points (e.g., Wright, Rossi and Daly 1983; *Gallup Poll Monthly* 330

March 1993, 5). And although reported gun ownership is roughly at the same level among westerners and midwesterners, people living in the West (and in the South) are substantially more likely to own two or more handguns than people living in the East or Midwest.

Figure 3.1 portrays the voting of representatives and senators by region. Four major voting outcomes are recorded in the figure: the Gun Control Act of 1968, the Firearms Owners' Protection Act of 1986, the Brady Act of 1993, and the assault weapons ban of 1994. The upper-left panel of the figure shows the proportion of southerners in each congressional house voting for each major bill. The Firearms Owners' Protection Act relaxed some provisions of the 1968 law and repealed

FIGURE 3.1
Regional Voting in Congress on Gun Control Legislation

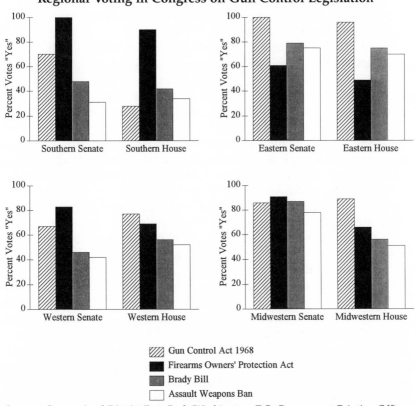

Sources: *Congressional District Data Book* (Washington, DC: Government Printing Office, 1967; *Congressional Districts in the 1980s* (Washington, DC: Congressional Quarterly, Inc., 1983); and *Congressional Districts in the 1990s* (Washington, DC: Congressional Quarterly, Inc., 1993).

others; all southern senators and 90 percent of southern House members voted for this legislation. Although a large majority of House southerners opposed the Gun Control Act, 70 percent of southern senators voted for firearms regulation. Only four months earlier these southern senators voted overwhelmingly against a similar measure proposed as an amendment to a crime bill. Their switch to support the Gun Control Act was largely a result of the public outcry for gun control immediately following the assassination of Senator Robert Kennedy (D-NY) in California.

In sharp contrast to the position of southern representatives and senators, members of Congress from the East have shown the strongest pro–gun control voting records (the upper-right panel of Figure 3.1). Large majorities of eastern senators favored all four pieces of gun legislation, although the fewest supported the 1986 bill watering down federal firearms regulation. A similar pattern prevailed among House easterners except that fewer than half voted for the legislation tempering the provisions of the Gun Control Act.

The pattern of support for the four legislative efforts on gun control was very similar among midwestern and western House members, as the bottom panels of Figure 3.1 show. Support for gun control by representatives from this part of the country fell between the strong support of easterners and the strong opposition of southerners in the House; and about two-thirds of House members from the West and Midwest supported the Firearms Owners' Protection Act. But midwestern senators took positions on gun control more like their eastern colleagues, and western senators voted akin to southerners. This regional difference between westerners and midwesterners developed largely out of political party differences. On the one hand, few western Republican senators voted for the Brady Bill and the assault weapons ban; on the other hand, midwestern Democratic senators voted overwhelmingly for all four gun bills (all midwestern Senate Democrats voted for the Brady Bill and the assault weapons ban, whereas only a fifth of western Senate Republicans favored these bills).

These regional differences in congressional voting on firearms legislation partly reflect urban-rural differences. Irrespective of regional and party differences, representatives from urban areas are much more likely to favor strict gun controls than are members of Congress from rural areas. The urban-rural difference mirrors the pattern of gun ownership: "All studies to have considered the matter report that weapons ownership is highest in rural areas and falls off as city size increases" (Wright, Rossi, and Daly 1983, 104). Far more guns are owned for hunting and other recreational purposes in open, rural areas than among city dwellers, and, not surprisingly, rural citizens are much less favorable to gun regulation than their city cousins. Because cities tend to have high rates of violent crime compared to rural America, members of Congress from cities tend to vote for gun controls in order to keep weapons out of the hands of criminals and, thereby, reduce violent crime. Accordingly, senators and House members who represent highly urban states and districts strongly tend to favor gun control measures. Almost 92 percent of House members from the nation's 20 largest cities voted in favor of the Gun Control Act of 1968 (*Congressional Quarterly Almanac* 1968, 554).

Figure 3.2 shows the striking differences between urban and rural representatives' voting on gun control measures. Overwhelming proportions of urban House members supported the Gun Control Act of 1968, the Brady Bill, and the assault weapons ban, and nearly three-fourths of the urban representatives opposed the Firearms Owners' Protection Act of 1986. In contrast, rural representatives strongly tended to oppose firearms regulation, and almost all rural members voted for the legislation weakening federal firearms controls. As Figure 3.2 indicates, the urban-rural split occurred within House party groups and withstands control for regional differences. Almost all urban House Democrats voted for the Gun Control Act, the Brady Bill, and the assault weapons ban and against the Firearms Owners' Protection Act. Although the gulf between House Democrats and Republicans shows up strongly in Figure 3.2, urban House Republicans were more inclined to support federal gun control legislation than were their rural colleagues. Moreover, Figure 3.2 displays urban-rural voting differences within each major region, indicating the expected relationships: urban-rural differences in gun control voting exist in all regions, although generally these differences are strongest in the South and West and weakest in the East and Midwest.

The role of political party cleavage in gun control politics has increased dramatically in recent years. In the 1960s, party affiliation was not a very reliable predictor of roll-call voting on gun control legislation. As Figure 3.3 indicates, overwhelming majorities of House and Senate members of both parties voted for the Gun Control Act of 1968. Indeed, a bipartisan coalition of conservative southern Democrats and Republicans—occasionally joined by a majority of midwestern and western Democrats—formed the core of the congressional opposition to gun control laws (see *Congressional Quarterly Weekly Report*, November 1, 1968, 2985). For instance, on May 16, 1968, the Senate voted on a gun control amendment that received nearly equal support from senators in both political parties: 34 percent support from Democrats and 31 percent support from Republicans. Regional differences prevailed over partisan cleavage. The measure won the support of fully 93 per-

FIGURE 3.2

Urban-Rural Voting in Congress on Gun Control Legislation, by Party and Region

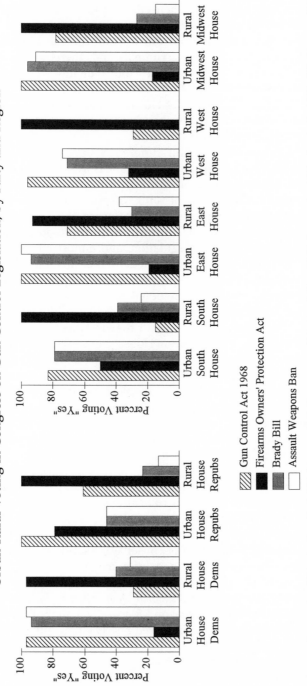

Source: Congressional District Data Book (Washington, DC: Government Printing Office, 1967; Congressional Districts in the 1980s (Washington, DC: Congressional Quarterly, Inc., 1983); and Congressional Districts in the 1990s (Washington, DC: Congressional Quarterly, Inc., 1993).

FIGURE 3.3
Party Voting in Congress on Gun Control Legislation

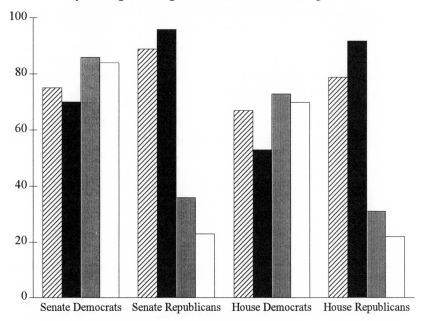

Gun Control Act 1968
Firearms Owners' Protection Act
Brady Bill
Assault Weapons Ban

Sources: Congressional District Data Book (Washington, DC: Government Printing Office, 1967; *Congressional Districts in the 1980s* (Washington, DC: Congressional Quarterly, Inc., 1983); and *Congressional Districts in the 1990s* (Washington, DC: Congressional Quarterly, Inc., 1993).

cent of eastern Democrats, but not a single western Democrat favored it; and only a fifth of southern Democrats voted for the measure (*Congressional Quarterly Almanac* 1968, 554).

Beginning in the 1970s, congressional voting on firearms regulation began to take on more distinctly partisan hues. Although the 1968 and 1972 Republican party platform provisions concerning gun control had acknowledged the need for some federal firearms regulation, after 1972 the party shifted to strong support for gun owners' rights, closely mirroring the stand of the National Rifle Association (Spitzer 1995, 123). In contrast, the Democratic party platform consistently supported gun control from 1968 onward, although that support, reflecting the varying views of its presidential candidates, vacillated between strong and lukewarm (Spitzer 1995, 124–125). As the national parties came to be more polarized on the issue of gun control (and other issues as well), roll-call voting reflected stronger party cleavage.

The party differences displayed in Figure 3.3 were especially sharp in voting on the Brady Bill and the assault weapons ban. Ironically, House and Senate Republicans were more favorable to the Gun Control Act of 1968 than Democrats and also much more supportive of diminishing its provisions through the Firearms Owners' Protection Act of 1986. Additionally, congressional voting on the Gun Control Act of 1968 failed to indicate a consistent cross-regional partisan cleavage. Although both House and Senate Republicans supported the bill by higher percentages than their Democratic counterparts, those margins—less than 15 percentage points—are attributable to strong regional and urban-rural differences.

Figure 3.4 shows House and Senate voting patterns by party and region. On the Gun Control Act vote, eastern and midwestern Republicans and Democrats from both chambers overwhelmingly supported the bill; among southerners, Republicans exhibited stronger support for the measure than Democrats. In the West, Democratic senators gave only 50 percent of their support to the bill, whereas their House colleagues and Republicans from both houses supported the measure by 71 percent of the vote and more. Clearer party voting emerged with the 1986 Firearms Owners' Protection Act. A majority of Democrats and Republicans in both houses favored the bill. But the Republican majorities favoring the bill were considerably larger: a difference of 38 percentage points in the House and 26 percentage points in the Senate. Voting patterns across regions and between rural and urban areas showed variation, but with the exception of the South a striking partisan influence on voting was evident.

By the 1990s, gun control voting in Congress—on the Brady Bill and the assault weapons ban—had become highly polarized, with Republicans predominantly opposing the measures or seeking repeal of existing controls and Democrats largely supporting gun control. House Democratic support for the Brady Bill and the assault weapons ban exceeded House Republican support by margins of 42 and 48 percentage points, respectively. Similarly, in Senate voting, Democratic support for the two proposals outstripped that of Republicans by 49 and 61 percentage points, respectively. These substantial party differences held up across regions. Although support for gun control in the South was lower overall than in other regions, the difference between the party's yea-vote percentages was greater than 30 points in both houses

FIGURE 3.4
Party and Regional Voting in Congress on Gun Control Legislation

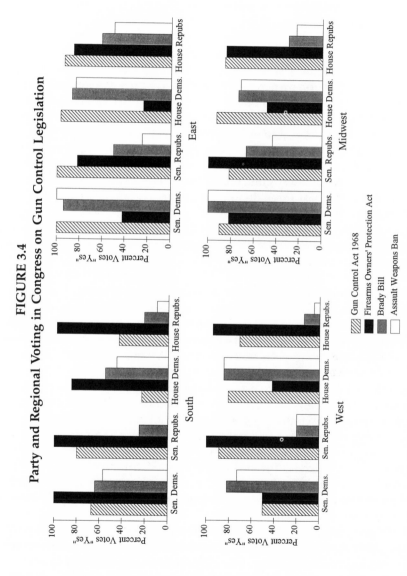

Sources: Congressional District Data Book (Washington, DC: Government Printing Office, 1967; *Congressional Districts in the 1990s* (Washington, DC: Congressional Quarterly, Inc., 1993).

of Congress. The gun control debate, along with health care, welfare, crime, and a host of other issues, now centers around unmistakable differences between Democrats and Republicans and helps to define the polarization of the two political parties.

The Continuing Dilemma

The ubiquity of gun ownership in the United States poses an enormous problem for congressional policymakers seeking to regulate the manufacture, sale, and distribution of weapons. The citizen culture of gun ownership is firmly established, and gun ownership is very widespread in this country. At the citizen level, resistance to governmental regulation and control of guns and gun ownership is significant indeed. Even the modest gun control laws that Congress has been able to enact in the past three decades were passed only after highly conflictual debate and heated lobbying campaigns. The passage of federal gun control legislation has been most likely when the president took up the cause actively and vigorously, putting his personal political reputation on the line.

Moreover, federal firearms regulation has become a matter of partisan disputation as political party polarization over the issue has grown and as both Republican and Democratic parties have come to take official party stands on gun control. Roll-call voting on gun control issues in the House of Representatives and in the Senate has grown increasingly divided along political party lines. Whereas 30 years ago there was something left of bipartisanship in these matters, with a significant number of southern and western Democrats opposing federal gun regulation and a significant number of northern suburban Republicans supporting gun control, today party divisiveness is much stronger. Changing patterns of party politics in the country and polarization of support for and opposition to a larger role for the federal government in regulating citizens' behavior have affected congressional coalition-building on gun control issues and on political issues generally. Today, gun control is a party issue, and decisionmaking evokes a highly partisan response in Congress.

At the same time, the 1996 congressional election outcomes were encouraging for gun control advocates. Nineteen of the staunchest supporters of the NRA's anti–gun control position lost their bids to be reelected to the House of Representatives, including freshman Steve Stockman (R-TX) and veteran Harold L. Volkmer (D-MO). Yet this 1996 loss of gun advocates in the House is not sufficient to tip the balance (the assault weapons ban of spring 1996 passed the House by a vote of

239 to 173). The $4.5 million spent by the NRA to elect its friends in 1996 appears to have preserved its capacity to prevent stronger gun control legislation in the 105th Congress, and its minimal losses in the 1996 election may encourage renewed efforts to pass repeal of the ban on assault weapons (see *New York Times*, December 24, 1996, A1, A7).

How effective can federal gun control laws be? Their modesty and limited applicability portend only a marginal impact (Kleck 1991, 431–445). Although one cannot dispute the value of restraining the distribution of dangerous weapons useless for sporting purposes or self-defense and although gun control is commonly associated with anti-crime legislation, it is not easy to demonstrate a substantial relationship between gun control and the reduction of crime (see Kleck 1991, 101–222). Gun ownership is so widespread in the United States that hope of eliminating most guns altogether is utopian even if this were deemed desirable (see Wright, Rossi, and Daly 1983 and the relevant essays in Nisbet 1990).

Although a very large majority of Americans favor effective government regulation of guns, few support the outright banning of guns altogether. Organized gun owners and users, led by the NRA, make for potent political influence. In short, as one scholar has noted, "the gun policy struggle is one where elephantine political forces battle over policy mice" (Spitzer 1995, 181). State and local regulation of guns and gun ownership is quite extensive and moderately effective. But further efforts to extend and strengthen federal regulation of firearms will undoubtedly reactivate the emotional struggle between regions, parties, and policymaking bodies that epitomizes gun control politics in the United States.

4

Madison's Mistake?
Judicial Construction
of the Second Amendment

Karen O'Connor and Graham Barron

The Bill of Rights was added to the Constitution in 1791. Since then, many of its guarantees have been the subject of literally hundreds of thousands of judicial opinions. Most readers, no doubt, are familiar with at least a few cases involving the scope of the First Amendment's free exercise, establishment, or press clauses. Similarly, the Fourth Amendment's search and seizure clause, the Sixth Amendment's right to a jury trial, and the Eighth Amendment's stricture against cruel and unusual punishments all are the subject of intense judicial as well as popular debate. Law school courses, in fact, often are taught about each of these clauses, and the existing case law concerning each can more than adequately fill an entire semester.

The Second Amendment to the U.S. Constitution reads: "A well regulated Militia, being necessary to the security of a free State, the right of the people to keep and bear Arms, shall not be infringed." It is not only "perhaps one of the worst drafted" of all constitutional provisions, but also one that has been the object of very little judicial interpretation (Levinson 1989, 643). Questions abound concerning whether the right to bear arms is a right tied to or based on membership in "a well regulated Militia," as well as whether a well-regulated militia means a government-sponsored militia or one of the informal militia groups that have gained so much attention in the wake of Ruby Ridge and the bombing in Oklahoma City. Today, new challenges face those who seek to limit access to handguns in the wake of the Supreme

Court's recent decision ruling portions of the Brady Bill unconstitutional (*Printz* v. *United States*).

In this chapter we trace the Supreme Court's treatment of the Second Amendment and discuss how the Court has handled state and national efforts to encourage or limit the citizenry's right "to keep and bear Arms." The first section presents a short history of the Second Amendment, including reasons for its inclusion in the Bill of Rights, how the Supreme Court dealt with state efforts to regulate firearms through the Civil War period, and post–Civil War efforts on the part of the southern states to limit the rights of newly freed slaves to own firearms. These efforts ultimately underscored the need for passage of the Fourteenth Amendment to the Constitution. This section also presents a discussion of the Supreme Court's treatment of restrictive state laws and of early congressional efforts to limit firearms, which began in the 1920s as a reaction to organized crime that flourished in the wake of Prohibition. The effects of the selective incorporation doctrine—which makes some of the guarantees contained in the Bill of Rights applicable to the states via the Fourteenth Amendment—on judicial resolution of state firearms restrictions are also reviewed in this section. In the second section we present modern judicial treatment of national and state efforts to regulate firearms and discuss the role of organized interests in presenting policy debates, questions of constitutional interpretation, and the Framers' intent to the Supreme Court. The final section concludes this analysis with a discussion of the two most recent U.S. Supreme Court decisions concerning federal efforts to regulate where guns can be carried and conditions of their sale. We also speculate on the constitutional limits of the right to keep and bear arms.

The Second Amendment and Early Efforts
to Regulate Possession of Firearms

During colonial times, the original settlers and then their heirs were imbued with a strong sense of distrust toward the English and English standing armies, which they believed infringed upon their personal liberties. Yet the need for a strong army to defend colonial outposts often led the British to deputize the entire white population in some areas (Cottrol 1992, 763; see also Cottrol 1994). Most colonies required by law that nearly all white men not only keep arms but carry them in local militias. The American Revolution, which was fought by men in state militias mobilized for the purpose of defending the colonies, reinforced colonial distrust of standing armies and the belief that a standing army was a direct reproach to liberty and individual security.

Once the Revolutionary War was won and a new Constitution was drafted, the drive for its ratification began. Anti-Federalists argued that the new Constitution would be used by a too powerful national government to infringe on the personal rights and liberties that colonists, as British citizens, had traditionally enjoyed. During the ratification conventions of many of the states, including New Hampshire, New York, and Rhode Island, explicit calls were made for an amendment in the future Bill of Rights to guarantee the public's right to bear arms, and these were more numerous than demands for explicit protection of the right to free speech or assembly.[1] Commentators believe the colonists were concerned over the propensity of the British to seize the arms of citizens (Kates 1983). In the seventeenth century, for example, following the absolutist regimes of France that tried to disarm the population to quell rebellion, the English Parliament passed the Games Acts, which effectively disarmed most of the population (see Halbrook 1994).

The Bill of Rights was a partial answer to these concerns. James Madison, the principal author of the Second Amendment, seemed to indicate that its specific purpose was to protect the arms of the population at large (see Halbrook 1994; Kates 1983; Malcom 1994). Even during the ratification debates about the new constitution, Madison argued in *Federalist No. 46* that the new national government need not be feared because Americans had "the advantage of being armed, which the Americans possess over the people of almost every other nation" (Rossiter 1961, 299; see also Reynolds 1995). Personal communication among Madison's contemporaries makes it clear that the Second Amendment was added because of concern over individual freedoms, not just out of a desire to protect the militia system (Kates 1983, 224).

Once the Bill of Rights was ratified, in spite of the poor wording of its Second Amendment, no cases were brought to the Supreme Court to test its scope or meaning prior to the Civil War (1861–1865). Some southern states enacted laws prohibiting slaves from carrying weapons. A few other states passed laws banning the carrying of concealed weapons, but those laws were not subject to Supreme Court review because the U.S. Supreme Court's decision in 1833 in *Barron* v. *Baltimore* held that the Bill of Rights constrained only the actions of the national government, not those of the states.

Although no actual case came before the Court involving firearms during the antebellum period, on more than one occasion a sitting justice of the high court noted his belief in the right to keep and carry arms. In his *Commentaries on the Constitution of the United States*, Justice (and noted constitutional scholar) Joseph Story wrote: "The right of the citizens to keep and bear arms has justly been considered as the palladium of the liberties of a republic, since it offers a strong moral check against the usurpation and arbitrary power of rulers, and will generally, even if these are successful in the first instance, enable the people to resist and triumph over them" (Story 1891, quoted in Reynolds 1995, 470). Similarly, in 1896 in *Dred Scott* v. *Sanford*, Chief Justice Taney enumerated the right to keep and bear arms as one of the essential rights of citizenship, noting: "It would give to persons of the negro race, who were recognized as citizens in any one State of the Union, the right to enter every other state whenever they pleased, . . . and it would give them the full liberty of speech in public and in private upon all subjects upon which its own citizens might speak, to hold public meetings upon political affairs, and to keep and carry arms whenever they went."

The Civil War and Its Aftermath

After the end of the war, southern state legislatures quickly enacted far-ranging laws called black codes. These new laws dramatically restricted the rights of the newly freed, including their right to own firearms. Southern passage of these black codes hastened passage and ratification of the Fourteenth Amendment, which was intended to restore basic civil rights to black citizens. During debate on its provisions, several members of Congress noted that the new amendment would require the states to uphold the protections contained in the Bill of Rights, including those guaranteed by the Second Amendment.[2] Senator Jacob Howard Meritt of Michigan, for example, specifically noted that once passed by Congress and ratified by the states, the Fourteenth Amendment would "restrain the power of the states" from abridging "the personal rights guaranteed and secured by the first eight amendments to the Constitution; such as . . . the right to keep and bear arms." (Congressional Globe 1865, 2765).

Although there was clear legislative support for the notion that the Fourteenth Amendment could require the Court to make the provisions of the Bill of Rights applicable to the states via the incorporation doctrine, the Supreme Court declined to do so, citing its decision in *Barron*. In a case decided not long after ratification of the Fourteenth Amendment, the Court was faced with a challenge to the constitutionality of the Enforcement Act of 1870, a federal law that prohibited conspiracies to deny the constitutional rights of any citizens. In 1873, three armed Ku Klux Klan members killed more than 100 black men in a dispute over a gubernatorial election. William Cruickshank and several others were charged with violating the rights of two black men to peaceably assemble and interfering with their right to bear arms. The defendants challenged their convictions on the ground that their indictments were unconstitutional. In *United States* v. *Cruickshank*, the Supreme Court held that the Second Amendment's right to keep and bear arms, along with the First Amendment's guarantee of the right of freedom of assembly, could not be enforced against the actions of private citizens in spite of passage of the Fourteenth Amendment. The Court held that the First and Second Amendments were limits only on the actions of Congress, not the states (*United States* v. *Cruickshank*).

A decade later, the Supreme Court decided *Presser* v. *Illinois* (1886), which more directly addressed the question of whether the Fourteenth Amendment limited state action in regard to guns. In *Presser*, the defendant organized and led a parade of sword- and rifle-bearing members of a German nationalist organization through town without first obtaining a permit as required by state law. The challenged Illinois statute barred any group of men—other than those officially recognized by the state as an organized voluntary militia—from parading with arms or associating in any kind of military organization. The Supreme Court rejected the defendant's Second Amendment arguments on the ground that the Second Amendment was not incorporated or made applicable to the states via the Fourteenth Amendment, citing the *Cruickshank* case. It noted that although Congress could not infringe on rights guaranteed by the Second Amendment, the state could legitimately limit parades by armed men.

Some commentators look at these cases as simply a logical judicial buildup to one of the worst cases ever decided by the Supreme Court, *Plessy* v. *Ferguson* (1896). In *Plessy*, the separate but equal doctrine in regard to race was enunciated for the first time. The "end result" of *Plessy*, argues law professor Glenn Harlan Reynolds, was "disarmed blacks who could look for protection only to the very state governments that were turning against and disenfranchising them" (Reynolds 1995, 498). Professors Robert Cottrol and Raymond Diamond further argue:

> The *Cruickshank* decision, which dealt a serious blow to Congress' ability to enforce the Fourteenth Amendment, was part of a larger campaign by the Court to ignore the original purpose of the Fourteenth Amendment. . . . The doctrine in *Cruickshank*, that blacks would have to look to state government for protection against criminal conspiracies, gave the green light to private forces, often with the assistance of state and local governments, that sought to subjugate the former slaves and their descendants. Private violence was instrumental in driving blacks from the ranks of voters. Its helped force many blacks into peonage, a virtual return to slavery, and was used to force many blacks into a state of ritualized subservience. (Cottrol and Diamond 1991, 347–348)

After *Plessy*, several southern states moved to prohibit blacks from owning guns; in the North, restrictions were enacted to prevent immigrants from purchasing or carrying weapons. In general, however, the right to bear arms was not an issue of concern to many legislators or commentators. The nation was largely agricultural and rural, and most lawmakers recognized the need for or desirability of gun ownership, especially for hunting. But as immigration continued and Prohibition was enacted, organized crime flourished and automatic weapons became the weapon of choice for bootleggers and others like Bonnie Parker, Clyde Barrow, and John Dillinger. Territorial warfare broke out in many cities over control of the illegal liquor trade, and the development of the Thompson submachine gun made it clear that guns were being developed to kill people, not to hunt for food.

The exploits of these gangsters and the damage their weapons could do were highlighted by the development of the motion picture industry. Every Saturday and Sunday afternoon millions of Americans saw newsreels of the devastation produced by "Tommy" guns and the first forms of urban warfare (Cottrol 1994, xxvii).

The National Firearms Act of 1934

Congress passed the National Firearms Act of 1934, which was proposed by the Roosevelt administration to deal with the violence and organized crime that began during national Prohibition. The Firearms Act called for the taxation and registration of gangster-associated weapons including automatic weapons and sawed-off shotguns. The constitutionality of this act soon was challenged in *United States* v. *Miller*. In *Miller*, the Court was presented with a single question: whether it was appropriate to take judicial notice of whether a sawed-off shotgun was a "militia weapon" and therefore protected by the Second Amendment or whether such a finding required evidentiary hearings. In defending the constitutionality of the law, U.S. Solicitor General Robert Jackson, a future justice of the Supreme Court, offered several reasons the federal law did not violate the U.S. Constitution: (1) Echoing *Cruickshank* and *Presser*, Jackson argued that the Second Amendment did not create a right to keep and bear arms—it merely recognized a preexisting common law right. Because common law rights always exist subject to a government's right to regulate for the public health and safety, this was what the government was doing here. (2) The Second Amendment guarantees a collective right to bear arms only to those who are members of a state militia. (3) The national government has the right to restrict weapons peculiarly adaptable for criminal purposes, such as the "weapons which form the arsenal of the gangster or desperado" targeted by Congress for its control (Cottrol 1994, xxvii).

In sending the case back to the district court for evidentiary hearings on the question of whether a sawed-off shotgun was a militia weapon, the Court noted:

> In the absence of any evidence tending to show that the possession or use of a "shotgun having a barrel of less than eighteen inches in length" at this time has some reasonable relationship to the preservation of efficiency of a well regulated militia, we cannot say that the Second Amendment guarantees the right to keep and bear such an instrument. Certainly it is not within judicial notice that this weapon is any part of the ordinary military equipment or that its use could contribute to the common defense. (*United States* v. *Miller*)

Thus, the Court again sidestepped a direct ruling on the meaning of the Second Amendment, indicating only that it was not likely to "protect" weapons clearly designed for unlawful purposes. Since *Miller*, "lower federal courts and state courts have unanimously held that regulation of the private ownership of firearms offends the Second Amendment only if it interferes with the arming of the state militia" (Hennigan 1991, 108).

The Muddled Modern Meaning of the Second Amendment

The Court's refusal to make the Second Amendment applicable to the states in *United States* v. *Cruickshank* is still cited as support for the proposition that the Second Amendment does not apply to the states. Many scholars and gun rights activists argue that reliance on *Cruickshank* is meaningless, however, because the Court had yet to begin making other rights contained in the Bill of Rights applicable to the states (see Halbrook 1982; Van Alystyne 1994). Many of the protections now enjoyed by criminal defendants, for example, did not come into existence until the 1960s.

The assassination of President John F. Kennedy in 1962 with a mail-order shotgun found through an advertisement in the back of the NRA's *American Rifleman* (Herz 1995), the shootings of Robert F. Kennedy and Martin Luther King Jr., and the race riots that erupted throughout the United States in the tumultuous decade of the 1960s, refocused attention on government regulation of firearms. Concerns about crime and violence then led to passage of the Omnibus Crime Control and Safe Streets Act of 1968.

It was not until 1980, however, that the U.S. Supreme Court addressed the constitutionality of certain provisions of the 1968 federal act. In *Lewis* v. *United States*, which was concerned with whether Congress could prohibit the possession of firearms by convicted felons, the Court failed to find that the right to bear arms was a fundamental right and thus subject to the Court's highest level of scrutiny—preferred freedoms. In *Lewis* v. *United States*, the Court applied its lowest level of judicial scrutiny—rational basis—in finding the ban on firearms ownership by convicted felons to be constitutional. The Court specifically noted that these kinds of restrictions "are neither based upon constitutionally suspect criteria, nor do they trench upon any constitutionally protected liberties" (*Lewis* v. *United States*, 66). The Court also reiterated its earlier holding in *Miller* as "the Second Amendment guarantees no right to keep and bear a firearm that does not have 'some reasonable relationship to the preservation or efficiency of a well-regulated militia.'"

After *Miller* and *Lewis*, through 1995, ten federal circuit courts "explicitly adopted a narrow reading of the right to bear arms, and one other seems similarly inclined" (Herz 1995, 73–74). Thus both federal and state courts have upheld myriad kinds of restrictions on the right to keep and bear arms, including record-keeping requirements, registration, dealer licensing, and prohibitions on felons.

Quilici v. *Village of Morton Grove*

Many commentators argue that the Court's failure to incorporate the Second Amendment in *Presser* or *Cruickshank* is meaningless because these decisions were rendered before the Court began to incorporate other liberties guaranteed in the first eight amendments. But as recently as 1983, the Supreme Court refused to hear *Quilici* v. *Village of Morton Grove*, a case in which a federal court of appeals upheld a village ban on the possession of handguns; village boundaries were also upheld, as was a ban on the possession of machine guns not lawfully owned prior to 1986.[3]

In 1981 the Village of Morton Grove, Illinois, enacted a ban on the possession of handguns to "promote and protect the health and safety and welfare of the public" (*Quilici* v. *Morton Grove*). In upholding the constitutionality of this ban against a Second Amendment challenge brought by the NRA, the Seventh Circuit Court of Appeals wrote: "Construing this language [of the Second Amendment] according to its plain meaning, it seems clear that the right to bear arms is inextricably connected to the preservation of a militia" (*Quilici* v. *Morton Grove*, 270).[4] And after *Quilici*, even the NRA opted not to bring an incorporation claim to the Supreme Court when the Ninth Circuit Court of Appeals upheld California's ban on assault weapons rejecting the NRA's challenge on the grounds that the Second Amendment does not apply to the states via the Fourteenth Amendment (*Fresno Rifle and Pistol Club* v. *Van de Kamp*).

The Second Amendment, Gun Control, and the Supreme Court

In 1990 Congress passed the Gun-Free School Zones Act to make it a federal offense for "any individual knowingly to possess a firearm at a place that the individual knows, or has reasonable cause to believe," is a school zone. The act further defined a school zone as the area within 1,000 feet of a school. In 1992, Alonso Lopez Jr., a twelfth-grade student at Edison High School in San Antonio, Texas, arrived at school carrying a concealed .38 caliber handgun and five bullets. Acting on an anonymous tip, school authorities confronted Lopez, who then admitted he was carrying the gun and ammunition. He was arrested and charged with violating a Texas law against firearms possession, but those charges were dismissed the next day after federal charges under the new law were brought against him. At the time of his arrest, Lopez was an average student, never had had disciplinary problems at school, and was scheduled to join the marines upon graduation.

The federal district court found Lopez guilty and sentenced him to six months in prison and two years supervised release. On appeal to the Supreme Court, Lopez challenged his conviction, arguing that the 1990 law was beyond the scope of Congress's power to legislate under the commerce clause. A narrow majority of the Court (5 to 4) agreed with him, noting the powers delegated to the "federal government are few and defined. Those which are to remain in the State governments are numerous and indefinite." After a careful survey of cases involving the scope of Congress's authority to regulate under the commerce clause, the majority rejected the government's contention that guns in schools pose a substantial threat to the educational process and thereby threaten the learning environment and have an adverse effect on the national economy. The five-justice majority simply found the connection too tenuous to swallow. To do so, the Court concluded, would force it to "pile inference upon inference in a manner that" would equate "congressional authority under the Commerce Clause to a general police power of the sort retained by the States" (*United States* v. *Lopez*, 19). Writing for the majority, Chief Justice William H. Rehnquist even noted that the act "by its terms has nothing to do with commerce or any sort of economic enterprise, however broadly one might define those terms."[5]

The four justices in the minority—John Paul Stevens, David Souter, Ruth Bader Ginsburg, and Stephen Breyer—opined that the Gun-Free School Zones Act should be upheld under the commerce clause. They also lamented the majority's lack of judicial restraint and the fact that the majority decision would call into question the legality of all sorts of federal criminal penalties, including those laws under which Timothy McVeigh was prosecuted for the Oklahoma City bombing. Nevertheless, *Lopez*, while invalidating the Gun-Free School Zones Act, did not offer much direction about how to interpret the Second Amendment. Instead, the Court ruled that Congress lacked the constitutional authority to legislate concerning weapons on or near schools under the commerce clause. Interpretation of the Second Amendment's meaning was left for another day.

Printz v. *United States*

Some believed that day had come when the Court announced it would hear the first challenge to what is known as the Brady Bill, named after the former White House press secretary James Brady, who nearly died from wounds suffered when John Hinkley Jr. attempted to assassinate President Reagan in 1981. In late 1993, President Clinton signed the Brady Handgun Violence Prevention Act, one of the most controversial gun control measures ever enacted, in a White House ceremony amid much fanfare. For several years, Brady's wife, Sarah, as head of the Washington, D.C., based Handgun Control, Inc., went head-to-head with powerful lobbyists from the National Rifle Association to enact into law a five-day waiting period for handgun purchases to provide time for a check of criminal records.

Soon after the law went into effect, two local county sheriffs from Arizona and Montana, assisted by the National Rifle Association, filed suit in federal court, alleging that the background-check requirement was too burdensome on local governments. Richard Mack, the sheriff of Graham County, Arizona, said that Congress and the president "should quit trying to micromanage the country. They are violating the Constitution and asking me to help. I won't do it" (Thomas 1994, A1).

Mack and several other sheriffs did not ground their challenge to the Brady Act in the Second Amendment's right to bear arms. Instead, they argued that the Brady Act was vague and violated the Tenth Amendment to the Constitution by encroaching on the authority of the states, forcing local or state officials to carry out federal mandates that cost money, took time, and could be taken on by federal personnel if the national government was really serious about gun control. A federal district court judge agreed with the sheriffs' arguments but was overruled by the Ninth Circuit Court of Appeals. In a nearly identical suit brought by sheriffs in Mississippi and Texas, however, the Fifth Circuit Court of Appeals struck down the law as unconstitutional. Both cases were appealed to the Supreme Court.

The NRA, which has lost many recent gun control fights in Congress, clearly changed its tactics as it challenged the Brady Act. Just like many other interest groups before it that had lost legislative battles, the NRA turned to the courts, hoping for a different outcome.[6] It was also shifting its target "from legislative battles to preserve gun ownership to judicial assaults on laws that restrict gun purchases" (Thomas 1994, A1). But instead of relying on the Second Amendment to support its position, the NRA began to attack restrictive national legislation as encroachments on state power, a line of argument that the states rights–oriented Rehnquist Supreme Court might be more likely to accept. Said Dennis Henigan, general counsel of Handgun Control, Inc., about the NRA's new strategy: "[They] knew if they mounted a frontal assault on the Second Amendment they'd lose, so they took an indirect approach" (Thomas 1994, A1).

In December 1996, the Supreme Court heard oral arguments in *Printz* v. *United States* and *Mack* v. *United States*. Both challenged the constitutionality of provisions of the Brady handgun law, which required local law enforcement officials to conduct background checks for prospective gun purchasers. It was the first time since *Miller* in 1939 that the Court had opted to address the constitutionality of a federal law regulating firearms.

Guns rights lawyer Stephen P. Halbrook represented the sheriffs who opposed the law (Herz 1995, n. 27; Mauro 1991). During oral argument he stressed the state sovereignty approach advocated by the NRA as he told the justices that the law allowed Congress to "commandeer the sheriffs' departments of this country," as they attempt to make a "reasonable effort" to check local, state, and federal records for any evidence that a prospective buyer of a handgun has a criminal record of any kind. In contrast, Acting U.S. Solicitor General Walter Dellinger tried to convince the justices that the law was eminently "reasonable" and that its burdens on local law enforcement officials were but minimal (*Printz* v. *United States*).

Several justices on the Rehnquist Court have very strong states-rights leanings, and these views were evident during the give-and-take in the Court during oral argument. Conservative Justice Antonin Scalia, for example, noted that the effect of the Brady Bill was to "make the states dance like marionettes on the fingers of the Federal Government."

Since 1992, the justices of the Supreme Court have been involved in a continuous reexamination of the constitutional nature of the federal-state relationship. They have often ruled in favor of states rights while limiting the powers of Congress, reflecting the apparent public desire to return power to the states. In 1992, for example, the Court ruled that it was unconstitutional for Congress to require states to provide for the disposal of low-level radioactive waste generated within their borders or to assume legal ownership of that waste (*New York* v. *United States*). Writing for the Court, Justice Sandra Day O'Connor noted that "state governments are neither regional offices nor administrative agencies of the federal government" in holding that the U.S. Congress could not "commandeer state governments into the service of Federal regulatory purposes" (*New York* v. *United States*). Thus in challenging the Brady Act, the NRA was simply trying to capitalize on the sentiments of several of the justices, including O'Connor and Scalia, who appeared to be increasingly sympathetic to the states and notions of state sovereignty in the federal system.

At the end of its 1996–1997 term, the justices announced their decision concerning the constitutionality of the Brady Act. In a 5 to 4 decision, the Supreme Court struck down as unconstitutional a key section of the Brady gun control law—the requirement that local law enforcement officials conduct background checks of prospective gun buyers. The decision, however, left intact the section of the act requiring a five-day waiting period. Writing for the majority, Justice Antonin Scalia noted that the national government could not force the states to administer this kind of a program because "such demands are fundamentally incompatible with our constitutional system of dual sovereignty." He went on to say, "The power of the federal government would be augmented immeasurably if it were able to impress into its service—at no cost to itself—the police officers of the 50 states" (*Printz* v. *United States*). The majority, however, did leave open the right of the states to voluntarily conduct background checks. Scalia and the majority clearly accepted the NRA's arguments and continued to build a state-centered jurisprudence denying powers to Congress and the national government.

Writing in dissent were Justices Stevens, Souter, Ginsburg, and Breyer, the same four justices who had dissented in *Lopez* two years earlier. Justice Stevens actually read his strongly worded dissent aloud, an unusual action. He argued that the Court should respect Congress's assessment of its constitutional power and likened the background check to requiring local law enforcement officials to report missing children to the federal government.

Reaction to the decision came quickly. The NRA announced that it was "vindicated by the decision." In contrast, President Clinton, whose administration had vigorously defended the constitutionality of the law, said, "I'm going to do everything I can to make sure we can keep guns out of the hands of people who shouldn't have them." He also noted that 27 states had their own background-check provisions and offered his belief that those states would continue to conduct background checks (Asseo 1997). Although Sarah Brady was "somewhat disappointed" by the decision, she was "very delighted" that the waiting period "remains intact" (Asseo 1997). Sheriff Mack, who along with Sheriff Printz had brought the challenge, was unavailable for comment. He was defeated in a primary election in January 1997.

Implications for the Continued Viability of the Second Amendment

The Second Amendment, although still part of the Bill of Rights, has been largely ignored in recent judicial contests over the scope of national and state attempts to limit the public's access to firearms. Since 1939, the Supreme Court has shied away from interpreting it, preferring to regard the constitutionality of gun restrictions through the lens of other constitutional provisions. The Court, as was the case in *Quilici* v. *Village of Morton Grove*, has repeatedly refused to hear any challenges to state firearms restrictions and has yet to rule that the Second Amendment's provisions have been made applicable to the states via the Fourteenth Amendment. Thus whereas "reasonable" state restrictions have been upheld by lower federal courts, challenges to congressional efforts to limit access to handguns and assault weapons have not fared nearly so well. Yet the Court has chosen not to rule these provisions inconsistent with the Second Amendment; instead, their constitutionality has been assessed as an issue of state sovereignty, echoing the mantra of the Republican-controlled Congress and, only recently, the National Rifle Association. Does the Second Amendment, then, have any real meaning in today's litigious world? The answer probably is, not much. But that is not to say that governmental efforts to regulate firearms will always pass constitutional muster. Most reasonable state efforts to limit access to guns will probably be immune from serious constitutional challenge; Congress will have a far more difficult time justifying any infringements—at least until (and if) President Clinton has the opportunity to replace at least one of the justices in the majority in *Lopez* and *Printz*.

Notes

1. The first call for a protection of the right to keep and bear arms was made in a failed motion at the Pennsylvania ratifying convention. There unsuccessful delegates attempted to take on a provisions to the Constitution specifying that "the people have a right to bear arms for the defense of themselves and their own state, or the United States, or for the purpose of killing game." This language undoubtedly influenced James Madison, who "worked from a reprint of state demands that included the Pennsylvania report" (see Bursor 1996, 1136).

2. See generally Van Alstyne (1994). For specific mention, see the remarks of Senator Jacob Meritt Howard, *Congressional Globe* 1865, 2765.

3. *Farmer* v. *Higgins*, 907 F. 2d 1041, 11th Circuit 1982; cert. denied, 498 U.S. 104, 1991. For a list of the cases denied certiorari see Herz (1995,.77).

4. 695 F. 2d at 270 (citing *Miller*).

5. 115 S. Ct. 1624, 1995.

6. See, for example, Vose (1958) and O'Connor (1980).

5

Gun Control Politics in California

Marcia L. Godwin and Jean Reith Schroedel

Since the late 1980s California has appeared to be a leader in the movement to enact gun control legislation. The California legislature's passage of an assault-weapons-control law in 1989 and a uniform 15-day waiting period for the purchase of weapons in 1990 predated both the Brady Handgun Violence Prevention Act and the federal assault weapons ban by several years. With Senator Dianne Feinstein's (D-CA) successful sponsorship of the 1994 federal assault weapons bill in Congress and the decade-long support of stricter gun regulations by a series of Republican governors, many believed California was destined to continue to be a model for gun control advocates. Yet in 1996 the California assembly approved preemptive legislation (Assembly Bill 638) to allow almost unlimited numbers of concealed-weapons permits, and the state legislature easily passed Senate Bill 2069 to prohibit local land-use controls over shooting ranges. Although neither bill was enacted into law,[1] these actions mirror national trends toward increased state preemption of local gun regulations and appear to signal a more favorable political climate for gun owners. However, we will argue that the California legislature continues to be torn by conflicting pressures and that substantive policymaking activity has devolved to local government entities.

This tension is consistent with the longer historical record of gun policy in California. Californians have had a long-standing love affair with guns, frontier justice, and individualism.[2] Yet the Golden State has had its share of political assassinations, riots, and lone-gunman massacres, triggering unease about the easy accessibility of guns. Within the state legislature the politics of guns shifted from the historical pattern of pro-gun dominance to a brief period in 1989 and 1990 when the supporters of gun control prevailed; this period was followed by intensified political conflict and policy stalemate. Local governments have stepped into the policy vacuum, initiating bans on Saturday night special handguns and experimenting with a variety of programs to limit urban gun violence.

State legislative actions closely follow John Kingdon's model (1995) on agenda setting and the development of policy alternatives. According to Kingdon, the process of focusing the policymaking agenda on particular issues results from the interaction of three separate streams: problems, policy, and politics. These streams must converge in order for policy windows to open; through these windows, policy entrepreneurs can guide the adoption of preferred alternatives (Kingdon 1995). The opening of policy windows and their duration can be random; success or failure in changing policy is due largely to happenstance or the skill of policy entrepreneurs (Kingdon 1995, 184–190). In retrospect, the support by the legislature for gun controls in the 1989–1990 session turned out to be a short-lived policy window resulting from an unstable convergence of political resources and public sentiment. Although proponents of stronger gun controls became better organized and funded in the 1990s, a more permanent shift in the policymaking environment at the state level has not yet emerged. Miniwindows have opened at the local level as gun control advocates have shifted their emphasis to local governments, especially in the wake of the Republican party's gaining a majority in the state assembly following the 1994 election.

Gun Control Emerges as an Issue: 1966–1989

The Problem Stream

The political assassinations of the 1960s had a major impact on the passage of new federal regulations on gun sales[3] but led only to the adoption of a 15-day waiting period for handgun purchases in California. In fact, the state legislature passed a law in 1969 to limit local government discretion in adopting gun control ordinances, in response to a San Francisco local ordinance to ban handgun ownership within its jurisdiction (Borland 1995, 40–41). State regulations on gun ownership remained relatively stable, and gun politics were dominated by gun rights supporters through the 1970s.[4]

The largest gun-related policy controversy in the 1970s was not over gun control per se but the overturning of the popular "use-a-gun-go-to-prison" law by the California Supreme Court in *People* v. *Tanner*[5] in

1978. The court considered the *Tanner* case while Chief Justice Rose Bird and three justices were up for confirmation by the California electorate. Prior to the election, several California newspapers alleged that the court had decided the case but was withholding the decision in order to avoid political fallout. When the *Tanner* decision was released just a month following the election, a very public investigation of alleged improprieties followed. The justices were cleared of wrongdoing by the Commission on Judicial Performance, but the controversy seriously damaged the credibility of the Bird court.[6]

Gun control issues emerged on the political agenda largely due to several mass killings by lone gunmen that attracted widespread media attention. The first major "focusing event," to use Kingdon's term,[7] was former San Francisco supervisor Dan White's 1978 killing of Mayor George Moscone and Supervisor Harvey Milk. Dianne Feinstein rose to national prominence in assuming the mayor's office and in exercising strong leadership in the ensuing period.[8] At least in part due to those murders, San Francisco in 1982 adopted a strict handgun control ordinance that would have banned handgun possession within the city limits, except under specialized circumstances and for peace officers, and would have required a minimum 30-day jail sentence for violations. Although the ordinance was subsequently ruled to be in violation of state law,[9] Feinstein earned a reputation as a champion of gun control. Feinstein's political viability was not undercut by her position because at that time she was one of the few state Democratic leaders who supported the death penalty. The identification of unrestricted gun ownership as a distinct problem, along with a weakening of the historic tie between advocates of the death penalty and gun rights supporters, was a key turning point in making gun control regulation politically feasible.

The 1984 slaying of 21 people in a McDonald's restaurant in San Ysidro served as another critical focusing event. The incident triggered the introduction of a bill in the state legislature to ban assault weapons with individual exceptions granted only by permit of the California attorney general. After passing out of committee by a single vote, the bill was defeated in the assembly (Ingram 1985). The media attention from the San Ysidro incident and subsequent legislative activity heightened public awareness of the problems caused by the growing number of AK-47 and similar semiautomatic assault weapons imported into California from China.[10]

The Policy Stream

The policy stream refers to the activities of "communities of specialists" who develop technical information and prepare policy proposals.

In order to advance onto the policymaking agenda and attract support, a policy proposal must be technically feasible, compatible with specialists' values, and perceived as adoptable within existing constraints. Policy entrepreneurs play important roles in consolidating ideas and "softening up" the political arena (Kingdon 1995, 116–144).

Beginning in the early 1980s, academic researchers began to publish studies that explored the interrelationship among guns, violence, public opinion, and policy responses. Researchers focused on the root causes of violence, the likely substitution effects if particular weapons were banned, and the difficulties of designing effective policy solutions.[11] However, the creation of policy alternatives and refinement within California took place largely because of the activities of politicized interest groups and elected officials rather than through a true community of specialists. Due to California's fragmented political structure, policy proposals have been initiated by state legislators, private citizens via the statewide initiative process, and local governments.[12] Early proposals, although not successful, served as trial balloons in the years prior to successful adoption of assault weapons legislation.

Proposition 15, a November 1982 ballot initiative, emerged as the first major gun control policy proposal in California. This statewide initiative was proposed after the San Francisco assassinations but prior to the San Ysidro killings. Attorney John Phillips and business leader Victor Palmieri, both from Los Angeles, sponsored Proposition 15, which would have banned sales of new handguns and limited handgun ownership to those pistols and revolvers owned on April 30, 1983. Proposition 15 was defeated, 63 percent to 37 percent. Gun rights organizations outspent proponents by over a two-to-one ratio, $5.8 to $2 million. Proposition 15 was defeated by a wider margin than another poorly funded initiative on the same ballot, indicating that campaign contributions probably were not decisive in its defeat (Brazil 1982). Given the perception that Proposition 15 was inherently unpopular, gun control supporters then focused on proposals that were much less expansive, as discussed later in this chapter.

The Political Stream

The political stream consists of those factors particular to the political arena: the public mood, organized political forces, and governmental officials. The ability to achieve consensus through bargaining and changes in a few key players can be critical in determining the policymaking agenda (Kingdon 1995, 145–164). Until the late 1980s, the so-called gun lobby dominated gun politics in the Golden State and was able to block gun control legislation from advancing to final vote. Although the NRA has a Sacramento office and has been a major contributor to political campaigns, the Gun Owners of California, Inc., (GOC) has been the most prominent interest group. The GOC accurately describes itself as the "hardest hitting, most effective, toughest fighting pro-gun organization in California."[13] The GOC cites its actions in the defeat of all gun control proposals in the state legislature during Democrat Jerry Brown's 1974 to 1982 tenure as governor, the defeat of Proposition 15, and the eventual defeat of "anti-death penalty and pro-criminal" Chief Justice Rose Bird in 1986.[14]

Much of the GOC's success is due to its close links to powerful figures in the California legislature, most notably its founder, state senator H. L. "Bill" Richardson (R-Arcadia). Richardson, who was first elected to the state senate in 1966,[15] created the first professional mass-mailing fundraising organization with ties to a sitting California legislator. In 1975 Richardson founded the GOC in response to proposed legislation to end handgun ownership. Richardson then used the GOC and his primary political action committee, the Law and Order Committee, to promote the election of allies to office and take positions on ballot measures. By the mid-1980s, Richardson had played a significant role in the election of at least a half-dozen Republican state legislators (Christensen and Gerston 1984, 46). Thus Richardson's leadership position as one of the most senior Republicans in the senate, along with the presence of his protégés in both chambers of the legislature, made it virtually impossible in the 1970s and early 1980s for any restrictive gun regulatory proposals to succeed. For example, a 1988 assault weapons bill sponsored by assembly member Mike Roos (D-Los Angeles) was easily defeated in the assembly. The gun lobby then successfully targeted assembly member Paul Zeltner (R-Los Angeles) for defeat in his reelection campaign (McDonald 1989, 319–320). By the mid-1980s, with gun rights apparently secure, donations for the GOC had fallen by about a half-million dollars per year, to $200,000 ("Richardson" 1985).

State senator David Roberti (D-San Fernando) who, like Richardson, represented a suburban southern California district, emerged in the 1980s as the legislature's strongest advocate of gun restrictions. Roberti became president pro tempore of the state senate in 1981, ousting previous president pro tem James Mills (D-San Diego), and ushering in a more partisan era.[16] Roberti consolidated his leadership by successfully increasing Democratic majorities in the state senate in 1982 and 1984 (Block 1994, 10).

The rise of Roberti's influence occurred about the same time that Richardson's power began to wane. Not only did donations to Richardson-affiliated political action committees decline but Richardson himself was unsuccessful in a 1986 campaign for lieutenant governor.[17] Richardson served out the remainder of his term in the state senate, but chose to retire at the end of the 1988 session.

Thus the policy environment by the late 1980s was very different than at the start of the decade. Senator Richardson had served a gatekeeper role for decades by opposing any gun control proposals, developing a core group of allies, and effectively going after political opponents. In spite of these efforts, Richardson was unable to significantly harm the Democratic leadership, and Senator Roberti was able to consolidate support for his position as speaker pro tempore. Ironically, Richardson's own pioneering efforts in mass media campaigning also resulted in a California legislature that was less insulated from outside pressures and more easily influenced by changes in public opinion.

A Policy Window Opens: 1989–1990

At the start of the 1989–1990 legislation session, few recognized that Richardson's retirement, declines in the gun lobby's financial resources, and backlash from its uncompromising positions had significantly undercut the gun lobby's political clout. Senator Roberti and assembly member Roos introduced similar assault weapons bills in their respective chambers at the start of the session, but no one expected either Senate Bill (SB) 292 or Assembly Bill (AB) 357 to make much headway.

Less than two weeks later, on January 17, 1989, the Stockton schoolyard massacre occurred, instantly causing a dramatic increase in public and elite support for an assault weapons ban. Patrick Purdy, a drifter with a history of mental illness and criminal activity, opened fire with an AK-47 in a playground in Stockton, located an hour from the state capital, Sacramento. Purdy killed 5 elementary school children and wounded 29 other children and a teacher before committing suicide with a handgun.[18] Although the AK-47 was purchased in neighboring Oregon, the media focused attention on Roberti's Senate Bill 292.

As speaker pro tempore of the state senate, Roberti had powerful institutional resources at his disposal to ensure that SB 292 came to vote in the senate. However, Roberti and his staff conducted lobbying efforts in public to take advantage of the perceived shift in public opinion and to attract media attention to undecided legislators. Roberti's press secretary coordinated a very focused media campaign that directly tied assault weapons to the Stockton incident. Roberti's office responded quickly to press releases by opponents and compiled a list of prominent organizations, local governments, and newspapers supporting the ban (Forsyth 1989). In addition, gun control interest groups spent about $175,000 in lobbying efforts in the few weeks before Roberti's and Roos's bills came to vote in the California legislature (Ingram 1989b). In contrast, the National Rifle Association had recently fired its California lobbyist and was unable to effectively campaign against gun control legislation (Jeffe 1989).

The active support of a broad coalition of governmental, educational, and law enforcement associations was key to the campaign to pass assault weapons legislation. The National Rifle Association's refusal to support a ban on armor-piercing bullets in the previous session resulted in the first public split between California law enforcement organizations and the gun lobby (McDonald 1989). The NRA's 1988 national media campaign, which aggressively attacked San Jose's chief of police, Joseph McNamara, for his support of gun control, further alienated law enforcement groups (Davidson 1993). With the strong support of the law enforcement community, pressure mounted on legislators from swing suburban districts to vote for restrictions on assault weapon ownership and sales (Jeffe 1989).

Governor George Deukmejian, a Republican in his second term and a former state attorney general, joined law enforcement in supporting the ban. Just two days after the Stockton incident, Deukmejian announced that he would sign assault weapons legislation, reversing longtime opposition to stricter gun controls (Ingram 1989a). By removing the threat of a gubernatorial veto, Deukmejian's support meant that gun control was politically feasible for the first time in California. Deukmejian's support also provided political cover that allowed undecided legislators to come out in favor of assault weapons legislation. However, by signaling that he favored a ban on specific weapons rather than general controls, Deukmejian was able to influence passage of weaker controls than Roberti had proposed (Ingram 1989a).

Approval of Assault Weapons Legislation

On March 9, 1989, the senate passed SB 292 by the surprisingly large margin of 27–12, with one abstention. Five of 15 Republicans, including 3 from suburban Orange County, voted for the ban; only two Democrats voted in opposition (Ingram 1989d). With chamber rules requiring absolute majorities on bills, the assembly passed a version of Roberti's bill on April 17 by a single vote, 41–34, with six Democrats in opposition and two Republicans voting for it (Ingram and Gillam

1989). The assembly version was then ratified by the senate by a 29–8 vote with the two Democrats previously in opposition voting for SB 292 and two Republicans not voting ("Roll Call" 1989).

The assembly passed Roos's AB 357 on March 13, 1989 (Ingram 1989b). This bill was eventually sent to a conference committee for technical amendments to ensure the governor's support. The revised bill, named the Roberti-Roos Assault Weapons Act of 1989, was then approved by the senate on a 27–11 vote and by the assembly by 41–35 (Walters 1990). The new law banned a list of assault weapons, allowed existing weapons to remain in private ownership if registered with the state, and created a procedure for the California attorney general to add copycat weapons to the list of banned assault guns (Ingram 1989c).

Approval of Waiting-Period Legislation on Rifles and Shotguns

A number of other bills opposed by the gun lobby also worked their way through the legislative process during the 1989–1990 session (McDonald 1989). Assemblyman Lloyd Connelly (D-Sacramento) sponsored the most significant proposal, Assembly Bill 497, to extend the 15-day waiting period on purchases of handguns to all other types of guns and prohibit gun ownership by people with a history of mental illness and those previously convicted of misdemeanor gun offenses (Ingram 1990d). The bill passed the assembly by 48–24 in 1989 but failed in the senate by 14–22 after gun interests rejuvenated their lobbying efforts (Ingram 1990f).

During the winter recess, legislators were influenced by continued acts of gun violence and constituent support for stricter controls on gun sales. In one well-publicized instance, a man killed his two daughters with a recently purchased shotgun in a community near the state capital. Gun control supporters linked this tragedy directly to the earlier defeat of AB 497 as they brought the bill forward for reconsideration at the start of the session; the gunman's widow prominently sat in the visitor's gallery as the legislation was voted upon (Ingram 1990f).[19]

The legislature reversed its previous decision and passed the waiting-period bill, AB 497, in February 1990. The senate passed the bill by 23–10 with the support of 18 Democrats, 4 Republicans, and an independent. Most notable was the vote for approval by conservative Ed Davis (R-Valencia), retired Los Angeles police chief and previously an avid gun rights supporter (Ingram 1990f). In the assembly, the bill was approved by 42–25 with the support of 41 Democrats and 1 Republican, Stan Stanham (R-Oak Run). Stanham represented a mostly rural district and was a gun owner, but his vote had been heavily courted by Handgun Control, Inc. Governor Deukmejian signed the legislation on the same day as he gave a radio broadcast calling it "a common sense approach to dealing with the criminal element in our society" (Ingram 1990c).

The assembly vote was particularly noteworthy because ten Republicans and one Democrat chose not to cast votes (Ingram 1990a). Just days prior to the legislative action, statewide poll results were released showing 81 percent public support for waiting-period legislation (Gunnison 1990a). Many assembly members were still opposed to the bill but decided to abstain from voting. Given assembly rules, these abstentions had the same effect as no votes but allowed legislators to avoid political fallout. Their abstention indicated that for the first time, legislators feared the consequences of not supporting gun control and were torn between competing pressures.

Veto of Firearm Safety Bill

The policy window began to close during consideration of Assembly Bill 1680, which would have required new handgun owners to complete a safety class before taking possession of their weapons. AB 1680 passed the assembly by 42–29 in 1989 and passed the senate by a vote of 21–16 in April 1990. The margin was much narrower than with the earlier assault weapons ban and waiting-period legislation. In fact, AB 1680 passed the senate only after Senator Lucy Killea (D-San Diego) returned briefly to Sacramento to cast her vote for the proposal while in the midst of a family medical emergency (Ingram 1990e). Governor Deukmejian cited the bill's vague statutory language and the apparent lack of a "compelling need" for the legislation in his decision to veto AB 1680. The bill's sponsor, Assemblyman Rusty Areias (D-Los Banos) and gun control supporters accused Deukmejian of vetoing the bill to pacify assembly Republicans and "throw a bone to the NRA" to soften the impact of his support for other gun control legislation (Ingram 1990b).

Deukmejian's veto marked the closing of the policy window for enacting gun control legislation at the state level. The policy window was open only from January 1989 to May 1990. Figure 5.1 summarizes the circumstances leading to the opening of the policy window and its subsequent closure. The short duration of the policy window and its very narrow range meant that change in gun policy was very limited. Furthermore, the legislation was adopted without a fully developed policy stream and reflected political compromises, resulting in an assault weapons ban that is largely symbolic and leaving legislation in place that does not effectively limit gun access by criminals.[20]

FIGURE 5.1
Kingdon's Policy Window Model and Gun Control Policy in California

Convergence of Streams	Policy Window	The Window Closes
		Firearms safety training legislation vetoed (1990)
Problem Stream San Francisco assassinations (1978) San Ysidro/McDonald's massacre (1984) Stockton schoolyard massacre (1989)	Assault weapons ban adopted (1989)	
Policy Stream Proposition 15 defeated (1982), trial balloon Assault weapons proposals unsuccessfully considered in California legislature Rise of Handgun Control, Inc.	Waiting-period requirement adopted (1990) Firearms safety training approved in legislature (1990)	Gun policy proposals stalemated in legislature
Political Stream David Roberti selected as Senate speaker pro tempore (1981) Gun lobby donations decline (mid-1980s) Senator H. L. Richardson retires (1988) Law enforcement community splits with NRA on armor-piercing bullets (1988) Governor Deukmejian announces support for assault weapons ban (1989)		Policymaking shifts to local governments

Source: Compiled by author.

The Policy Primeval Soup: 1991–1996

Although a number of policy proposals have been introduced into the California legislature, another policy window has not opened. There is insufficient support in the state legislature to either strengthen gun controls or return to the earlier pro-gun status. Kingdon uses a modified garbage can model to describe the policy environment during periods when policy windows are closed. The problem, policy, and political streams diverge and problems and solutions mix in the policy environment, symbolically represented as a garbage can (Kingdon 1995, 83–89). Kingdon's description of the policy stream as a "primeval soup" with ideas floating in a fragmented way across policy communities aptly reflects the legislative environment for gun policy proposals in California from 1991 to 1996 (Kingdon 1995, 116–131). Proposals have surfaced in each legislative session and some technical legislation has been approved, but significant policy changes have not been adopted.

Although state law appears to prohibit local bans on gun ownership, local governments have initiated several new gun policies. Interested groups favoring gun controls have intensified their efforts to influence policymaking by venue shopping for receptive cities and counties (Baumgartner and Jones 1993, 216–234). Local ordinances banning Saturday night specials have been adopted both in the Bay Area and in Los Angeles, encompassing much of the state's population. Because of the prominence of these regions, the success of their local regulations has the potential to influence not only the direction of state lawmaking activity but also policies across the nation. This prevalence of localized regulations has also resulted in a patchwork quilt of decentralized policies.

The Problem Stream: Conflicting Focusing Events

The successful passage of gun control legislation in California has been closely linked with focusing events. Periodically, massacre-type events have occurred and have been followed by increased support for stricter gun controls. For example, the July 1, 1993, killing of nine people at a San Francisco law firm by a former client led to the California Bar Association three months later to endorse additional gun control measures to protect the legal community and to study the revision of all gun-related laws (Paddock 1993).[21] This pattern within California is consistent with national polling data, which has documented dramatic short-term public opinion changes due to "highly publicized acts of gun violence, with support increasing sharply immediately after the event and then dropping as memory of the event fades" (Kleck 1991, 367).[22]

However, the apparent evolution of gun control policy toward more restrictions on gun sales and ownership was disrupted by the 1992 Los Angeles riots. Sales of handguns, which had increased at a steady rate every year since 1986 except for 1991, skyrocketed in the wake of the riots. Many citizens became first-time gun owners as handgun purchases went from 311,154 in 1991 to 367,375 in 1992 and then to 448,247 in 1993 (Ingram 1994). Total gun purchases reached 665,229 in 1993, an almost 19 percent increase from the previous year.[23] With the market at saturation point and lower crime rates, gun sales began dropping in 1994 and plummeted in 1995 with total sales of 411,668, 254,626 of which were handguns (Ingram 1996a; Gunnison 1996).

With about half of all Californians now owning guns, one might expect public opinion to turn away from support of additional restrictions on gun ownership. However, at the same time that gun ownership was increasing, law enforcement and public health activists began to aggressively support gun controls (see next section). California polling data do indicate sharp differences in responses between gun owners and nonowners; a majority of gun owners surveyed in 1994 felt that having guns made them feel safer and reduced their chances of becoming crime victims, compared to less than a third of nonowners. Interestingly, though, both owners (76%) and nonowners (91%) favored requirements for registering guns with law enforcement agencies. In addition, the poll showed that a majority of the population feared becoming a victim of a serious crime, up a significant percentage from 1992 (DiCamillo and Field 1994, Field Institute 1994). Thus Californians appear ready to support additional regulations on guns if they keep weapons out of the hands of criminals, but public opinion is divided on proposals that could affect gun ownership by law-abiding private citizens.

The Policy Stream: Policy Entrepreneurs

Policy proposals have continued to be generated by policy entrepreneurs and interest groups. The California attorney general is an elected office, and the last two attorneys general, Democrat John Van de Kamp and Republican Dan Lungren, have used the powers of office to push for more restrictive gun regulations. Interest groups have taken the lead in initiating policy alternatives rather than simply reacting to proposals sponsored by legislators. Interest groups often have focused on problems with existing gun policy and on different constituency groups, which has resulted in apparently incompatible policy alternatives being advanced simultaneously in the California legislature (Baumgartner and Jones 1993, 201–215).[24] See Table 5.1 for a summary of interest groups and their positions on gun regulation.

The National Rifle Association has sponsored legislation in states across the country, including California, on concealed-weapons permits. The NRA also has tried to expand its constituent base through its "Don't Be a Victim" advertising campaign encouraging female gun ownership. The NRA has claimed that the number of women owning guns increased from 12 million to 17 million from the mid-1980s to the mid-1990s. In contrast, a University of Chicago opinion poll found that gun ownership patterns had remained largely unchanged. Informal media surveys of gun shops indicate that there have been increases in female ownership within California, but the magnitude is impossible to calculate (Japenga 1984; Montgomery 1994).

The law enforcement community has been increasingly vocal in advocating more restrictive gun regulations. Los Angeles area law enforcement officials have publicly supported a ban on Saturday night special handguns (Riccardi 1994). In addition, the California Police Chiefs Association has taken an extremely strong position for strict gun control measures through a 1995 position paper entitled "Confronting the American Tragedy: The Need to Better Regulate Firearms" (California Police Chiefs Association 1995).

A most intriguing development has been the recent sponsorship by the California Wellness Foundation of a five-year, $35 million educational program on handgun violence.[25] The California Wellness Foundation used statistics from the national Centers for Disease Control and more specific California statistics to categorize handgun violence as a major health care concern.[26] The foundation has underwritten the activities of the Campaign to Prevent Handgun Violence Against Kids, based in northern California. The campaign has developed and distributed sophisticated citizen-involvement kits to encourage bans on Saturday night specials, regulation of handguns as consumer products, maintenance of restrictions on concealed-weapons permits, and increased "home rule" for local governments to enact their own handgun regulations.[27]

In addition, the foundation commissioned a series of 1996 public opinion polls in selected metropolitan areas on attitudes before and after being shown statistics about gun violence. Although many questions were rather leading, voters opposed proposals to make it easier to obtain concealed-weapons permits and supported a ban on Saturday night specials (EDK Associates 1996). See Table 5.2 for a sampling of survey questions and results.

The California Wellness Foundation has provided funding to over a

TABLE 5.1
Interest Groups

Gun Rights Organizations	*Description/Position(s)*
National Rifle Association	Most prominent gun-owner association in the US; maintains a Sacramento office and lobbyist.
Gun Owners of California	Most strident organization promoting gun rights in California.

Organizations Favoring Gun Controls	*Description/Position(s)*
Handgun Control, Inc./Center to Prevent Handgun Violence	Most prominent national organization favoring additional restrictions on gun ownership and sales; maintains regional office in Los Angeles and satellite offices in San Francisco and San Diego.
California Police Chiefs Association	Law enforcement association that has supported the most stringent gun control measures; issued 1995 position paper entitled "Confronting the American Tragedy--The Need to Better Regulate Firearms."
California State Sheriffs Association	Association representing county sheriffs; opposed concealed-weapons-permit legislation but also issued statement reaffirming its support of private gun ownership.
California League of Cities	Endorsed the Police Chiefs Association position paper and opposed proposed concealed-weapons- permit legislation.
California Bar Association	Passed statements in 1993 calling for additional gun control measures.
California Wellness Foundation	$600 million foundation endowed by Health Net; has awarded $35 million in grants related to gun violence education and research.
The Campaign to Prevent Handgun Violence Against Kids	Recipient of California Wellness Foundation grant; supports Saturday night special ban, regulation of handguns as a consumer product, local control over handgun regulation, and increased penalties for carrying concealed weapons without a permit.

Source: Compiled by author.

TABLE 5.2
California Wellness Foundation-Sponsored Public Opinion Poll Results from Selected Questions

(Question relating to liberalizing laws for concealed-weapon permitting) Do you favor or oppose this bill? [Is that strongly favor / strongly oppose?]

	Los Angeles	Orange County	Sacramento	San Diego
Strongly favor	9%	10%	14%	7%
Favor	12	16	22	19
Oppose	35	26	26	35
Strongly Oppose	38	44	32	32
Don't Know	6	5	7	8

Do you favor or oppose banning the sale and possession of poorly made, cheap to buy and easy to conceal handguns known as "Saturday Night Specials?" [is that strongly favor / strongly oppose?]

	Los Angeles	Orange County	Sacramento	San Diego
Strongly favor	46%	40%	39%	44%
Favor	12	13	22	28
Oppose	21	16	19	15
Strongly Oppose	15	28	14	9
Don't Know	6	3	6	4

[Two Southern California cities] have both banned the sale and use of "Saturday Night Specials." Would you be in favor of your city banning the sale and use of "Saturday Night Specials?"

	Los Angeles	Orange County	Sacramento	San Diego
Yes, in favor	88%	84%	78%	84%
No, not in favor	7	13	17	13
Don't Know	5	4	5	3

Source: EDK Associates, New York, Spring 1996.

dozen community organizations working on youth violence issues and over $6 million to a trauma organization affiliated with the politically active Pacific Center for Violence Prevention. This serious commitment has the potential to direct the course of public opinion and alter the political environment regarding gun regulation. The Gun Owners of California has strongly criticized the effort for essentially being funded by businesses and patients using Health Net, the foundation's sponsor, as its health maintenance organization (Herbertson 1996).

The foundation's work with grassroots organizations is part of the growth in policy entrepreneurship at the local level. Gun control advocates have successfully promoted local regulations, but in response to this success, gun rights organizations now have increased their local lobbying efforts. A number of competing interest groups have now formed that lobby local city councils and communicate with their local state legislators. For example, Simi Valley Council member Sandi Webb, an extremely vocal gun rights supporter, heads up the Second Amendment Caucus and scheduled a meeting during the annual League of California Cities conference.[28]

The Political Stream: Legislative Turmoil

In the 1990s the California legislature has failed to enact any major legislative proposals. The reapportionment process has led to an increasing number of "safe" districts dominated by one party, resulting in the election of candidates who hold more partisan views (Jeffe 1992). With gun control generally favored by Democratic elected officials and gun rights supported by conservative Republicans, gun issues have been part of the broader, bitterly partisan gridlock that has characterized the legislature in the 1980s and 1990s. In 1996, after a year with three assembly speakers and two successful recall campaigns by conservative Republicans against incumbent moderate Republicans, assembly Republicans held a majority for the first time since 1970. Under the leadership of Assemblyman Curt Pringle (R-Garden Grove), the assembly has supported a deeply conservative, partisan legislative agenda (Borland 1996, Bailey, Warren, and Filkins 1996).

Assemblyman Pete Knight (R-Palmdale) introduced AB 638 in February 1995 to require local governments to issue concealed weapons to all individuals who pass a background check and demonstrate firearm competence. This proposal was similar to concealed-weapons legislation that passed in a majority of states with the strong support of the National Rifle Association from 1987 through 1996 (Dean 1996). However, law enforcement organizations vigorously opposed the proposal. The opposition by law enforcement was especially strong in Los Angeles County, where it was expected that up to 500,000 permits would be issued. Local governments, which maintain strong links to law enforcement groups, also saw the bill as unwanted state preemption of a traditional local government responsibility.

Assembly Bill 638 received limited committee support in 1995 but quickly passed the assembly by a 42–33 vote in early 1996 under the direction of the new Republican leadership. Not only had the partisan majority changed but less than 20 percent of the overall assembly membership had been in office in the 1989–1990 session. Regardless, the vote on AB 638 was deeply partisan with only one Republican, Steve Kuykendall (R-Rancho Palos Verdes) voting in opposition. Likewise, the only two Democrats who supported AB 638 were concealed-weapons permit holder Denise Ducheny (D-San Diego) and Willard Murray (D-Los Angeles), a longtime gun rights supporter.[29] In the Democratic-controlled senate, the Criminal Procedure Committee voted 6–1 not to report the bill out of committee. The image of frontier justice was invoked to oppose the bill, with memorable testimony by the president of the California Police Chiefs Association that "the citizens of this state do not want a return to the Tombstone era, when disputes were settled, not by rational discussion, but by who had the quickest draw" (Ingram 1996b).

Ironically, the evidence suggests that a less partisan approach could have resulted in the passage of a concealed-weapons reform bill. A 1986 assembly study had found that concealed-weapon policies were inconsistently applied by local jurisdictions and that state laws were confusing and lacked coherence (State of California Assembly Office of Research 1986). Senate leader Bill Lockyer (D-Hayward) admitted that he would support a bill that set uniform standards while preserving most local police and sheriff discretion (Vellinga 1996). The paradoxical example of Isleton, a small community in Sacramento County, highlights the need for reform while giving credence to predictions that legislation like AB 638 would lead to unacceptable numbers of permits being issued. Isleton's leaders decided to market concealed-weapons permits as a revenue-generating program; with a population of only about 1,000 citizens, Isleton plans to issue 700 permits a year to county residents and has a waiting list of 6,000 people (Borland 1995). Some opponents of AB 638 may be willing to sacrifice some local autonomy and support increases in numbers of permits in some locations if more rational standards can be enacted and cases like Isleton eliminated.

Public opinion and recent legislative history suggest that majority support may be possible in the California legislature for a mix of pro- and antigun bills. Proposals such as AB 638 and calls for bans on Saturday night specials have emerged on the political agenda at the same time as proposals that have received less political attention. For example, the state legislature easily passed a bill in 1996, Senate Bill 2069, to preempt local land-use controls over shooting ranges. Although Governor Pete Wilson vetoed the bill, the NRA effectively promoted SB 2069 in the state legislature as necessary to protect the right of gun owners to have practice sites, similar to "right to farm" regulations that have been widely adopted at the state and local levels of government (League of California Cities 1996). During the same session the legislature passed AB 632, sponsored by Assemblyman Richard Katz (D-Los Angeles), which increases the penalties for carrying concealed weapons without a permit. AB 632 easily passed both chambers with final votes of 26–5 in the senate and 56–11 in the assembly and was signed into law by Governor Wilson in September 1996. Although all of the votes in opposition were by Republicans, it is notable that assembly Republicans supported AB 632 by over two to one; assembly Republicans apparently did not consider support of AB 632 to be inconsistent with support of the NRA's concealed-weapons-permit proposal, perhaps because AB 632 relates to criminal penalties for the illegal use of concealed weapons rather than the conditions for issuing permits.

The Political Stream: Statewide Offices

The diversity of California as a whole has meant that statewide elections have been more personality driven, and candidates who are perceived as being too extremist have been unsuccessful in gaining statewide offices. The two most prominent gun rights supporters in California, state senator Richardson and Assemblyman Tom McClintock, who both espouse very conservative political views, have been defeated in runs for statewide offices.[30] Los Angeles mayor Tom Bradley's narrow defeat by George Deukmejian for governor in 1982 may have been due to Bradley's support of Proposition 15 to restrict handguns, along with unusually high voter turnout from rural, conservative gun rights supporters (Brazil 1982, 444; Clayton 1986). Support for gun control usually has not been a critical factor in more recent statewide elections.

It is notable that gun rights supporters mobilized around a district-level recall election against state senator Roberti in his last year of office rather than simply opposing his concurrent campaign for state treasurer. The recall effort failed by 59 percent to 41 percent and was described by the popular media as a major defeat for the gun lobby (Scott 1994). However, in the longer term the gun lobby triumphed because the diversion of campaign funds away from his treasurer's race contributed to Roberti's defeat in the Democratic primary (Block 1994).

At this time it is likely that the governor's office will continue to be occupied by individuals who are supportive of at least some additional gun controls. Deukmejian's successor, Republican Pete Wilson, has a fairly moderate political record and has voiced support of "reasonable controls" on guns (Ingram 1991) while also aggressively pursuing anticrime legislation and supportint gun ownership (Chavez 1993). Attorney General Dan Lungren, the most likely Republican gubernatorial candidate in 1998, has sided with law enforcement officials supporting gun control and announced his opposition to the concealed-weapons-permit bill, AB 638, whereas Wilson has remained neutral (Bernstein 1996). Possible Democratic candidates such as Lieutenant Governor Gray Davis, Controller Kathleen Connell, and Senator Feinstein also would be expected to support stricter gun control laws.

Prospects for Policy Windows

Local Government Policy

State policymaking on gun control has remained at a standstill since 1990, but a number of local governments have adopted ordinances and programs to limit gun ownership and use. In 1993, San Francisco, Oakland, and Los Angeles sponsored gun-exchange programs. In these urbanized areas, the programs were a moderate success; the Los Angeles program gathered 412 guns in a five-day program that provided tickets for concerts and sporting events in exchange for weapons (Johnson 1993). In 1994, Contra Costa County therapists, in cooperation with local police, initiated an especially innovative program to offer three hours of therapy to anyone bringing in a gun (Paddock 1994).

In recent years, several local communities have approved restrictions on ammunition sales as a way of controlling weapons use without directly banning weapons. In March 1995, the city of Pasadena pioneered this policy option in southern California by requiring registration of ammunition purchasers (Winton and Holguin 1995). Several other Los Angeles County cities passed similar ordinances, but they have not been successful in lowering crime rates or in making crime solving easier (Riccardi and Brazil 1996).

Local governments now are adopting ordinances to ban sales of Saturday night specials, although gun rights organizations have filed suit on the basis that state law preempts such ordinances ("West Hollywood" 1995). In southern California, West Hollywood adopted a ban in 1995 and the Los Angeles City Council voted 13–0 in September 1996 to approve a similar ordinance (Riccardi and Brazil 1996; Ferrell and Zamichow 1996). In the Bay Area, the large cities of San Francisco, San Jose, and Oakland all have adopted Saturday night special ordinances (Johnson 1996).

These actions suggest that the momentum to open a policy window can be promoted by trying other political venues. It may be possible to create enough miniwindows at the local level to increase pressure on decisionmakers at high levels of government. Local innovation may show that merging of the problem, policy, and political streams is feasible at a higher level of government in the absence of cataclysmic focusing events. In Los Angeles, supporters of the Saturday night special ban have recognized concerns about the substitutability of other firearms and the likely ineffective nature of a single-city ban, but they see it as a first step. As Councilman Nate Holden stated, "We can't ban all guns . . . but we can ban Saturday night specials as we did with Uzis and AK47s. And when we took that action, Sacramento listened, and then Washington."[31] This optimism about Saturday night specials is at least partially justified; California senator Barbara Boxer introduced a bill to prohibit production of Saturday night specials nationwide and to extend an existing ban on imports (Hefland 1996).

Statewide Policy Windows

With term limits going into effect in the late 1990s, the membership of the state legislature is expected to undergo rapid turnover.[32] Term limits and the return of open primaries in 1998 make it difficult to predict the composition of the state legislature as we move into the twenty-first century. However, the public's shift away from the extreme conservatism of the 1994 elections and the heightened entrepreneurship of antigun interest groups make it unlikely that the California legislature will reverse previous gun control legislation. As a result of the 1996 elections, the Democrats outnumber the Republicans by 44 to 36 in the state assembly, which should give extra political strength to those who seek to maintain current regulations. There is a possibility, though, that state-level policymaking will remain gridlocked. The intensity of involvement by law enforcement and health organizations and their ability to link policy proposals to public opinion will be critical in determining the course of gun control legislation in California.

Notes

1. The concealed-weapons bill was defeated by committee in the state senate. The shooting-range bill was vetoed by Governor Pete Wilson.

2. For a detailed discussion of the Wild West legend and its role in popular culture and politics, see Slotkin (1992).

3. The assassination of President John F. Kennedy in 1963 and especially the killings of civil rights leader Martin Luther King and presidential candidate Robert Kennedy in 1968 are credited with helping to bring about passage of the federal Gun Control Act of 1968 after several years of debate in Congress (see Kennett and Anderson (1975, 243; Robin 1991, 19–23).

4. For a summary of California laws see Wright, Rossi, and Daly (1983, 250–267).

5. California Supreme Court, *People* v. *Tanner*, 151 Cal. Rptr. 299, December 22, 1978. A revised decision was later issued upon rehearing. *People v. Tanner*, 156 Cal. Rptr. 450, June 14, 1979.

6. The 1978 election confirmed Chief Justice Rose Bird for the remaining 8 years of a 12-year term. See Christensen and Gerston (1984, 168–174).

7. According to Kingdon (1995, 94–100), a focusing event is a crisis, disaster, personal experience, or symbol that reinforces a trend, focuses attention, or increases awareness of a policy problem.

8. San Francisco is both the fourth most populous city and the only combination city and county in California, giving its mayor special visibility.

9. Court of Appeals of California, First Appellate District, Division Three, *Doe* v. *City and County of San Francisco*, 186 Cal. Rptr. 380, October 13, 1982.

10. Dianne Feinstein, in a speech ten years later, cited the San Ysidro incident as one of several violent acts that strengthened her views on gun control and the only event that took place outside her northern California political base (see "Decision '94"). For a summary of the assault weapons import problem, see Robin (1991).

11. For book-length discussions see Wright, Rossi, and Daly (1983) and Kates (1984). For more recent research see Kleck (1991) and Wright and Rossi (1994). For more normative approaches see Kopel (1995).

12. California was one of the leaders of the Progressive Movement and its state constitution provides for statewide initiatives and referenda. State and local politics follow the principle known as Dillon's rule, whereby the state government reserves all powers not explicitly delegated to local governments. In practice, local governments, especially those designated as charter cities, are given considerable latitude to enact their own regulations and ordinances. The initiative and referendum processes also may be used at the local level.

13. Gun Owners of California, Inc., membership brochure, 1996.

14. Gun Owners of California, Inc., "Dear Friend" letter, 1996.

15. In 1966 California voters adopted Proposition 1A, which established a full-time professionalized legislature.

16. Ironically, the leadership change was sparked by alarm at Senator Richardson's successful sponsorship of a protégé against the 20-year senate incumbent, breaking an unwritten norm against outside-district campaigning (see Christensen and Gerston 1984, 136–138).

17. Richardson lost handily to former lieutenant governor and record producer Mike Curb. Curb lost the general election to Democrat Leo McCarthy.

18. See Robin (1991, 81). For an in-depth account of Patrick Edward "Eddie" Purdy's background and the events in Stockton, see Davidson (1993, 3–19).

19. Incidents also had taken place in Sacramento and Los Angeles. See Gunnison (1990b).

20. For a gun rights critique of California's legislation see Kopel (1994, 23–36). For a critique in support of tougher gun controls see "Taming the Gun Monster: Local Crusades," (*Los Angeles Times*, December 3, 1993). For thought-

ful discussion of the flaws of assault weapons legislation generally see Kleck (1991, 70–82). Wright, Rossi, and Daly (1983, 307–308) also make the point that gun legislation has lacked "basic knowledge about the connections between crime and gun usage, the distribution system through which guns are circulated, and the ways in which criminal justice systems in this country operate."

21. See also "After Long Debate, Gun Control Measures Pass Bar Conference," *Recorder* October 12, 1993.

22. Kleck reviewed polling data that documented changes following the 1963 assassination of President John Kennedy, the 1981 assassination attempt on President Ronald Reagan, and the 1980 killing of John Lennon.

23. Purchasers were not tracked by gender, but anecdotal evidence suggests that the number of women gun owners increased greatly following the Los Angeles riots. See Chou (1993) and Seligman (1994).

24. Baumgartner and Jones (1993) demonstrate through analysis of case studies of congressional activity that competing interest groups frequently use different jurisdictional venues and advocate completely different ideologies, in effect talking past each other.

25. The California Wellness Foundation was endowed by Health Net, one of the largest health maintenance organizations in the United States as part of court settlements and has had assets approaching $800 million. The Violence Prevention Initiative was funded in 1992 with an initial commitment of $25 million, which has since been increased to $35 million. For a summary of the decision to fund violence prevention programs see Leovy (1983).

26. See the Campaign to Prevent Handgun Violence Against Kids, "Handguns Are the #1 Killer of California Kids," in *Fact Sheet*, 1996. For an example of a research article concluding that health care professions should become actively involved in efforts to support gun control, see Wintemute, Teret, and Kraus (1987).

27. The campaign's literature includes a series of fact sheets on handgun violence and policy proposals (updated in March 1996), the Public Service Announcement Organizing Kit, the Community Leader Portfolio, and the Citizen Involvement Kit. Public service announcement videos also are available for broadcast.

28. Council member Webb has received an unusually high amount of media attention because she made an obscene gesture at Senator Feinstein to protest Feinstein's support of gun control during a public gathering.

29. Murray had originally been elected over an incumbent Republican due to NRA support. For information on the assembly vote see Morain and Vanzi (1996) and Sweeney (1986).

30. As noted previously, Richardson was defeated in the Republican primary election for lieutenant governor in 1986. McClintock was successful in the Republican primary for controller in 1994 but lost in the general election to Democrat Kathleen Connell. For a profile of McClintock see Barber (1994).

31. Nate Holden, September 4, 1996, cited in Ferrell and Zamichow (1996).

32. In 1990, California voters passed an initiative, Proposition 140, that sets

lifetime limits of three two-year terms for the assembly and two four-year terms for the senate. Even before the limits became effective, there were unusually high numbers of special elections and turnover because state legislators ran for other offices. See Ross (1996, 189–190).

6

The Structure of Public Support for Gun Control: The 1988 Battle over Question 3 in Maryland

James G. Gimpel and Robin M. Wolpert

In 1989, the killing of five schoolchildren by a gun-toting maniac in Stockton, California, raised the salience of gun control and spurred a spate of new restrictive laws across the nation. Even before the Stockton killings, however, the Democratic-dominated Maryland legislature had already taken the lead on gun control by proposing a ban on sales in its spring 1988 session. Maryland has a history of progressive legislation on gun control. The state passed a criminal background check and seven-day waiting period for the purchase of handguns in 1966, at least ten years in advance of other states. But a waiting period is considerably less restrictive than a ban on sales. Although many cities and the District of Columbia had passed handgun control laws, no state had even come close to banning the sale of handguns since the failure of a gun control referendum in California (Proposition 15) in 1982.

The bill proposed by the Maryland state legislature in 1988 would set up a nine-member board to decide which small handguns could be sold within the state. Known as the Handgun Roster Board, the group would be made up of law enforcement officials, public citizens, a representative from a handgun control group and from the NRA, and two members from the gun industry. They would determine which handguns could be used legitimately for recreation, law enforcement, or self-protection. The goal of the legislation was to outlaw cheap and poorly manufactured handguns known as Saturday night specials that were purportedly used in many street crimes (Barnes and Goldstein 1988; Schmidt and Goldstein 1988; Lancaster 1988a).

The bill was passed by a comfortable margin and signed into law by Governor William Donald Schaefer in May. Less than six weeks later, however, anti–gun control activists, with the support of the National Rifle Association (NRA), gathered the necessary 34,000 signatures to place the law on the general election ballot in November. Known as Question 3, the gun ban referendum would turn into the most intensely fought political campaign in Maryland that year.

Scholars have noted that the intensity of preference for gun rights is far greater among opponents of gun control than the preference for gun restrictions is among proponents of gun control (Schuman and Presser 1981; Kleck 1991). It was predictable, then, that the NRA and its allies would wage a far stronger campaign against the law than the supporters would in favor of it. The NRA launched a high-profile effort on the airwaves to defeat the legislation, spending nearly $5 million on advertising and grassroots mobilization. Gun rights advocates hired the same campaign manager, George Young, who had helped defeat California's Proposition 15 by 2 to 1 six years earlier. Young organized an operation that included a paid staff of 30 people, a large phonebank operation, and thousands of NRA volunteers (Lancaster 1988b, 1988c). The thrust of the NRA message in TV spots was that the Handgun Roster Board would have the power to outlaw all handguns, thereby denying Maryland citizens the right to defend themselves against crime. The NRA's campaign also focused on the complaint that it was impossible to determine which guns had "legitimate" purposes and which did not and attempted to raise fears that the board would be stacked in favor of gun control advocates.

Supporters of the gun ban, though not nearly so well financed, included most of Maryland's prominent political elites such as the governor, key legislative leaders, and officials from the state's main law enforcement agencies. In addition to these well-placed proponents, a grassroots group, Citizens for Eliminating Saturday Night Specials, organized to counter the NRA campaign. Run on a shoestring budget and a paid staff of six (Lancaster 1988c), the organization was able to place ads, financed on a budget of $275,000, only very late in the contest. Although the supporters of the gun ban had far less money than those who sought to overturn it, public opinion in Maryland was running on their side. Early polls indicated that Marylanders favored the law by 3 to 1, especially in the more urban areas of the state between Washington and Baltimore (Montgomery, Howard, and Prince George's Counties) (Lancaster 1988b).

By the end of the race, however, the NRA-backed forces were closing the public opinion gap. In the last week of October, a *Washington Post* poll indicated that the gun law was favored by a tiny margin—49 to 44 percent—a statistical dead heat (Lancaster and Morin 1988). Several days before the election, a Baltimore *Sun* poll indicated an even closer 48 percent to 47 percent edge in favor of the law, with 5 percent undecided (Bock 1988). The *Post* poll showed that in the Washington suburbs, voters were evenly split, but the *Sun* poll, taken about a week later, showed that the Washington suburbs had moved into the favorable column. Opposition to the law was concentrated in rural western and southern Maryland and on the eastern shore. The city of Baltimore and the Baltimore suburbs were evenly split.

Even more surprising was that blacks were evenly divided, with more black voters than white voters claiming to be undecided. The gun rights campaign had specifically targeted the black community with the message that gun control advocacy was a racial issue—that the new law would ban affordable guns for self-protection and black voters would be less able to protect themselves against crime than affluent suburban white voters. The NRA had purchased advertising on black radio stations and paid volunteers $6 an hour to heavily canvass black neighborhoods in the Washington suburbs and in Baltimore (Lancaster 1988a). In the waning days of the campaign, the gun lobby had even hired black activists as consultants in Baltimore to put out the message that the gun ban would disarm poor blacks and allow wealthy whites to keep their guns.

The Election Outcome: A Defeat for the NRA

When the votes came in on election day, the gun control law was upheld by 58 to 42 percent. Even though the NRA outspent the opposition by 10 to 1, it failed to convince voters in the most populated areas of the state. In affluent Montgomery County, the law was decisively upheld by 72 to 28 percent, and in Baltimore, it was upheld 69 to 31 percent. The distribution of support for the law across the state's 24 counties is depicted in Map 6.1. The darkly shaded areas show the counties in the highest-support quartile. Heavily urbanized central Maryland stands out as an island of support sandwiched between rural counties that opposed the legislation. The law found its strongest support in Montgomery County and the greatest opposition in rural Garrett County, where a mere 13.7 percent voted to uphold the ban.

Supporters and opponents alike argued that the campaign had turned into a referendum on the NRA itself (Lancaster 1988d). Media analysts as well as politicians attributed the victory to the fact that

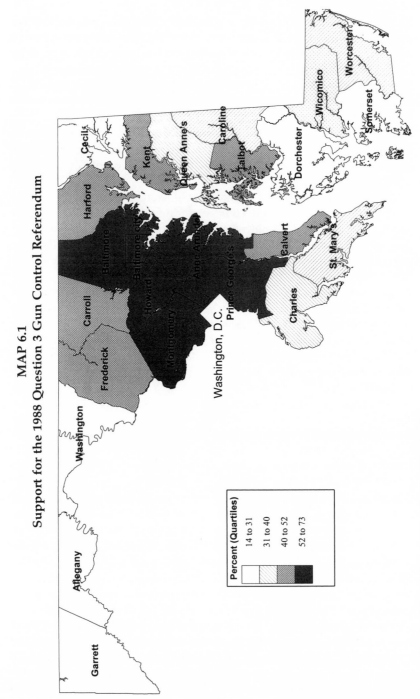

MAP 6.1

Support for the 1988 Question 3 Gun Control Referendum

Percent (Quartiles)

14 to 31

31 to 40

40 to 52

52 to 73

Source: Maryland State Administrative Board of Election Laws

Marylanders resented the interference of well-financed outsiders trying to overturn popularly supported state laws. From the beginning, the gun rights forces faced long odds, and their campaign was remarkable for making the contest as close as it turned out. But with a high proportion of residents living so close to Washington, D.C., "the murder capital of the world," it is little wonder that the gun control forces prevailed. Montgomery and Prince George's Counties receive all of their local television news from Washington-based stations. Day after day, the intense criminal activity in Washington's poorer neighborhoods enters these homes through the evening news.

The Structure of Support for Gun Control Legislation

Table 6.1 provides the breakdown of support for the legislation from exit polls taken on election day by CBS News and the *New York Times.* For comparison purposes, polling data from the California gun control referendum in 1982 are also shown. Support for gun control is uniformly higher across all demographic categories in Maryland than in California. Aside from this obvious fact, however, there are some striking differences. First, support for the Maryland law increased with age; in California, support decreased slightly as voters became older. Second, racial differences in support for the legislation were greater in Maryland than in California. Sixty-four percent of blacks ultimately supported Question 3's ban, compared to 52 percent of whites, a difference of 12 percentage points. In California, however, there was only a 3 percent difference in support. Finally, there was a far wider gap between support from the lowest- and highest-income groups in Maryland than in California. Apparently, the Maryland gun law contained a component of class cleavage, with wealthier voters favoring the law and poorer voters opposing it. The California law did not divide voters along class lines to nearly the same extent.

What explains the structure of public support for Question 3 in Maryland? For further insight into this issue, we performed a multivariate analysis to evaluate the outcome of the vote. There are obvious rural-urban differences evident in Map 6.1. Gun enthusiasts are more likely to live in rural areas, where guns, hunting, and sport shooting activities are more common (Wright and Marston 1975; Bankston and Thompson 1989). Crime rates are also far higher in urban and suburban areas than in rural areas, so support for gun control legislation as a means of protection from criminals may be lower in rural areas.

Race and class are relevant explanatory variables because the NRA's campaign deliberately set out to divide the state by class, building

TABLE 6.1

**Support for the 1988 Maryland Gun Ban Referendum and the 1982
California Gun Ban Referendum by Selected Characteristics**

Variable	Voted For MD Gun Ban	Voted For CA Gun Ban
Male	56.5	35.1
Female	52.6	42.2
Age 18-29	48.2	44.3
30-44	58.6	42.0
45-59	53.4	32.1
60-older	60.2	36.4
White	51.9	38.2
Black	63.9	41.4
Hispanic	62.5	39.7
Republican	46.5	28.0
Democrat	60.0	47.6
Independent	53.2	38.4
Conservative	45.4	24.8
Moderate	53.8	37.9
Liberal	68.9	59.0
Less than HS	47.9	-
High School Graduate	42.6	-
College Graduate	65.1	-
Lowest Income	47.6	34.0
Highest Income	70.4	45.4
Bush (Reagan) Voters	40.9	26.8
Dukakis (Carter) Voters	66.6	51.3
Gun owners	31.9	-
Baltimore City	57.1	-
Baltimore Suburbs	51.4	-
Washington Suburbs	70.7	-
Rural Maryland	35.2	-

Source: CBS News/*New York Times* Election Day Exit Polls, 1988; CBS News/*New York
Times* Election Day Surveys 1982.

black support for repeal of the gun ban. This strategy had some prima
facie plausibility because although the black community in urban areas
is often victimized by gun violence, it is also less likely to have competent police protection. At least one study shows that defensive-weap-
ons ownership rises when citizens perceive police services to be
ineffective (Smith and Uchida 1988). Fear of crime is also highly related
to the purchase of firearms for protection (McDowall and Loftin 1983;

Lizotte and Bordua 1980). Therefore, the perceived need for handguns as a means for self-defense might be higher in inner-city neighborhoods than in the affluent suburbs, which have much higher levels of public service. It is also well known that blacks are far less trusting of the local police than whites. Tensions between the black community and local police forces are widespread not just in large cities but in many smaller ones. Thus, pro–gun rights advocates could persuasively argue that Question 3 was an attempt by wealthy white suburbanites and predominantly white police forces to disarm poor blacks.

Partisanship and ideology may also be relevant in explaining support for gun control. Republicans in Congress and at the state level have been more supportive of gun rights than Democrats, who have usually led the charge to restrict access to firearms; and conservatives, including many conservative Democrats, have opposed restrictive gun laws, whereas liberals have been at the forefront of gun control efforts. Since women are less likely to be gun owners than men, we expect that women are more likely to support gun control legislation than men (Young 1986; Bankston et al. 1990; Branscombe and Owen 1991; Sheley et al. 1994). Similarly, since older people are more likely to be gun owners than younger ones (Sheley et al. 1994), we expect that support for restrictive gun laws will decrease with age. Finally, we add a control variable for gun ownership, hypothesizing that gun owners are far more likely to vote against Question 3 than nongun owners because gun owners have a direct stake in the outcome (Kleck 1991, 365).

Results in Maryland

The results for a logistic regression model predicting opposition to the Maryland gun control law are presented in Table 6.2. For comparison purposes, we present two models, one excluding region, the other including region. In the model excluding region (Maryland 1), five variables are significant predictors of the vote: race, ideology, income, age, and gun ownership. Of these, gun ownership and income have the greatest impact. Gun owners were about 33 percent more likely to vote against the gun ban than those not owning guns. Those in the wealthiest category (>$100,000) were 36 percent more likely to vote for the ban than those in the lowest-income cohort (<$12,500). Ideology was also an important influence; conservatives were about 20 percent less likely to vote for gun control than liberals. Finally, blacks and older people were more likely to vote for the ban than whites and younger voters.

The second model (Maryland 2) shows that once region is taken into

TABLE 6.2

Influences on Opposition to the Question 3 Gun Control Legislation in Maryland and Proposition 15 in California

Variable	Maryland 1 MLEb (Std. Error)	Maryland 2 MLEb (Std. Error)	California MLEb (Std. Error)
Black	-.51** (.21)	-.37 (.26)	.02** (.16)
Effect	-12.1	-6.5	.45
Hispanic	-.02 (.83)	.09 (.87)	.02 (.20)
Effect	-.5	2.2	.47
Democrat	-.18 (.23)	-.22 (.23)	-.37** (.12)
Effect	-4.4	-5.4	-8.7
Republican	-.07 (.25)	-.11 (.26)	.23* (.13)
Effect	-1.7	-2.7	5.4
Female	.11 (.17)	.13 (.17)	-.27** (.08)
Effect	2.7	3.2	-6.3
Ideology	-.42** (.12)	-.38** (.13)	-.61** (.07)
Effect	-20.2	-18.3	-28.2
Income	-.31** (.07)	-.29** (.07)	-.16** (.04)
Effect	-36.4	-34.0	-14.5
Age	-.19** (.08)	-.15* (.09)	.11** (.04)
Effect	-13.8	-10.9	7.7
Gun owner	1.35** (.20)	1.13** (.21)	--
Effect	32.5	27.5	--
Washington Suburbs	--	-.58** (.24)	--
Effect	--	-13.9	--
Baltimore City	--	-.11 (.31)	--
Effect	--	-2.7	--
Rural Maryland	--	.44* (.25)	--
Effect	--	10.9	--
Constant	0.46	0.56	-.05
N	698	698	2609
% Correct	66.8	67.9	66.2
Null Model	54.7	54.7	61.0
Model χ^2,df	97.2, 9	117.9, 12	228.9, 8
Significance	p<.0001	p<.0001	p<.0001

Source: CBS News/New York Times Election Day Exit Polls, 1988.
*P<.10; **p<.05
Notes: Dep. variable: 0 = Voted For Gun Control, 1 = Voted Against Gun Control.
Effect = Change in the odds of voting against the gun control by moving each x variable from its lowest to highest value while all holding all other x variables constant at their sample means.

account, the impact of race diminishes considerably and the impact of income remains about the same as in the first model. The effects for gun ownership, ideology, and age change only slightly. The influence of region is shown in the coefficients for the Washington suburbs, Baltimore, and rural Maryland. Washington suburban voters were about 14 percent less likely to vote against the ban than those elsewhere in the state. Conversely, voters in rural Maryland opposed the ban even if related variables are controlled. Those in the city of Baltimore showed no decisive tendency to support or oppose the legislation.

Contrary to expectations, party identification had very little discernible impact on the vote. Apparently, Question 3 cross-cut party lines because so many affluent Republicans voted for the ban and many Democrats opposed it. Women were slightly more likely to vote against gun control than were men, although the difference was not statistically significant.

The structure of support for Question 3 by county indicates that gun control is a class rather than a racial issue in Maryland. In Figure 6.1, a scatterplot illustrates the relationship between median family income and the percentage of each county voting for the ban. The association

FIGURE 6.1
Income Cleavage on Question 3, by County

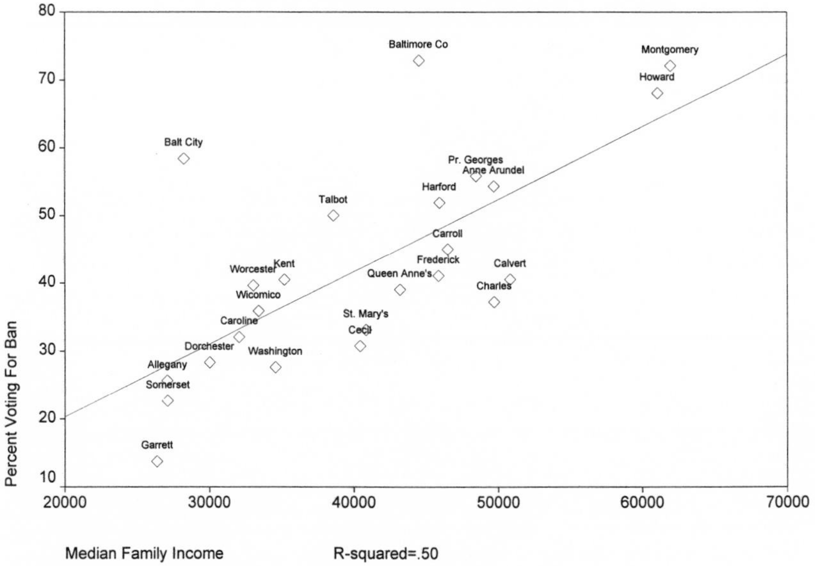

Median Family Income   R-squared=.50

Source: Maryland Board of Elections

between these two variables is quite strong. At one extreme, the wealthiest counties, Howard and Montgomery, voted strongly in favor of the ban. At the other extreme, in the poorer rural counties, the ban found very little support. Income alone explains about half the aggregate countywide variation in the vote. The county-level data also reinforce the notion that the ban did not cleave the state along racial lines. In Figure 6.2, the scatterplot shows that there was very little difference in support for the ban across counties with varying proportions of black voters. Several of the counties that were most supportive contain small percentages of minorities; some of those with large black populations were hostile to its passage.

In evaluating the extent of urban-rural cleavage on Question 3 across Maryland, we find that urban-rural differences do explain some of the differences in levels of public support, but not nearly as much as class differences do (see Figure 6.3). The city of Baltimore is an especially influential point in Figure 6.3, standing alone as the most urbanized jurisdiction in the state. Despite Baltimore's dense population, support for the ban did not run as high as in several less urbanized suburban counties. Urbanization is not the best predictor of support for Question

FIGURE 6.2
Racial Cleavage on Question 3, by County

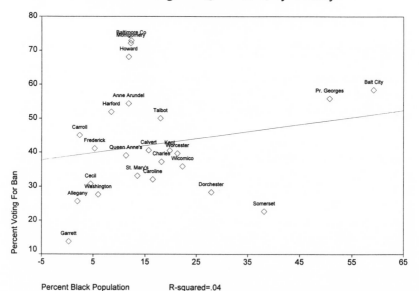

Percent Black Population   R-squared=.04

Source: Maryland Board of Elections

FIGURE 6.3
Urban-Rural Cleavage on Question 3, by County

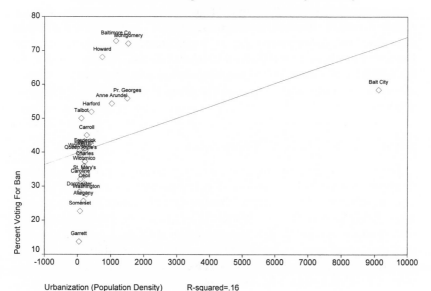

Urbanization (Population Density)   R-squared=.16

Source: Maryland Board of Elections

3, suggesting that the NRA's strategy of campaigning heavily in black-inner city neighborhoods paid substantial dividends.

Results in California

The vote on California's Proposition 15 is evaluated with the logistic regression model presented in the fourth column of Table 6.2. This model differs from the one for Maryland in the third column because there was no variable for the California poll reflecting gun owner-ship—a crucial omission but one we cannot change. Even so, some striking similarities and differences emerge from the analysis. First, the vote on the California gun control measure was far more partisan than in Maryland. In California, Democrats voted for gun control and Re-publicans voted against it. Second, gender was an influence in Califor-nia, with women being 6 percent more likely to vote for gun control than men. In Maryland, there was no statistically significant difference between men and women. The third major difference is that age had a different impact in California than it had in Maryland. Older voters opposed the gun control law in California while supporting it in the Free State.

There are also similarities across the two referenda. There is a strong component of ideology in the vote; conservatives in California were 28 percent more likely to vote against gun control than liberals. Income divides voters in both states in the same way. In California, those in the wealthiest cohort were about 15 percent more likely to vote for the law than those in the poorest bracket. Most important, there is no significant racial cleavage in the outcome of the Proposition 15 vote. Blacks were about evenly split on the issue after controlling for other variables.

Discussion: Gun Control, a Class Issue

The most striking finding in the multivariate analysis of the vote on Question 3 and on Proposition 15 is the pronounced impact of class and the minimal impact of race. Wealthy people, white and black, were more likely to vote for gun control than poorer people. In Maryland, class had an even stronger impact on the vote than gun ownership! And once region is controlled for, race makes no difference. Why is this so? First, gun control may be a class issue because poor people are more likely to live in high-crime areas and therefore more likely to purchase weapons for self-protection. Fear of crime and gun owner-ship for self-protection go hand in hand, and those with low incomes are more likely to fear crime than those with higher incomes (Lizotte and Bordua 1980, 241; 1981). In addition, the lack of racial cleavage in the vote has to do with the support of blacks for gun rights in places like Baltimore, who see the police and courts as ineffective and who face crime as a regular threat. A related fact is that more Baltimore residents are gun owners (17.5 percent) than are residents of the D.C. suburbs (13.5 percent); the highest rate of gun ownership is in rural Maryland (43 percent). Rural weaponry could be seen as having recre-ational uses, but the logic of firearms ownership in cities is not so clear (Wright and Marston 1975, 99). In big-city neighborhoods, guns are more likely to be used for protection than sport. Residents of wealthy suburbs may fear crime, but the threat is not as immediate as for inner-city residents. They are more comfortable with their level of police pro-tection and would seek to alleviate their fears of crime less through the purchase of a gun than through laws aimed at disarming the criminal element.

That the gun control issue was not a partisan contest in Maryland is both surprising and revealing. The NRA has long been thought to stand with Republicans for gun rights. Republicans have consistently opposed gun control initiatives in Congress, including the Brady Bill and the assault weapons ban. Yet among the rank and file in Maryland, the faithful of both parties were divided. The respondent's sex was not significant in the Maryland case either, and this is also surprising. Most surveys have shown that men are far more likely to be gun owners than women, and this is true in Maryland, where 31 percent of men reported owning guns compared to only 15 percent of women. There are signs that this gender gap in gun ownership may be closing; more women are reportedly buying guns for self-protection (Stange 1995). The results here show that women and men supported or opposed the gun control legislation for reasons quite aside from gender.

In both California and Maryland, the NRA made a case that a gun ban would restrict the rights of law-abiding citizens. What is especially interesting about the structure of support for gun control is that lower-income people were more likely to go along with the NRA than the wealthy. Although both the poor and the wealthy fear crime equally, they are not touched by it to the same extent in the areas where they live. Nor are the poor and wealthy equal in the extent to which they can rely upon local police to protect them from crime. The response of the poor and the affluent to fears of crime sends the two groups in completely opposite policy directions. The wealthy turn to public policy as a means of disarming criminals. The poor, having less confidence in public institutions, would rather turn to self-protection through the purchase of weapons.

Is gun control racist, as the NRA argued during the campaign? Certainly gun rights advocates in the black community are convinced that guns are necessary for self-defense. However, the Maryland law was shepherded through the legislature by two of the state's most prominent black politicians: Elijah Cummings (D-Baltimore) and Albert Wynn (D-Prince George's, now in Congress). A study of the votes shows that the black community's support was highly contingent on class. Middle- and upper-income blacks voted 3 to 1 in favor of the ban; lower-income blacks were about evenly divided.

Conclusion

The Maryland gun control referendum was widely heralded as the NRA's Waterloo, representing the vaunted lobby's first major defeat in a statewide contest. Although this assessment may be exaggerated, the outcome on Question 3 did embolden other states to enact similar measures. Within a few years, Virginia, Florida, Oregon, Massachusetts, and California enacted waiting periods for the purchase of handguns. California's Republican governor George Deukmejian signed an assault weapons ban into law after the Stockton killings in 1989. New

Jersey, Connecticut, and Hawaii enacted assault weapons bans soon thereafter. Even conservative, rural South Carolina followed Maryland by enacting its own Saturday night special law. Maryland added a waiting period for the purchase of assault weapons in 1989 followed by an assault weapons ban in 1994. Congress went on to pass the Brady Bill (imposing a waiting period before a handgun can be purchased) in November 1993 and an assault weapons ban in August 1994. Although the NRA was credited with defeating several Democratic incumbents in the 1994 election, including Judiciary Committee Chair Jack Brooks (D-TX), attempts by the lobby to get the Republican Congress to repeal the assault weapons ban failed.

In Maryland, however, the actions of the Handgun Roster Board have failed to live up to the hopes of gun control advocates or verify the fears of the NRA. By 1990, only 10 handguns had made the board's list of weapons prohibited for sale within the state. By 1994, the list of banned guns had jumped to 29, but the list of approved weapons stood at nearly 1,300. The law does require gun companies to petition the board to sell their guns within the state, but some companies have not done so; and the law has done next to nothing to limit the supply of deadly weapons. In the years following passage of the law, more handguns were sold in Maryland than in prior years. Reports suggested that guns were rejected because they were of low quality rather than because they were popular with criminals (Schneider 1990). Large gun manufacturers, including one manufacturing plant within the state, were especially likely to have their weapons approved. Governor William Donald Schaefer pressed for more precise standards for determining which handguns should be banned, but by the time he left office in 1995, those standards were not in place. More disappointing for gun control proponents is the fact that gun-related homicides have not been significantly reduced by the modest legislation Maryland has adopted. Serious attempts to put a dent in gun violence will require a more aggressive ban, which is likely to increase the polarization of the state's population by class and region.

7

Virginia: The Politics of Concealed Weapons

Harry L. Wilson and Mark J. Rozell

In 1993 Virginia governor L. Douglas Wilder attracted national attention for his successful effort to promote a law limiting gun purchases by state residents to one per month. Prior to the passage of the limit, a coalition of powerful gun-owners groups lobbied state legislators to reject the initiative. That Wilder succeeded in a conservative state with a strong tradition of limited government and a large rural base of voters in favor of gun owners' rights was testimony not only to his leadership savvy but also to changing demographic and political patterns in the state. The one-gun-per-month limit was very popular in the growing urban corridor from northern Virginia to the southeast coastal Tidewater region.

In that same year, Virginians elected to the governorship George Allen, an unabashed defender of gun owners and opponent of the one-gun-per-month limit. Although Democrats characterized Allen as an extremist on gun control issues, voters overwhelmingly elected him over the pro–gun control candidate, incumbent attorney general Mary Sue Terry. Republicans also made an important gain in the state legislature, winning enough seats in both chambers to be within striking distance of control of the general assembly for the first time since Reconstruction.

Although Allen, many Republican legislators, and some rural conservative Democrats openly advocated fewer gun restrictions, there did not appear to be any major movement toward revising state laws. Nonetheless, gun-owners groups were preparing to take aim at Virginia's laws regarding the issuing of permits to carry a concealed handgun.

These groups achieved high-profile public attention to their issue in August 1994, when a Clarke County circuit court judge refused to renew the concealed-weapons permit of Republican U.S. Senate nominee Oliver L. North. Judge James L. Berry denied the renewal "on the ground that the applicant is not of good character." Berry cited North's convictions (which were overturned) in the Iran-Contra scandal. Yet two years earlier, Berry had renewed North's permit without comment. North and his supporters charged that the denial was politically motivated (Jenkins 1994).

Whether or not this charge was accurate, the revocation of North's permit drew widespread publicity to the controversial concealed-weapons law, which gave enormous discretion to judges in determining if individuals qualified for a permit. Jeff Freeman, the NRA lobbyist who led the organization's campaign to revise the concealed-weapons law, stated that the lack of uniformity in implementation—and even arbitrariness—mandated change (Freeman 1996). The NRA skillfully made a case for more uniform and fair procedures—a tack that drew attention away from the more controversial notion of allowing greater ease of access to concealed-weapons permits.

In 1995, two years after attracting national attention to Virginia by voting to restrict gun purchases to one per month, the general assembly moved in a different direction by dramatically relaxing the concealed-weapons law. As gun owners touted the revision as a victory for the rights of individuals, gun control advocates warned of the ominous consequences of so many citizens carrying concealed weapons. The debates in the state legislature shed light on the forces that led to the changed law, and the new provisions make it clear why the legislature's action was so controversial.

Guns and the Policy Process

The changing politics of gun control in Virginia is evidence of the variable nature of the agenda-setting process. Scholars of the policy process identify the factors that lead to changes in agenda priorities: media coverage, election politics, changes in leadership, dramatic events, interest-group mobilization, and skillful issue framing, among others (Cobb and Elder 1972).

In early 1993, national news stories reported that an unusually large percentage of homicides in urban areas from Washington, D.C., to New York City were being committed with handguns purchased in Virginia. Public embarrassment and even outrage in Virginia enabled a pro–gun control governor to seize the opportunity to promote what he characterized as a reasonable limitation on the number of guns purchased in the state. And when Wilder asked how limiting individuals to 12 gun purchases every year infringed on their basic rights, gun owners could invoke only a weak slippery-slope argument that any limit, however reasonable, might open the door to a ban on gun ownership.[1] With public opinion and a Democrat-controlled legislature on his side, Wilder prevailed.

Later that year the context had changed. Virginia elected as its governor a pro–gun rights conservative who had skillfully avoided debating gun control in his campaign but instead emphasized a tough-on-crime message. The election of Allen and more Republican legislators in 1993, media coverage of the concealed-weapons controversy in light of North's denied permit in 1994, public fear of crime, and savvy framing of the issue by pro-gun lobbyists in 1995 created a policy environment that favored a changed policy direction.

Yet much of the public remains dubious about the concealed-weapons law, and changed conditions could lead once again to policy revision. For an issue as emotion-ridden and volatile as gun control, the question is not whether more policy change is on the horizon but rather whose interests will be favored when change does occur.

In what follows we describe and analyze the conditions that led to the successful enactment of the concealed-weapons law in Virginia. We assess some of the consequences of the law and speculate about the likelihood of future changes in the policy environment.

Senate Action

In January 1995 Senators Virgil H. Goode Jr., a Democrat from rural Rocky Mount in southwestern Virginia, and Kenneth W. Stolle, a Republican from Virginia Beach, introduced similar concealed-weapons bills. The major focus of both bills was to eliminate the judicial discretion that existed under the old regulation: applicants had to demonstrate both that they needed to carry a weapon for protection and that they were of good character. According to the bills' sponsors and supporters, these requirements led to major disparities in the issuance of permits. Even some opponents agreed that disparities existed. The question was how to remedy the inequities.

It was generally much easier to obtain a permit in rural southern Virginia than it was in the more heavily populated northern Virginia suburbs near Washington, D.C. A state police study cited by the Law Enforcement Alliance of America, a group that supported the changes, revealed that no permits had been issued in 18 months in Alexandria or Prince William County, one each in Fairfax and in Loudoun County, and 23 in Arlington. About 8,000 permits had been issued statewide during that same period (Baker 1995). According to the NRA's Jeff Freeman, Fairfax County issued fewer than ten permits for each of ten years prior to the law's change (Freeman 1996).

To eliminate the disparity, the bills' sponsors targeted for removal both the demonstrated-need and good-character conditions of the existing legislation. Those conditions were to be replaced by specific enumerated disqualifiers including having a felony conviction, being a foreign national, or having been involuntarily committed to a mental health or drug rehabilitation facility. Further, the bills stated that judges may require that the applicant demonstrate competence in using a handgun. Competence was to be demonstrated by completion of any court-approved firearms training or safety course.

According to bill sponsor Goode, the purpose of the legislation was to restore the original intent of the existing law and "to have a uniform set of standards a person would have to meet to get a concealed weapons permit" (Goode 1996). Advocates of reformed procedures also cited the disparities in both the process and the outcomes in various jurisdictions. "Many judges didn't like guns, period. They just didn't give them [permits] to anyone," said Republican delegate H. Morgan Griffith of Salem. He and others cited northern Virginia as the area in which it was most difficult to obtain a permit, but "there was some disgruntlement with some of the judges in the Roanoke Valley" (Griffith 1996).

Goode concurred, noting that it was easier to obtain permits in some jurisdictions than in others and that it was difficult in some areas for women to obtain permits. He also agreed that the "problems" were not exclusively in northern Virginia, citing Tazewell County in southwestern Virginia as a "difficult" jurisdiction (Goode 1996).

Although the ultimate fate of the bills was not really in question, there were failed attempts at amending the legislation, about a dozen of which were proposed by Madison E. Marye, a Democrat and life member of the National Rifle Association from Montgomery County, and Richard L. Saslaw, a Democrat from Fairfax County. One of the amendments would have required that permit applicants demonstrate competence in using the weapon.

The Goode bill passed both the Courts of Justice and Finance Committees, which had heard testimony during hearings that might be best described as emanating from the "usual suspects." Representatives of the commonwealth's attorneys, the Virginia Association of Chiefs of Police, and gun control groups criticized the bill, claiming it would only contribute to an escalation of gun proliferation, crime, and violence.

The senators also heard from citizens who felt that they had been unjustly denied the right to protect themselves when their permit applications had been denied by judges. One woman said that she had been terrorized and threatened by a woman who was obsessed with her husband and that she felt vulnerable whenever she left her home.

Suzanna Gratia came from Texas to testify that she had been unable to protect her parents, who were killed during a mass murder in a restaurant. She urged Virginia lawmakers to learn from her experience and allow commonwealth residents to protect themselves ("Gun Toting" 1995).

Final debate on the floor of the senate lasted almost two hours, and the bill was passed by 24–16 on February 7, 1995. According to Goode, the issue cut across both party and regional lines. "There was bipartisan support and bipartisan opposition," he said. "Proportionately, there was more opposition from Senators representing Northern Virginia, but there was opposition from Southwestern Virginia and South side as well." Goode summarized the bill's passage. "It was difficult to get it passed. Some people thought we wouldn't get anything passed, but we did" (Goode 1996).

Although the senate vote may not be described as purely partisan, the bill received the support of a significantly greater proportion of Republicans (16 of 18) than Democrats (8 of 22). In short, minority Democratic support was necessary for the passage of the bill, but it was primarily a Republican piece of legislation.

There were also regional differences in the level of support. In the Tidewater area, including Norfolk and Newport News, six senators voted in favor of the bill and four were opposed. Senators from the Richmond area were evenly split (two supported, two opposed); seven of the ten senators from northern Virginia were opposed. Those representing the remainder of the state, including the more rural areas of southern Virginia, central Virginia, and southwestern Virginia, voted strongly in favor of the bill (13 supported, 3 opposed).

Opposition focused on some of the senate bill's provisions, most prominently one backed by Governor Allen that would permit people to carry concealed weapons into restaurants and bars. This provision prompted editorial mockery from the *Washington Post*: "Better not order a shot in a Virginia saloon. . . . Cheers—here's aiming at you. Why on earth does someone in a bar need a hidden firearm?" ("Drink and Pack Heat" 1996, A26). A leading opponent of the legislation, Senator Richard Saslaw of Fairfax, best characterized the absurdity of the provision: "You can't drink and drive, you can't drink and fly a plane, but you can drink and pack heat" ("Drink and Pack Heat" 1996, A26). Goode's bill did allow owners of establishments that disapproved to post a sign stating that it was not permissible to carry a gun on the premises.

The House of Delegates Moves on the Bill

A preliminary skirmish that presaged the concealed-weapons debate took place in the house of delegates one day after the senate voted to change the law. The house of delegates narrowly defeated an effort to amend Roanoke's city charter to permit the city council to enact a ban on all guns in city parks, exempting police officers and those with con-cealed-weapons permits. The bill had been unanimously endorsed by the city council and had passed the house Cities, Counties and Towns Committee, but it failed the full house when it garnered only 62 of the necessary 67 votes (a two-thirds majority is required for this legisla-tion).

Despite being from a neighboring city, Delegate Griffith opposed the charter amendment. He said it would make someone driving through a park with a weapon in his or her car a felon. Although he admitted prosecution was unlikely, it was possible: "Maybe I'm too skeptical because I'm a defense attorney," he said (Griffith 1996).

The house Courts of Justice Committee heard many of the same ar-guments that were made before its senate counterpart. Both sides pre-sented victims of gun-related violence and their families to bolster support, but the "big gun" of those opposed to the law was left for later.

The real significance in the committee was not found in the testi-mony but in the amendments that were added to the bill. "On an issue as powerful as this in which everyone has thought out their position, debate makes no difference," said Griffith (Griffith 1996).

More than 30 amendments were adopted at this time, however. Most focused on adding categories to the list of disqualifiers for permits, including those who had been convicted of driving under the influence of alcohol or of public drunkenness in the previous three years. Other amendments included requirements that permits be carried at all times and presented on demand to police and that a computerized list of those granted permits be kept by police. One represented a new at-tempt to grant Roanoke City Council the authority to ban handguns in city parks.

The committee rejected raising the minimum age to obtain a permit from 21 to 25 (the minimum age in the senate version was 18) as well as permitting restaurants and shops to ban concealed weapons on their property. In addition, it did not modify the requirement that the state pay the costs incurred by an applicant who successfully appealed an initial denial of a permit. The Courts of Justice Committee passed the bill by a 16–6 vote on February 20.

Debate before the full house of delegates lasted over three hours and was watched by James S. Brady, President Ronald Reagan's press secretary who was wounded during the assassination attempt on the president. Brady received a standing ovation from the delegates when he was introduced (Hsu 1995). Yet Brady's presence made no difference to the outcome, according to Griffith. "All the gun laws passed so far would have made no difference to James Brady . . . waiting period, registration, criminal background checks" (Griffith 1996).

Some additional changes were made to the legislation on the floor, including stripping the provision that would have allowed Roanoke to ban guns in its parks but inserting permission for restaurants and other establishments that serve alcohol to ban handguns on the premises. Griffith opposed this latter change, arguing that "we are setting people up for an armed robbery outside of a restaurant because the criminals know they won't be carrying [a concealed handgun]" (Griffith 1996). The final version of the bill passed overwhelmingly by a vote of 69–29 on February 22.

The partisan breakdown of the house of delegates vote is similar to that of the senate. Republicans were almost unanimous in their support of the legislation (44–1 with two not voting); Democrats were more evenly split (24–28). The house's lone independent voted in favor of the bill.

The regional analysis reveals slight differences from the senate vote. Tidewater delegates were slightly more supportive (16–9). Those from Richmond were more likely to be opposed (two supported, four opposed, one not voting), and northern Virginia delegates supported the legislation (16–11–1). Not surprisingly, representatives from the remainder of the state were very likely to vote in favor of the bill (35–5).

All that remained was for the senate to approve the house version of the bill and send it along to Governor Allen for his approval. This was accomplished on a 25–13 vote on February 23. Senator Goode had tacked his original bill on to an unrelated house measure on February 22, but the house removed the amendment.

The Governor's Amendments and Final Passage

Governor Allen, exercising his constitutional authority, proposed amendments to the concealed-handgun-permit legislation to be considered by the general assembly during its veto session on April 5. He rejected a request by Richmond mayor Leonidas B. Young to exempt Virginia's capital from the legislation, but he did offer several amendments. The most prominent of these was the removal of the so-called saloon amendment, which permitted establishments that serve alcohol to ban concealed handguns by posting a sign. He also suggested that the number of drunk-driving convictions necessary for permit disqualification be raised from one to two.

Both amendments were rejected by the house of delegates, the first on a 53–42 vote following its passage by the senate by 21–19, the second by a resounding 93–7 on April 6. Allen ultimately signed the bill into law on May 5, 1995.

Major Provisions of the New Law

Following are the major provisions of Virginia's concealed-handgun law as enacted by the general assembly and signed by the governor.

Any person 21 years of age or older may apply for a two-year permit to carry a concealed handgun. Under the previous law, there was no age requirement for a permit to carry any type of concealed weapon. The permit will be issued within 45 days of receipt of the completed application unless the applicant is disqualified. Previously there was no time limit, and the applicant had to demonstrate a need to carry a concealed weapon and be of good character.

The major categories of those disqualified are any convicted felon who has completed his sentence in the previous five years, anyone who has received mental health or substance abuse treatment in a residential setting in the previous five years, anyone convicted of driving under the influence of alcohol or public drunkenness in the previous three years, anyone convicted of assault or battery or of illegally discharging or brandishing a firearm in the past three years, anyone ever convicted of stalking, and anyone who is addicted to any controlled substance.

Also disqualified are illegal aliens, anyone convicted of an offense as a juvenile that would have been considered a felony if committed by an adult in the past 16 years, and anyone dishonorably discharged from the military.

In addition, the sheriff, chief of police, or the commonwealth's attorney may write a statement that the applicant "is likely to use a weapon unlawfully or negligently to endanger others" to incur a disqualification. There were no specific disqualifiers in the previous legislation. A report from the Central Criminal Records Exchange and a consultation with local law enforcement authorities constitute a check for possible disqualifications.

The court may require proof that the applicant has demonstrated competence in using a handgun. Competence may be demonstrated by completion of any court-approved firearms training or safety course. It appears that in practice most, if not all, judges have exercised this option.

Permits shall be renewed upon application "unless there is good cause shown for refusing to reissue a permit." The denied applicant has a right to appeal the decision. If the applicant wins the appeal, the commonwealth will pay his or her costs. Costs were previously paid by the applicant.

No concealed handgun may be carried in a place of business or special event that has a state license to sell alcoholic beverages. Concealed weapons could be carried in these establishments under the old law.

The total cost of the permit may not exceed $50, including $10 for processing, $35 for the background check, and $5 for state police processing. The previous maximum fee was $25.

Effects of the Law

Despite the law's implementation date of July 1, applications for permits increased dramatically beginning in January 1995, when the bill began to receive publicity. In fact, by mid-June, in several jurisdictions the number of applications received exceeded the number of permits granted in the previous year. Those applications and any others returned before July 1 were processed under the old law, but the approaching effective date of the new law caused court clerks across the commonwealth to be inundated with inquiries concerning the law and its application (Loan 1995a).

County courthouses were flooded as the new law went into effect. People rushed to pick up and, in some cases, even complete applications on the spot. Fairfax County distributed nearly 200 applications and fingerprinted more than 150 people for background-check purposes. Roanoke County distributed over 180 applications (Loan 1995c; Lipton 1995).

By mid-July the rush for permits seemed to be slowing. The long lines were gone, and although a large number of applications had been picked up, many fewer had been returned. In Prince William County, where over 2,000 applications had been distributed, only 342 had been completed. Part of the time lag was attributed to the time required to obtain the required firearms training (Fountain 1995b).

Not surprisingly, there were logistical problems with implementation. A Tazewell County judge made the independent decision that applicants wishing to obtain a permit had to undergo a psychological examination. The state attacked the ruling as improper and said that the judge exceeded his authority in mandating such a requirement ("Judge's Handgun" 1995).

Some residents complained that some of the information being requested was unnecessary. For example, Fairfax County residents were asked for names and addresses for every neighbor since age 18. The chief judge of the circuit court eliminated this requirement (Fountain 1995a).

The required criminal background check also added to the confusion. There was a question about whether checks had to be completed by the FBI, the state police, or local authorities. Some counties were sending fingerprints to the FBI, others were telling applicants to send the information to the state police, and some were conducting checks locally (Loan 1995b).

On July 1, 1996, the FBI stopped processing fingerprint checks for permits in Virginia. The FBI had provided the checks during a one-year grace period. The general assembly did not pass legislation authorizing the checks, and without additional authorization, the FBI will process fingerprints only as part of a criminal investigation ("FBI Stops" 1996).

The key issue with the end of the FBI fingerprint checks was that these checks are useful in determining whether an applicant has ever committed a felony under a different name, information not necessarily available to local and state police. According to Fairfax County's attorney, Robert F. Horan Jr., "With the FBI dropping out, it's just not as accurate a system. . . . Depending on what jurisdiction someone committed a crime in, we may or may not pick it up" (Finn 1996, B1). The Fairfax County sheriff, Carl R. Peed, said that people who should not get permits were getting them because the law was too "lax" (Finn 1996, B1).

Perhaps the greatest impact of the new law, however, was on the number of concealed-handgun permits issued in Virginia. Under the old law, about 8,000 permits were issued annually. That compares with a total of 37,629 permits issued between the new law's effective date of July 1, 1995, and June 30, 1996.

More than 4,500 permits were issued in September 1995; the figures for both October and November topped the 5,000 mark. March, April, and May 1996 all were above 3,000, but in June the number of permits issued dropped below 2,000. By March 1996, there was a three-month backlog of permits waiting to be entered into the statewide computer system. The overwhelming number of permit requests combined with Governor Allen's cutbacks in the state workforce caused a huge backlog. The state police firearms transaction center had to hire numerous part-time employees merely to handle the paperwork (McNair 1996).

Preliminary indications are that during the first year, only one person with a concealed-handgun permit was involved in a homicide, and there is no evidence that the concealed weapon was involved in the crime (Hayden-Snider 1996).

In December 1995, Governor Allen said he would oppose any attempt to repeal the legislation (Hardy 1995). A *Richmond Times-Dispatch*/Channel 12 News poll conducted in September 1995 showed that those who believed the new law would contribute to violent crime in the commonwealth outnumbered those who said it would improve public safety by 2 to 1 (56 percent to 28 percent, with 16 percent having no opinion).[2] Yet there remained only a weak grassroots effort to pressure legislators to repeal the law.

Politically, there was little fallout from the legislation in its first year. During the 1996 general assembly session there were three bills introduced in the senate and one in the general assembly that dealt with this issue.

A bill that would have overturned the law was killed in the senate, as was a bill that would have allowed court clerks to issue permits to qualified applicants rather than waiting for a judge to issue the permit. The logic behind this legislation was that the issuance of permits was now more of an administrative function than one of real decisionmaking authority. An attempt to revive the debate over allowing Roanoke City to ban guns in its parks was killed in the house. Efforts to authorize FBI background checks failed because the provisions were attached to other proposals that the legislature had rejected.

According to one legislator, there was an informal agreement in at least one chamber that no bills dealing with concealed weapons would be handled in this session. It was possible, although not stated explicitly, he said, that the consensus was that debate had been too acrimonious and that the legislature had not looked good. It was believed, then, that a cooling-off period would be beneficial. The situation was different in 1997, however. "Then there will be no holds barred, and once you have one bill [dealing with concealed handguns], then you've opened up the whole thing again."[3] That statement was only partly prophetic. Three bills related to concealed weapons were passed by the general assembly in 1997. Bills that authorized some localities to adopt ordinances prohibiting possession of a dangerous weapon in publicly owned recreation or community centers or in police stations were vetoed by Governor Allen. Both vetoes were upheld, although the attorney general later issued an opinion that concealed weapons could be banned from any property—private or public. A bill that made some technical clarifications to the concealed-weapon law (increasing the duration of permits from two to five years, requiring the state police to prepare the application form, and requiring fingerprinting of applicants to facilitate a national background check) was passed and accepted by Allen.

With the election of the new governor, the legislature is expected to focus on the personal property tax, general fiscal matters, and possible reorganization in 1998. One legislator commented, however, that wholesale changes were possible if, because of a shift in power from the Democrats to the Republicans, committee composition in the house of delegates were reorganized to more accurately reflect the almost even split between the two parties. He went so far as to say that an attempt to repeal the gun purchase limit was possible, although unlikely. In short, 1998 amendments are more likely to originate with the "conservatives."

Goode said there was no such deal in the senate in 1997, but obviously, whatever was sent over to the house of delegates would be killed. He declined to speculate on either the content or likely success of future bills, although he did say he expected the issue was not yet settled (Goode 1996).

Who Gets the Permits?

Limited data are available regarding the profiles of gun owners. In northern Virginia, for example, only Prince William County tracks data on the age, race, and gender of concealed-weapons holders. During the first ten months of the law, there were about 1,500 applications for permits in that county. Of these, fewer than 10 percent were filed by minorities and 11 percent by women. Most applicants were between the ages of 31 and 50 (Morris 1996, 1).

A *Washington Post* analysis of permit applicants in the northern Virginia region produced similar findings.[4] Women composed only 9 percent of all applicants and minorities only 8 percent. Most of the applicants were in their thirties, forties, and fifties. Perhaps most telling, the overwhelmingly largest number of applications came from the more rural communities in northern Virginia, farther away from the District of Columbia. Gun rights group representatives commented that these data were not surprising, although the popularity of concealed weapons among women appears to be growing steadily (Fountain 1996).

Conclusion

A number of factors were crucial to the success of the revised concealed-weapons law: the election of a sympathetic and very popular governor, increased GOP membership in the general assembly, and the influence of some senior, conservative rural Democrats in the house and senate. But ultimately, the law was not easy to sell to a skeptical public. For the latter achievement, much credit goes to the lobbying efforts of the NRA, which was savvy enough to focus on the issues of fairness and equity in implementation rather than on its desire to make access to gun permits easier.

NRA lobbyist Freeman said it was undeniable that jurisdictions for years had implemented the law in an inconsistent manner. The NRA argued that the organization's members merely wanted to "tighten up the law and make it more uniform." It portrayed its effort as promoting a "strengthened law" with consistent criteria for the issuance of permits. Finally, it argued that many other states have similar laws and presented compelling testimony backed by data showing that the laws had worked as intended (Freeman 1996). A gun control organization, Handgun Control, Inc., countered with data from a University of Maryland study suggesting that homicides increased in four of every five urban areas that allowed citizens to carry concealed weapons. The study did not establish a causal link (Gordon 1996).

Very telling was the fact that one state senator, Democrat Bernard Cohen of Alexandria, was an advocate of gun control yet voted for the new procedures on the basis of the fairness issue. Delegate Griffith admitted that he had never owned a gun, believed that gun ownership was potentially dangerous, yet favored the new law because he believed the Constitution grants citizens the right to own and carry guns (Griffith 1996).

Several key legislators interviewed for this study said that the grassroots support generated by the NRA and other pro-gun groups was crucial to the outcome. A strong letter-writing campaign backed by large numbers of constituent phone calls to legislators bolstered the legislation. Lobbyists focused their efforts on key committee leaders and swing votes in both chambers. The pro-gun groups were better organized, better funded, and more politically savvy than their opponents.[5]

According to the NRA, there are now 31 states that have concealed-weapons laws similar to the one in Virginia. Freeman said that he has witnessed a "sea change" across the country on this issue in 1994–1996, with a number of states following Virginia's lead, including North Carolina, South Carolina, West Virginia, Louisiana, Texas, and Oklahoma (with Tennessee updating its law) (Freeman 1996).

Yet there is no denying that the Virginia concealed-weapons law is unpopular and ripe for future challenge. This is made more likely by the election of the conservative incumbent attorney general James Gilmore as governor in 1997. While Gilmore's campaign focused on tax issues, his administration will certainly oppose any additional restrictions in the commonwealth's concealed-weapons law. Indeed, his tenure may oversee the elimination of nearly all restrictions on concealed weapons.

The general assembly is almost evenly split between the parties, but, perhaps more important, some longtime rural pro-gun legislators may retire or seek other offices. If the Democrats stage a political comeback in the state, there is strong enough sentiment along the urban corridor to change the concealed-weapons law once again to tighten up the requirements for obtaining a permit. Much too will depend on whether the dire projections of handgun advocates come true and some innocent citizens become victims of senseless acts committed by concealed-weapons holders. Indeed, policymaking is an ongoing process of accommodation and change. The politics of guns in Virginia clearly demonstrate the variable, fluctuating nature of the policy process, and we can conclude with certainty that change is on the horizon, although we cannot say in which direction.

Notes

1. A popular bumper sticker among gun owners in Virginia today reads: "Buy one gun per month. It's the law."

2. The survey was conducted with 508 residents of Virginia. The margin of error was + / - 4.5 percent.

3. The legislator who made this comment wishes to remain anonymous.

4.. Northern Virginia was defined as Prince William County, Manassas and Manassas Park, Loudon County, Fairfax County, Fairfax City, Falls Church, Alexandria, and Arlington County.

5. One legislator said that whereas the NRA played the game very smart, the more militant Virginia-based Gun Owners of America sometimes pushed too hard and alienated people, including some key legislators. The NRA had shown why it is such an effective organization, and the Gun Owners of America came across as politically naive.

8

Gun Control Laws in the States: Political and Apolitical Influences

John M. Bruce and Clyde Wilcox

The laws that govern the sale, transport, and possession of firearms are the result of a complex web of federal, state, and local activity. Although national legislation receives the most media attention, state and local governments have enacted a wide variety of laws regulating the sale, possession, and discharge of firearms, and as a consequence gun control laws differ widely across regions, states, and localities. The case studies included in this volume (Chapters 5, 6, and 7) show the dynamics and political context of gun control battles in three states. In this chapter, we focus on the variation in gun control laws in all 50 states. We begin by documenting the range of gun laws in the states and then attempt to explain the differences in laws across the states. Our purpose is not to examine the effectiveness of these laws (see Spitzer 1995; see also, among many others, Cook 1981; Kleck 1991; Wright, Rossi, and Daly 1983; Zimring 1991); rather we seek to understand the sources of state differences in the regulation of firearms.

State Laws Regarding Firearms

Any attempt to understand state differences in gun laws must begin with a description of the range of laws currently on the books. Although we describe the main categories of state laws in this section, it is important to note that most states have passed statutes that differ in subtle and not-so-subtle ways from similar laws in other states. Sometimes these differences are important, and in these instances we note distinctions among similar bills, but more generally we focus only on whether a state has passed a particular type of regulation, ignoring, for example, different provisions for precisely where a citizen can carry a concealed weapon. We also exclude from this analysis laws dealing with the discharge of the weapon.

In this analysis, we are concerned with 14 types of laws. Each of these types is described below.[1]

Purchase and Possession

Record of Sale. This type of law requires the seller to keep a record of information about firearms buyers (or some subset thereof). This information is retained by the seller and not relayed to any official agency. At present, 25 states require records of sale.

Registration. In the more stringent form, these laws require gun owners to register guns by serial number and type with the police. In the more limited form, these laws require documentation only of sales. Currently 13 states have some form of registration; 3 of those are of the more stringent type.

Licensing or Permit to Purchase. Some states have passed licensing or permit laws that limit the ability to purchase or receive a firearm to those who have met the conditions of the law. These may include background checks, training or safety courses, or fingerprinting. The extent of the permit requirements varies from state to state. Fifteen states presently have some version of this law.

Waiting Period for Handgun Purchase. The waiting period is the time between the purchase of the gun and possession. The federal Brady Act requires either a five-day waiting period or instant background checks. Some states have opted for each of these options to satisfy the law; others have their own, longer waiting period associated with the permit process.

Secondary or Private Sales. Unlike with firearms sales by a licensed dealer, federal law does not restrict secondary sales. Some states have passed laws that attempt to limit sales of weapons to individuals who would not be able to purchase a gun from a licensed dealer. Some 20 states currently regulate private sales to varying degrees.

One Gun a Month. These laws limit the purchase of firearms (usually handguns) to one per month per individual. These laws, exclusively enacted on the East Coast, were aimed at disturbing the illegal movement of guns from states with lenient control laws to those with more stringent laws. Currently, three states have limited gun purchases to one per month.

Ban on Saturday Night Specials. The Saturday night special is an easily concealed, inexpensive handgun that is generally of such low quality that it is unacceptable to sportsmen. These cheap guns have very often been used in crimes. Five states have prohibited the sale of such guns.

Ban on Assault Weapons. The federal government has limited certain assault weapons, and some states have also done so. These laws prohibit or restrict the possession of certain nonsporting assault weapons. Five states presently have such bans.

Carrying Concealed Weapons

The carrying concealed weapons (CCW) laws regulate the conditions under which a resident of the state may carry a concealed weapon. These laws fall into two general types. In some states, no one is allowed to carry a concealed weapon, or a permit for such action is difficult to obtain. A state with either of these alternatives can be described as having more restrictive CCW laws. Currently 7 states prohibit carrying concealed weapons, and 13 have "may issue" permit laws in which the burden is typically on applicants to show why they need the gun. Other states have more lenient controls on concealed weapons or none at all. One state currently requires no CCW permit, and 29 states have "shall issue" permit laws, in which the burden is on the state to show why any given applicant should not carry a concealed weapon. Shall-issue laws generally result in many more permits being issued than in the may-issue states.

Juveniles

Juvenile Possession. The federal government prohibits the possession of handguns by minors. States can pass their own laws that limit minors access to handguns or long-barrel weapons. Thirty states have some form of juvenile-possession law.

Juvenile Sale. Firearms dealers licensed by the federal government are prohibited from selling to those under 21. Private sales to those under 18 are also illegal under federal law. Forty-six states have some version of a juvenile-sale law.

Specific Issues

Child Access Prevention (CAP). These laws are aimed at eliminating accidental or uncontrolled access to a firearm by a child. Generally these laws require gun owners to store the gun in an inaccessible location or use some restriction device (such as a trigger lock). Currently 15 states have CAP laws.

Gun-Free Schools. These laws prohibit the possession of a firearm in all schools—public, private, or religious. All states have these laws.

Firearms Preemption. These laws limit the ability of the local governments in a state to regulate firearms. These limitations vary in their restrictiveness. Because cities and counties occasionally pass quite restrictive gun control laws, preemption laws are favored by the NRA and other pro-gun groups as a way of limiting local gun control. Preemption laws are present in 39 states.

This chapter focuses on state differences in the adoption of these laws. Table 8.1 shows the status of each of these laws in every state.[2]

There are several points worth noting in the data in Table 8.1. First, all states have laws banning guns in schools, and most have laws banning the sale of guns to minors. Because there is national legislation on both these points, these laws have mostly symbolic value, although in a few cases they go beyond the national standard. Clearly gun control is most likely to pass at the state level when it is seen as explicitly protecting children, especially from violence from other juveniles.

Second, the Brady Bill mandated a five-day waiting period for handgun purchases or instant background checks, and this forced a number of states to implement waiting periods. The Supreme Court's decisions in *Printz* v. *United States* and *Mack* v. *United States* did not overturn the waiting-period portion of the Brady Bill, and thus states that do not implement instant background checks are required to enforce a waiting period. Many states that have implemented this law have done so only to be consistent with federal requirements.

Finally, the most notable recent trend has been for states to relax requirements for carrying concealed weapons. Since 1987, at least 19 states have made it easier to carry concealed weapons, and bills have been introduced into the legislatures of several other states. The NRA has made concealed-weapons laws a top priority, and it seems likely that the concentrated lobbying by NRA members and other gun enthusiasts has had an impact. In Chapter 7 of this volume, Harry Wilson and Mark Rozell detail the politics of the passage of a concealed-weapons law in Virginia. Concealed-weapons laws often list specific places where guns cannot be carried: in Virginia, Governor Allen unsuccessfully fought to allow guns in bars throughout the state and in recreational facilities in the suburbs of Washington, D.C.

Variations in Gun Control Laws

In order to better understand the variation in gun control laws, we have created an additive index of gun control laws in each state; higher

TABLE 8.1
State Gun Laws Summary

State	Record of Sale	Reg.	Purchase Permit	Waiting Period	Private Sales	Gun a Month	Sat. Night Specials	Assault Weapons	CCW	Juv. Poss.	Juv. Sales	CAP	Gun Free Schools	Pre-emption
AL	•			5	•				May	•	•		•	•
AZ				5					Shall	•	•		•	•
AR				5					Shall	•	•		•	•
CA	•			10	•			•	May	•	•	•	•	•
CO	•			0					Shall		•		•	
CT	•		•	Permit	•			•	May	•	•	•	•	
DE	•			0					May		•		•	
DC	•		•	Permit	•				May	•	•		•	
FL				3					Shall	•	•	•	•	•
GA				0					May		•		•	•
ID				0					Shall		•		•	•
IL	•		•	Permit	•		•		None	•	•		•	•
IN	•		•	7	•				Shall	•	•		•	•
IA			•	Permit	•				May		•		•	•
KS				5					None		•		•	•
KY				5					Shall	•	•		•	
LA	•	•		5					Shall	•	•		•	•
ME	•			7		•			Shall		•		•	•
MD	•			Permit	•	•	•	•	May	•	•		•	•
MA	•		•	Permit	•				May		•		•	•
MI	•		•	Permit	•				May	•	•		•	•
MN	•			Permit			•		May	•	•	•	•	•

Source: Firearms legislation summary produced by Handgun Control, Inc. for 1996.

Note: A dot indicate that the state had some version of that law on the books in 1996. The waiting period is specified in days except for those states that indicate a waiting period as a part of the permit process. The carrying of concealed weapons is coded as follows: none = no carry allowed; may = the state has a "may issue" permit system; shall = the state has a "shall issue" permit system; and all = no permit required.

TABLE 8.1 (Continued)

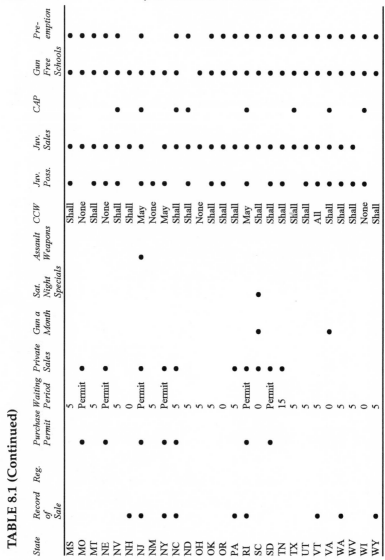

State	Record of Sale	Reg.	Purchase Permit	Waiting Period	Private Sales	Gun a Month	Sat. Night Specials	Assault Weapons	CCW	Juv. Poss.	Juv. Sales	CAP	Gun Free Schools	Pre-emption
MS				5					Shall	●	●		●	●
MO	●		●	Permit	●				None		●		●	●
MT	●			5					Shall	●	●		●	●
NE			●	Permit	●				None	●	●		●	●
NV				5					Shall		●	●	●	●
NH				0	●				Shall	●	●		●	
NJ			●	Permit				●	May	●			●	●
NM	●			5	●				None	●	●		●	
NY	●		●	Permit	●				May	●	●			
NC				5					Shall		●	●	●	●
ND				5					Shall		●	●	●	●
OH				5					None				●	
OK				0					Shall	●	●		●	
OR				5					Shall	●	●	●	●	
PA				5	●				Shall	●	●		●	●
RI	●		●	Permit	●				May	●	●		●	●
SC	●			0	●	●			Shall		●		●	●
SD			●	Permit					Shall	●	●		●	●
TN				15			●		Shall	●	●		●	●
TX				5					Shall		●		●	●
UT	●			5					All	●	●		●	●
VT				5					Shall	●	●		●	●
VA	●			0		●			Shall	●	●		●	●
WA				5					Shall	●		●	●	●
WV				5					Shall			●	●	●
WI				0					None				●	●
WY	●			5					Shall				●	●

scores indicate more restrictive firearms laws.[3] Scores could in theory range from 0, indicating no restrictive laws, to a possible high of 17 for a state that had adopted all existing restrictions. In practice the range was from a low of 4 to a high of 13, with the average state adopting roughly 7 laws.[4]

In Map 8.1 we show overall state laws by region. States in the mid-Atlantic region and in the West North Central and East North Central

MAP 8.1
Mean Scores on Gun Control Index, by Region

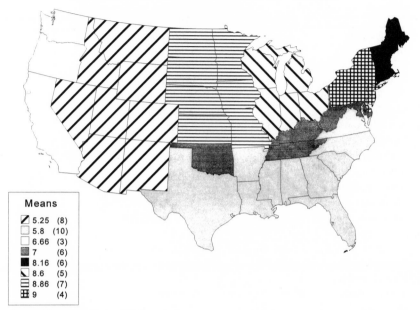

Means	
5.25	(8)
5.8	(10)
6.66	(3)
7	(6)
8.16	(6)
8.6	(5)
8.86	(7)
9	(4)

Source: Computed by authors.

regions have adopted the most restrictive laws; those in the South and mountain regions are distinctive in their less restrictive laws. That the Northeast has stricter gun laws than the South is certainly not surprising, but there are several possible explanations for these differences. First, these regional differences may be due to other demographic differences—in urbanization, racial distributions, or crime rates. Second, they may be due to long-standing cultural differences in politics (Elazar 1966; Sharkansky 1968). We will explore possible causes for this variation in greater detail later in this chapter.

Table 8.2 lists the states from most restrictive to least restrictive gun laws. The distribution of scores shows that most states have not adopted significant gun control laws. Fully 18 states are concentrated in the two lowest scores (4 or 5); the top 18 states are spread across the highest six scores (13 to 8). The data in Table 8.2 show considerable variation in state laws within regions. In New England, Connecticut leads with 13 restrictions, but neighboring New Hampshire and Vermont have only 5 laws each. On the West Coast, California is one of the more restrictive states with 10 laws, but Washington has only 6 and Oregon only 4. Within-region variation appears to vary with urbaniza-

TABLE 8.2
State Scores on Gun Control Index

State	Index Score	State	Index Score
Connecticut	13	Pennsylvania	6
Illinois	13	South Carolina	6
Minnesota	12	Tennessee	6
New Jersey	12	Virginia	6
District of Columbia	11	Washington	6
Maryland	11	Wisconsin	5
New York	11	Arizona	5
Rhode Island	11	Arkansas	5
California	10	Florida	5
Iowa	10	Maine	5
Massachusetts	10	Mississippi	5
Michigan	10	Montana	5
Nebraska	10	New Hampshire	5
Missouri	9	North Dakota	5
Alabama	8	Oklahoma	5
Kansas	8	Texas	5
North Carolina	8	Utah	5
South Dakota	8	Vermont	5
Delaware	7	West Virginia	5
Indiana	7	Georgia	4
New Mexico	7	Idaho	4
Ohio	7	Kentucky	4
Colorado	6	Oregon	4
Louisiana	6	Wyoming	4
Nevada	6		

Source: Computed by authors.

tion: Connecticut includes substantial stretches that qualify as New York suburbs, and California contains two of the largest cities in the nation.

Although many states have adopted few laws regulating guns and a few have adopted several, the correlations between the various laws are not generally strong. Knowing that a state has adopted one law is not especially useful in predicting whether the state has adopted a different law. The exception is laws regulating the purchase of firearms, which do tend to vary together. States that require a permit or license to purchase a gun are more likely to require a record of sale and to have a longer waiting period to buy the gun. Similarly, states that limit the number of guns purchased to one a month are more likely to have a ban on the sale of cheap handguns. Overall, however, these gun control laws are unrelated to each other and seem to represent a collection of diverse policies from which state lawmakers may shop. This suggests the possibility that when states pass additional regulations, legislators who desire stronger regulations may choose the policies that are most likely to be able to muster a majority in relevant committees or win the support of legislative leaders.

Explaining Variations in State Gun Control Laws

What leads some states to adopt a set of relatively stringent gun laws and others to adopt only minimal regulations? Chapters 5 to 7 in this volume provide a detailed analysis of the politics of adoption of specific laws in three states. In this section we attempt to explain the broader pattern of state adoption of gun laws. We will test a series of statistical models of gun policies, exploring the role of cultural, demographic, and political variables.

Why might legislators pass new gun laws? The case studies suggest that the impetus for action varies. In some cases, states may adopt regulations in the face of highly visible failures of past gun policy. California limited access to assault weapons after a well-publicized tragedy (see Godwin and Schroedel, Chapter 5). In other cases, an interest group may mount a coordinated mobilization of members to pressure legislators to act or not act. Patterson and Eakins in Chapter 3 trace much of the inaction of Congress on gun control to pressure from the NRA. Of course, part of the interest mobilization may involve an effort to convince citizens and elites that a current law is not working: in Virginia the NRA argued effectively that existing laws regulating the right to carry concealed weapons were applied unevenly across the state (Wilson and Rozell, Chapter 7).

In the analysis that follows, we approach the problem somewhat differently, focusing on three successive models—one that includes demographic factors, another that focuses on sociological factors such as crime rates and gun ownership, and a third that explores the impact of political variables.

A Demographic Model

It may be that states pass gun laws at least partially as a result of their demographic characteristics. In this case, we examine differences between urban and rural states, those with large and small numbers of

African Americans, and states in different regions of the country. Each of these factors is a likely source of gun control laws.

First, urban areas are crowded with people, and traffic and have higher crime rates. In cities, guns are not used for hunting but for crime and the hope of deterring or preventing crime. In rural states, in contrast, long guns are common on farms and ranches. Guns are used for hunting and for protecting livestock from predators. It seems likely that support for gun control is greater in urban areas.

We also explore the impact of the racial mix of the population on gun control laws. There are several reasons to consider race as a predictor variable. First, urban blacks tend to be supportive of gun control laws, presumably because of high crime rates in inner-city areas. Moreover, white suburbanites fear crime by young black men with guns, and thus racial threat may activate racial stereotypes and produce more support for gun control or, conversely, more support for the right to carry guns for protection.

We have also added two variables identifying the southern and mountain states, where gun control laws are less restrictive. By holding constant urbanization and racial composition, we can determine whether the modest gun control in these states is because of their rural composition or racial mix or whether political culture explains these differences.

To examine the relationship between gun control laws and these three demographic variables, we regressed the gun control index on measures of the percent of the state population that is urban and the percent of the population that is African American and whether the state is in the southern or mountain regions. The resulting equation,[5] with standard errors noted in parentheses, was

$$Gun\ Control\ Index = 2.22 + 0.08\ Urban + 0.03\ Black\ -2.31\ South\ -3.11\ Mountain$$
$$\qquad\qquad\quad (0.02)\qquad\quad (0.03)\qquad (0.79)\qquad\quad (0.67)$$

Greater levels of urbanization are associated with stricter gun laws. If we control for the effects of race and region, an increase in urbanization by 25 percent would be predicted to increase that state's score on the index by 2 points. The racial mix of the population is not a significant predictor of gun laws. Even after controls for urbanization and race, southern and mountain states are much less likely to have gun control laws than are states with similar levels of urbanization and African American populations.

The impact of region suggests that political culture may influence gun laws. Daniel Elazar (1966) classified states into traditionalistic, moralistic, and individualistic cultures, and his classification has been widely used in studies of state politics and policymaking. Yet although many southern states had traditionalistic cultures in Elazar's formulation and many western states had individualistic cultures, there is no significant correlation between any of Elazar's measures and gun control laws. We estimated a series of models, contrasting individualistic and traditionalistic states with those Elazar labeled moralistic. Individualistic states were not significantly different from moralistic ones, but traditionalistic states are less likely to adopt gun control regulations. Nearly all southern states were classified by Elazar as traditionalistic, and thus these measures are highly correlated. Because we believe that the cultural context of gun policy is somewhat different than the broader political culture that Elazar described, we present the model that includes measures of region and not Elazar's typology.

A Limited Sociological Model

If urbanization and region influence gun control laws, this may be because of sociological factors such as gun ownership and crime rates. Legislators in urban states may adopt gun control as a means of controlling violent crime; in rural states they may not do so because a substantial portion of the population owns guns and uses them for hunting.

Our measure of gun ownership is simply the percentage of individuals in the state who report having a firearm in their household. We make no distinction between those who report owning a rifle or shotgun and those who report owning a handgun; nor are there distinctions for those with multiple guns. State-level assessment of gun ownership is not an easy task. Firearms sales (including secondary sales) are not universally reported to any single reporting source. The lack of any comprehensive registration laws means there is often no public record of gun ownership to which we can turn. There have been a number of national surveys that asked about gun ownership, but no surveys of random samples of the residents in each state. In this analysis, we rely primarily on national exit polls to estimate statewide gun ownership. In a national presidential election exit poll conducted by Voter News Service (VNS) in 1994, half the respondents (5,000) were asked a question about gun ownership.[6] Nationwide, 25.4 percent of voters reported having a firearm in their household.[7] We broke these respondents down by state (covering 42 states) and generated measures of gun ownership by state. However, the sample size in some of these states was small, so we used data from the 19 state exit polls that had included the gun-ownership question. These state polls contained many more respondents per state (at least 1,000), which increases confidence in the quality of the estimate. These measures of gun ownership built from the state polls were very strongly related to those estimates from the national exit poll.[8] Thus, we use the estimates of state-level gun ownership from the national exit poll in order to expand the number of states under consideration.[9]

Our expectations for the level of gun ownership are simple: the more citizens in a state who own guns, the more lenient will be the gun laws. Of course, part of this may be because it is easier to buy guns in states with few regulations, but given the substantial base of gun ownership in America, it seems likely that the causal arrow mostly flies the other way—gun owners oppose stricter gun laws.

We also test whether the rate of violent crime predicts gun ownership. Our prediction is that states with high rates of violent crime will adopt a wide range of laws to deal with the problem, one of which will be stricter gun control. Gun control advocates frequently use violent crime as the justification for advocating more limited access to guns.[10] Our measure of this is merely the federal government's tally of crimes using any sort of firearm (mostly handguns). Our expectation is that high rates of violent crime (measured as crimes per 1,000 population) will be associated with more restrictive gun laws.

The results of the limited sociological model are reported below. In this model, our gun control index score was regressed on the percent of the state that reports a weapon in the home and the rate of violent crime involving a gun.[11]

$$Gun\ Control\ Index = 8.53 - 7.90\ Pct\ Guns + 0.002\ Violent\ Crime$$
$$(2.81) \qquad\qquad (0.002)$$

The percentage of the population that reported owning a gun has a significant relationship to the level of gun control in the state. A 10 percent increase in the population with a gun in the household is associated, on average, with a reduction of almost 0.8 in the control index. Violent crime appears to have no meaningful relationship to the level of gun control. This suggests that the mere presence of a high crime rate does not produce gun control.

It is very possible that lawmakers do not respond to the absolute violent-crime rate, but rather the level of attention paid to the sensational crimes that constitute that rate. A dramatic event, such as the shooting at a McDonald's in California, may do more to prompt action on gun control than hundreds or thousands of less visible crimes involving guns. It is also possible that high crime rates produce demand among frightened citizens for the right to own firearms for protection.

A Political Model

In contrast to the apolitical elements of demographics and sociological forces, it is possible that gun control laws are a function of explicitly political forces. In this model we include a measure of the state political ideology, past voting patterns for president and governor, party strength in the state legislature, and a measure of membership in the NRA in each state. Each of these terms taps some aspect of political life in the state.

Our measure of political ideology is drawn from the work of Wright, Erikson, and McIver (1985), who compiled data from national surveys over an extended period. We expect that states with more conservative citizens will adopt fewer gun restrictions. In addition, we assess more contemporary measures of partisan politics: the percentage of the vote in a state that went for the Democratic presidential candidate in 1992, and the percentage of the vote that went for the Democratic candidate for governor in the most recent election. We also assess the percentage of Democrats seated in the upper and lower legislative chambers in each state. Our expectations with these contemporary partisan measures is straightfoward: the more Democratic the citizenry and the state legislature, the greater the likelihood that there will be a higher level of gun control in that state. Taken together, these ideological and partisan measures allow us to explore the impact of opinion and of party control on state gun laws.[12]

Of course, what often matters in legislatures is not opinion but organized opinion. The National Rifle Association is organized in all 50 states and is especially effective in mobilizing grassroots pressure on legislators (see Shaiko and Wallace, Chapter 9). The NRA refused to provide us with membership figures by state, but we have approximated state membership by the numbers of *American Rifleman* magazine mailed to each state. Although this is not the optimal arrangement, this measure does allow us to get some sense of the critical state-by-state variation in NRA membership. Our expectation in this case is obvious: states with greater levels of NRA membership will have lower levels of gun control. The image of the NRA as a powerful mobilizer of political grassroots activity strongly suggests that this should be so.

The results of this political analysis are as follows.[13]

$$\text{Gun Control Index} = 13.03 + 0.20 \text{ Ideology} - 0.05 \text{ House} + 0.02 \text{ Senate}$$
$$\qquad\qquad\qquad\qquad (0.05) \qquad\quad (0.04) \qquad\quad (0.04)$$

$$-0.02 \text{ Gubernatorial} + 0.07 \text{ Presidential} - 0.60 \text{ NRA}$$
$$\quad (0.03) \qquad\qquad\qquad (0.09) \qquad\qquad\quad (0.17)$$

Clearly state gun laws are a product of political forces. The ideology of state citizens is a significant predictor: shifting the state's ideology to the left 1 point produces an average increase on the gun control

index of 0.2. In addition, our estimate of NRA membership is a strong
predictor of gun laws. An increase by one of the number of subscriptions mailed per 1,000 residents results in an average decrease in the
gun control index of 0.6. The substantive importance of the results for
the level of NRA membership in each state should not be underesti-
mated. States with many NRA members are significantly less likely to
pass gun control laws than those in which the organization has fewer
members.

Measures of recent partisan voting and of party control of legislatures are all poor explanatory variables. It may be that gun laws, which
have been adopted over the course of decades, are better predicted by
long-term ideology and NRA membership, which is also likely to be
quite stable, than by more recent trends in partisan voting. It is also
possible that gun control is not as partisan an issue in state legislatures
as it has become in the Congress. Rural Democrats in the South and
West may be just as likely to oppose gun control laws as their Republican counterparts, and urban Republicans in the Northeast may support
gun control to slow the crime rate as often as do Democrats.

A Combined Model of Gun Control

Considered separately, urbanization, gun ownership, and NRA
membership all predict gun laws, along with state ideology and region.
It is important to estimate a model with all of these variables simultaneously: it may be that urbanization is significant because of the higher
rates of gun ownership in rural areas or that gun ownership is significant only because there are usually more NRA members in states with
more guns.

We include in this consolidated model the variables that were statistically significant predictors in the demographic, sociological, or political models—urbanization, region, percentage of households with
guns, state ideology, and NRA membership. The results of the equation are as follows:[14]

$$Gun\ Control\ Index = 11.84 + 0.02\ Urban + .28\ Pct\ Guns - .60\ NRA$$
$$(0.03) \qquad (3.63) \qquad (.30)$$

$$+ 0.14\ Ideology - 1.95\ South - 1.39\ Mountain$$
$$(0.06) \qquad (.85) \qquad (1.14)$$

In this combined model, urbanization and gun ownership are no
longer significant predictors of gun laws, but ideology and estimated
NRA membership are strong.[15] Southern states remain distinctive, but
mountain states are no longer distinctively less likely to adopt gun
control laws. In this rather minimalist test of a variety of forces that

could influence the level of gun control in a state, we find that the political elements show the greatest utility. States with larger numbers of liberal citizens, outside the South, and with fewer NRA members adopt more restrictive gun laws.

Conclusion

In this chapter, we have attempted to account for variations in level of gun control across the states. The results presented here confirm much of the conventional wisdom: the NRA is a powerful force in state politics, the ideology of state citizens affects policy, and the South remains a distinctive region, at least in the area of gun policy. The significant predictors of gun control policy are not at all surprising, but we believe that some of the variables that do *not* predict state gun laws are worthy of note.

Gun control laws do not appear to be a function of the rate of violent crime, of racial threat, or of urbanization. Moreover, it is not a broad base of gun owners that prevents gun control legislation but rather a base organized through a powerful political organization. Finally, at the state level it appears that gun control policy is not yet a partisan issue. In Chapter 1 we argued that gun control may be becoming a partisan issue as national legislators begin to take sharply different positions that may signal to voters the new party alignment on the issue. If this is true, gun control politics in another decade or two may be partisan at the state level as well.

The importance of NRA membership in predicting gun control laws may indicate that strongly organized gun control groups at the grass roots could produce stronger gun legislation. To date, the NRA has an enormous organizational advantage in state legislatures. Until that changes, it seems unlikely that the states will move aggressively in the near future to regulate guns.

Notes

1. The law summaries were compiled using information obtained from the National Rifle Association and Handgun Control, Inc. The same information in a much more cumbersome format is available from the BATF in its report on state firearm laws (*Firearms: State Laws and Published Ordinances*).

2. Due to data limitations, we do not include Alaska or Hawaii in the study, but we do add the District of Columbia. These state summaries represent the status of the law as of the latter part of 1996.

3. We coded the waiting-period variable as 0 if the waiting period was less

than five days, 1 if the waiting period was a specified period of at least five days, and 2 if the waiting period was an unspecified period during which a permit would be processed. The concealed-carry law was coded 0 if no permit was required, 1 if the state had a shall-issue law, 2 if the state had a may-issue law, and 3 if no concealed weapons could be carried. All other variables were coded 1 if the restrictive law was present, 0 if not. Note that states with pre-emption laws are coded 0, and states without such laws are coded 1, for the purpose of preemption laws is to limit and in some cases even repeal local gun control ordinances. The gun-free-schools variable was excluded from the analysis, since all states have adopted this law.

4. The reliability of this index is 0.67.

5. The R^2 in this model was 48.6; the root mean square error was 2.00.

6. Of this 5,000, a small percentage failed to complete the back of the form. Only those who completed the form (both sides) are used in this calculation.

7. This figure is smaller than the number cited by Spitzer (1995, 6), who reports that an average of 47 percent of households have a gun. Our estimate is much closer to that calculated using an estimate of 60 million gun owners in the United States (a number cited by the NRA), which has a population of 250 million. This produces an estimate of 24 percent of the population having a gun. At least part of this difference stems from comparing households and individuals.

8. The correlation between the 19 states in both the state and national surveys was 0.86.

9. One possible problem with this measure is the likelihood that gun owners are more likely to vote than nongun owners. Any potential problem with bias here, however, is more than outweighed by the lack of alternative data sources.

10. Of course, not all agree with this view. For example, the NRA makes the argument that gun control hurts only law-abiding citizens. Rather than limiting guns, it says, provide for a well-armed public. The argument is that criminals will be less willing to attack someone if there is a significant chance that person is armed.

11. The R^2 for this equation was 0.22; the root mean square error was 2.44.

12. The linkages among these terms are not as strong as might be expected. The correlations average 0.42. The strongest relationship ($r = 0.83$) is between house and senate votes; the relationship between gubernatorial and senate votes is the weakest ($r = 0.07$).

13. The R^2 in this equation was 0.47; the root mean square error was 2.08.

14. The equation shows the unstandardized coefficients with robust standard errors in parentheses. The R^2 of this equation was 0.45; the root mean square error was 2.10.

15. A number of more comprehensive models were examined, including the use of all the terms used in the demographic, sociological, and political models. The results were largely the same.

9

Going Hunting Where the Ducks Are: The National Rifle Association and the Grass Roots

Ronald G. Shaiko and Marc A. Wallace

What makes the National Rifle Association a powerful force in American politics today? The answer, in a word, is grass roots. This term has many meanings in the contemporary political lexicon, but it is most commonly used to refer to the membership base of an organized interest group, social movement, or political party. It may also include a larger attentive public without any direct membership affiliation that views a particular political issue or policy arena as important. The ability of an organization to mobilize its membership and the sympathetic elements of the general public provide some organizations with substantial grassroots power. Some organizations attempt to manufacture the appearance of grassroots presence despite their lack of a coherent membership base or an organized, attentive public. Elected officials generally can tell the difference between real and manufactured grassroots pressure. In fact, a decade ago, Lloyd Bentsen, then a U.S. senator from Texas, used the term "astroturf" to refer to the ersatz grassroots campaigns conducted by interest groups with no real membership base of support.

Whether one strongly supports or vigorously opposes the political efforts of the National Rifle Association, it should be clear that the successes of the NRA in the electoral campaigns and in legislative arenas across the United States are largely attributable to its real grassroots prowess. Unlike many organized interest groups in contemporary American politics, the NRA benefits from a large, readily mobilizable membership base as well as an even larger public constituency that is attentive to issues relating to government regulation of firearms and firearms ownership. As the NRA celebrates its 125th anniversary, its financial position has been weakened by membership volatility as well as the purchase of a new national headquarters building in suburban Washington, D.C. (Vobejda 1996). Despite the internal tensions that have resulted from the ongoing reorganization, its grassroots efforts remain its strength. With approximately 3 million members nationwide, the NRA has created and maintained a variety of linking mechanisms that serve to connect membership with the organization in meaningful ways.

Rather than presenting the more commonplace journalistic exposé approach to the analysis of the NRA (see, e.g., Dreyfuss 1996; Anderson 1996; Sugarmann 1992; Loftus 1994, 87–104; cf. Davidson 1993), we will analyze the grassroots operations of the NRA in a dispassionate manner in order to assess the strengths and weaknesses of the organizational connections between NRA leadership and its membership and the larger attentive public. The bulk of the media attention garnered by the NRA is focused on the political dimension of the organization— the NRA Institute for Legislative Action, its lobbying arm, and the NRA Political Victory Fund, its political action committee. Whereas both entities play an integral role in the grassroots mobilization efforts of the organization as well as in the volatility of the membership base, the essence of the leadership-membership connection in the NRA lies in the broader attributes of the organization.

The NRA as Service Organization

For many members of the NRA, membership entails an economic transaction with little connection to the political dimension of the organization. For an annual membership fee of $35 (with direct-mail application, discounts of $10 are offered), members receive a variety of premiums, benefits, or selective incentives for belonging to the organization. For example, members receive a 12-month magazine subscription to either the *American Rifleman, American Hunter,* or *American Guardian,* a variety of insurance packages, discounts on Hertz and National car rentals, discounts on moving expenses through North American Van Lines, discounts at Choice Hotels International (Clarion, Quality, Comfort, Sleep, Rodeway, EconoLodge, Friendship), an affinity NRA VISA card, and NRA member discounts at selected gun stores, outfitters, and even car dealers. Members also gain access to the line of merchandise sold by the NRA through its catalog or at the NRA Store located at NRA headquarters. Finally, some members may qualify for the NRA Education Loan Program. It should be noted that NRA leaders, although stressing these selective incentives, conclude their proselytizing messages in the following manner: "The most important benefit of NRA membership, however, is the defense of your Constitutional right to keep and bear arms." Nonetheless, these selective incentives alone may be sufficient to maintain hundreds of thousands of members. These members simply view the NRA as a provider of useful goods and services.

Beyond the selective incentives, NRA members have the opportunity to participate in the vast array of membership programs offered that connect them with the organization in a nonpolitical manner but also serve to train and educate the larger gun-owning public through NRA volunteer efforts. These programs are provided to serve the needs of the NRA membership in their communities across the nation. The NRA Competitions Program, for example, sponsors more than 10,000 formal competitive events at the local, state, regional, national, and international levels and conducts over 80 national shooting championships each year. The Recreational Shooting, Training, and Ranges (RSTAR) programs serve as the training grounds for future competitors as well as for those who wish to be responsible shooters. The NRA provides a nationwide network of more than 36,000 certified instructors to train members in proper shooting technique and safety. This program also provides assistance in the proper development of shooting ranges. In addition to shooting events and programs, NRA Field Operations Programs include a network of more than 11,000 affiliated clubs and associations; the Business Alliance, made up of commercial organizations that support the NRA and its members; and the Friends of NRA program, which links local volunteers with full-time NRA field representatives in efforts to raise funds for the NRA Foundation, a tax-exempt education, safety, and training entity.

With more than 2 million hunters in its membership base, the NRA ranks as the largest hunting organization in the nation. As such, it provides many training and educational services for its hunting membership. The Hunter Services Department supports programs on youth hunter education and the general rules of hunter conduct as well as volunteer programs targeted at promoting proper stewardship of public lands through its Environment, Conservation, and Hunting Outreach (ECHO) program.

Whereas each of these programs is designed to serve the NRA membership in many important ways, the NRA Safety and Education Programs have the widest audience. Throughout the 125-year history of the NRA, firearms safety and education have been the core elements of the organizational mission. Each year more than 4 million people receive firearms safety training and educational materials from the NRA. For children, the Eddie Eagle Gun Safety Program has served as an effective educational tool. Eddie Eagle operates on a simple principle—"If you see a gun: STOP! Don't Touch. Leave the Area. Tell an Adult." The NRA mascot may not appear where firearms are being used, sold, or displayed. This program has reached more than 9 million children from preschool through grade 6 across the United States. There are many additional firearms safety courses for older children and adults, including programs directed at women through the Women's Issues Department, created in 1990. Through all of these programs, the NRA disseminates literally millions of brochures, books, videos, and informational documents to members and interested citizens across the country.

The educational, safety, and training programs continue to be the cornerstones of NRA operations. To most interested observers, these programs are uncontroversial. In fact, many of the NRA educational and safety programs have received accolades from a variety of sources including police, educational, and service organizations. For much of its existence, the NRA focused almost exclusively on these programs. In fact, until the late 1970s, the NRA had only sporadically entered into the political fray through direct lobbying efforts (see Spitzer 1995, 99–103; Davidson 1993, 20–36). In the 1930s, the NRA organized a successful nationwide letter-writing campaign to oppose a number of regulations included in the National Firearms Act of 1934. Three decades later, the NRA began a slow process of reorganizing its priorities, following the passage of the Gun Control Act of 1968. A growing number of NRA activists were becoming dissatisfied with the lack of political leadership at the NRA headquarters. By 1975, a new perspective on political leadership was advanced by Harlon Carter. That year, the Institute for Legislative Action was established as the lobbying arm of the NRA, with Carter directing. Its political action committee, the NRA Political Victory Fund (NRA-PVF), was established a year later, for the 1976 elections. After a series of internal battles that ended in a dramatic leadership shift in 1977, the organization had undergone a significant transformation. "The NRA became more than a rifle club. It became the Gun Lobby" (Davidson 1993, 36).

The NRA as Gun Lobby

Since the late 1970s, the NRA leadership has sought to incorporate political advocacy into the overall mission of organization with uneven results. The direction and intensity of political advocacy within the

NRA has always been hotly contested. The most recent manifestation of the internal debate over its advocacy mission occurred at the annual meeting of the 76-member board of directors in May 1997 in Seattle, Washington. Neal Knox, one of the few NRA leaders with ties to the Carter reorganization period in the late 1970s, attempted to replace executive vice president Wayne LaPierre through a year-long insurgency campaign. He slated a field of candidates to challenge the leadership.

LaPierre withstood the challenge by defeating Knox-supported candidate Donna Dianchi. Knox lost his seat as first vice president to a longtime NRA member and national NRA spokesperson, actor Charlton Heston. Marion Hammer, ceremonial head of the NRA and the first woman elected as its president (in 1996), was reelected (Claiborne 1997, A3). Together, LaPierre, Hammer, and Heston, along with Tanya Metaksa, executive director of the Institute for Legislative Action (NRA-ILA), serve as the core leaders of the NRA.

From a political perspective, NRA leaders view their members in a slightly different manner. Rather than recipients of organizational goods and services, members are viewed as political resources. Tanya Metaksa clearly states the political nature of the NRA leader-member relationship: "Grassroots is the central nervous system of NRA member clout" (NRA 1996b). Maintaining this central nervous system entails nourishing the political ties between leaders and members through an elaborate communications network. In addition, organized outreach efforts link the larger attentive public to the organization. Glen Caroline, manager of the ILA Grassroots Division, views NRA grass roots as members and "natural resources"—firearms owners that are not members of the NRA. For Caroline and Metaksa, along with the ILA lobbying team, "the gun lobby is people."

Connecting with NRA members and the larger attentive constituency on a political level in a meaningful way is not an easy task. The first decade of politicization of the NRA, from the mid-1970s to the mid-1980s, was generally a positive experience for the organization. In 1977, the NRA had just over 1 million members; by the mid-1980s, the membership had almost tripled to 2.8 million. Since that time, the NRA membership base has fluctuated significantly, reaching more than 3.5 million members only to decline by several hundred thousand members in recent years. The membership volatility in recent years is due in no small part to political efforts and public statements of some of the NRA leadership.[1]

Nonetheless, Metaksa and the ILA staff have recognized that a sizable bloc of the NRA membership is not only receptive to political information but also readily mobilizable for political purposes. As a result the NRA has developed the most elaborate grassroots operation in the country today. No interest group, association, labor union, or political party can match the number, quality, and effectiveness of NRA grassroots programs, not even the American Association of Retired Persons. The NRA has reached its level of success because its membership and attentive public is so like-minded on issues relating to firearms. Even though senior citizens have common political interests, they are not nearly as cohesive as the NRA membership—albeit on a much more concise issue agenda.

The NRA Institute for Legislative Action, under the direction of Tanya Metaksa, has an annual operating budget of approximately $25 million and a staff of more than 80 employees, including seven full-time lobbyists in Washington, D.C., and nine state liaisons. The entire NRA membership receives some level of political information through the monthly magazines *American Rifleman, American Hunter,* and *American Guardian,* but the bulk of NRA grassroots activities are targeted at approximately 250,000 "legislative volunteers" across the nation who form the Grassroots Network.

This network reaches NRA members in every state and congressional district; it may also be activated at the state legislative level to rally support or opposition across the country. Supported by the research, analysis, and information files managed by the ILA Research and Information Division, the Grassroots Division seeks to inform and mobilize NRA activists in a timely fashion. A variety of mechanisms exist to facilitate the rapid communications process. The ILA remains reliant on the U.S. Postal Service to deliver its messages to many of its volunteers. For example, *NRA Grassfire,* the newsletter for ILA volunteers, is delivered to 50,000 households through the mail. More timely contacts are made through the NRA-ILA Fax Alert Network, capable of disseminating 10,000 fax messages in a matter of hours. The ILA also maintains an 800 number for direct contacts with the Grassroots Division as well as a phonebank capable of generating 5,000 calls during a single weekend. The ILA has also developed an e-mail list of 23,000 NRA activists to communicate through the Internet.

Beyond communicating with activist members, the ILA seeks to mobilize them for political purposes. These members form the core of any NRA mobilization effort whether it involves financial contributions to NRA-PVF, writing letters to or calling members of Congress, or organizing get-out-the-vote efforts. The ILA Grassroots Division staff spends a significant amount of time conducting training sessions around the country, instructing activists in grassroots development, including establishing local grassroots networks, starting a phone tree, writing effective letters to elected officials, meeting directly with elected officials, attending town meetings, writing letters to the editor and guest editorials, and cultivating the broadcast media.

The ILA also publishes and circulates *The NRA-ILA Legislative and Election Action Manual*, a very thorough document that outlines the methods through which activists may help elect pro-gun lawmakers to office as well as affect the outcome of legislation through lobbying, media contacts, and grassroots activities. A recent manifestation of ILA grassroots activism is the creation of NRA member councils. These councils operate at the city or county level in order to monitor, organize, and mobilize for political purposes NRA members and gun owners at the local levels. By the end of 1996, more than 40 councils had been created, many of which are in California. The ILA has also conducted nationwide voter-registration campaigns during the past two election cycles.

In addition to these broad grassroots efforts, the ILA focuses specifically on mobilizing support for criminal justice reform and victims' rights through its Crime Strike program. For example, the NRA Keep Killers in Jail and the Silent No More projects target convicted murderers across the country who are eligible for parole and attempt to mobilize the relatives of victims of their violent crimes in order to prolong their prison sentences. The grassroots efforts of the NRA-ILA inform and mobilize NRA members but also serve to alert the larger public constituency that is supportive of the NRA agenda.

Cultivating the Pro-Gun Public: The Media and the Internet

Today, there are more than 60 million gun owners in the United States. Each one of these citizens is a potential advocate of the NRA. In reality, NRA leaders have found through internal polling that "between 22 and 27 million citizens in the United States identify with the NRA agenda" (Caroline 1996). In any political context, this places the NRA in an enviable position, particularly when these citizens are organized and when the majority of Americans who disagree with the positions of the NRA are largely unorganized. Glen Caroline characterizes the NRA's large attentive public as a "diverse group, but singularly focused" (Caroline 1996). This public is certainly more diverse than the stereotypical portrayal of NRA members—rural, uneducated, white males who drive pickup trucks. Reaching out to their geographically dispersed and demographically diverse attentive public involves a broader grassroots strategy.

The NRA-ILA uses all of the traditional media outlets to inform and energize its wider attentive public, both for influencing legislative outcomes and for electoral purposes. On the electoral front, the NRA-PVF has consistently ranked as one of the biggest spenders in congressional elections in terms of overall PAC contributions and independent expenditures. The bulk of NRA independent expenditures takes the form of campaign commercials on radio and television in support of NRA-endorsed candidates or against NRA opponents. These campaign messages reach broad voter constituencies but may be directed at particular audiences through targeted purchases of airtime on a variety of network and cable television stations and radio outlets. The NRA-ILA also conducts independent expenditure campaigns through direct-mail communications wherein targeted audiences are identified (e.g., citizens issued hunting licenses in a state or district, subscribers to *Field and Stream* magazine) and sent campaign literature that supports or opposes candidates based on their positions on firearms. Finally, paid newspaper advertisements as well as letters to the editor and guest editorials are also used to inform and activate voters.

Beyond the electioneering efforts conducted through the NRA-PVF, the ILA maintains a communications network that may be quickly activated for purposes of issue advocacy at the local, state, or national levels. Rather than relying on paid media for all of its outreach efforts, the NRA-ILA is closely linked to a number of syndicated radio shows that regularly serve as outlets for NRA messages. Perhaps the most comprehensive media network for issue advocacy is the radio linkage to the NRA attentive public. On more than 50 stations in 30 states, *The Wayne LaPierre Show* may be heard on the Westwood One Entertainment Network on Sundays from 8:00 to 10:00 P.M. While the media markets tend to be small, LaPierre is heard weekly in cities such as Tucson, Arizona; Washington, D.C.; Raleigh/Durham, North Carolina; Las Vegas, Nevada; Salt Lake City, Utah; and Norfolk, Virginia. Attentive citizens in 36 states, through almost 100 radio stations, may listen to *Tom Gresham's Gun Talk* on Sundays from 3:00 to 5:00 P.M. Each Sunday at 4:00, Tanya Metaksa joins Gresham's show to present the latest NRA-ILA legislative alerts.

Broadcasting out of the nation's capital, G. Gordon Liddy and Oliver North have daily syndicated radio talk shows that are decidedly pro-gun, but each show does cover a broad range of political topics. Together, these radio outlets reach several million listeners on a weekly basis. The NRA-ILA also runs a weekly television show on National Empowerment Television cable network that reaches several million households. This enterprise is an expensive undertaking for the organization; under the current financial conditions, the 1997 television production budget may be cut or eliminated (Vobejda 1996).

Beyond communications through direct mail, newspapers, radio, and television, the NRA-ILA embarked on a new mission to reach its members and larger alliance of citizens in 1994 by launching the NRA Web site on the Internet—http://www.nra.org/. Linking members and their attentive public on the World Wide Web has proven to be a successful enterprise for the ILA. According to Tanya Metaksa, "electronic communication is fast becoming the most powerful tool NRA members have in defending their right to keep and bear arms. Thousands of NRA members receive their legislative alerts daily through the Internet, and they are using the Internet to stay informed, communicate with legislators, and support our grassroots efforts" (Metaksa 1996a). When Metaksa took over as executive director of the NRA-ILA in 1994, she made the linkage to the Internet her major priority. Since that time the NRA Web site has become one of the premier showcases in the interest-group community. Under the management of Jim Manown, the site has won multiple awards from industry publications, such as the Point Top 5% Award, the Magellan 3 Star Site, and the IWAY 500 Winner.

The NRA Web site is clearly one of the most comprehensive among organized interest groups in the United States. *Mother Jones* magazine, not exactly known for its support of the NRA, acknowledges its comprehensiveness: "One of the best places to learn about the NRA short of actually joining is its Web site" (Dreyfuss 1996, 73). The site offers more than 3,500 separate document files to be downloaded. Today it generates significant attention on the Web with more than 30,000 contacts each day. Each month approximately 3 million information files are downloaded from the NRA Web site. Whereas it is difficult to identify the Web traffic hitting the NRA Web site, Manown and the ILA staff know, from the contacts through e-mail and other means, that their audience is a mix of NRA members, attentive citizens, Web surfers, and the media. The media audience has generated news stories as a result of documents and information downloaded from the NRA Web site; public affairs staffers have fielded numerous calls from journalists seeking comment or clarification on items posted on the site.

The next step for the NRA Web site involves adding multimedia components such as on-line audio files and full-motion video files. Upon completion of this project, interested browsers may download a speech delivered by president Marion Hammer, listen to an NRA press conference, or tune in to *Tom Gresham's Gun Talk* on the NRA site. (Gresham's show is already available live on the Internet through http://www.cp-tel.net/~guntalk/). The final step will be to include the video component in order to complete the multimedia presentation. In order to attract more of its members to the Internet, the NRA-ILA entered into an agreement with NETCOM to distribute its Net-

Cruiser computer software, specially customized for the NRA Web site. NRA members pay NETCOM a monthly Internet access fee of $19.95, a portion of which is turned over to the NRA-ILA.

Cultivating an attentive public, largely through political messages delivered via the media outlets discussed, while maintaining a multi-million-member organization has often caused difficulties for the NRA-ILA. Serving the dual needs of NRA members as both a service organization and the gun lobby is crucial to organizational mainte-nance. If those needs happen to conflict with the efforts of the political leadership to inform and activate members and the larger public, it is likely that dissatisfied members may leave the organization (Hirsch-man 1970). In recent years, such conflicts have resulted in the loss of several hundred thousand members. Such tensions have also driven up the costs of maintaining existing members and soliciting new members through direct mail. Nonetheless, the NRA-ILA has maintained its focus on utilizing the NRA grass roots in its electoral and issue-advo-cacy campaigns across the country with a significant degree of success.

Leaders of the NRA-ILA understand the political meaning of the title of this chapter—going hunting where the ducks are—as well as its various applications. This old adage is most often applied to political campaigning; that is, candidates should spend their time and money campaigning in neighborhoods, precincts, and towns where they be-lieve they have many potential or proven supporters. But the adage applies to the NRA and its grass roots as well, not only in the context of electioneering but also in the context of mobilizing grassroots sup-port in issue-advocacy efforts.

At the outset, the NRA is hunting for members. It is important that the membership-development team understand where its potential "ducks" are and, as important, what ammunition is best suited to hunt them. As was discussed in the earlier sections of this chapter, many members of the NRA conceive of the organization as a service pro-vider; yet others join the NRA to support the gun lobby. In its efforts to inform and activate the NRA grass roots, the NRA-ILA takes into consideration the dual nature of the membership base. Next, in the electoral context, the NRA is hunting for voters, but also for candidates to support or oppose. From a grassroots perspective, cultivating vot-ers—both NRA members and the larger attentive public—requires that the NRA-ILA inform potential voters of the candidates and their posi-tions on firearms issues and activate them to vote accordingly. For the NRA, the NRA-PVF serves the dual role of selecting candidates for support or opposition and presenting the NRA choice to its grassroots support base. The latter role is often undertaken through independent expenditure campaigns. On election day, the NRA must then demonstrate its real grassroots support through organized get-out-the-vote drives in districts across the nation.

Finally, when the elections are over, the NRA is hunting for advocates to support or oppose legislative initiatives introduced in city and county councils, in state legislatures, and in the U.S. Congress. In this context, there need not be as many "ducks" as in the electoral context, but these NRA advocates must be knowledgeable, credible, and vigilant. In many state legislative chambers across the nation as well as in Congress, the NRA has demonstrated, often successfully, its ability to mobilize and unleash its grassroots support.

NRA Grass Roots: Electoral Consequences

In the 1995–1996 election cycle, the NRA Political Victory Fund surpassed its 1993–1994 total expenditures of $5.9 million by raising and spending more than $6.6 million in PAC contributions and independent expenditures. The strategic allocation of PVF funds in more than 200 congressional races reaped rewards for the NRA in 1996. On the day after the election, the NRA issued a press release that stated, in part: "Based on the declared congressional races, 92 percent of Congressmen who voted for the repeal of the Clinton gun ban and who ran for reelection were returned to office" (NRA 1996a). The PVF expenditures, although significant in their magnitude and important in their impacts on elections and the policymaking process (Langbein and Lotwis 1990; Langbein 1993), often overshadow the real grassroots impact of the NRA in electing or defeating candidates for office.

An important case from recent electoral history illustrates the importance of grassroots mobilization in electoral success for the NRA. The case involves the 1994 Tennessee races for the U.S. Senate, in particular the contest between the incumbent Democrat, Jim Sasser, first elected to the Senate in 1976, and the Republican challenger, Bill Frist, a doctor with no previous political experience. In the other Senate race, Rep. Jim Cooper, a Democrat, was pitted against Fred Thompson, a Republican, known more widely for his motion picture acting than his political background. The Cooper-Thompson special election was conducted to complete the final two years of the Senate term vacated by Vice President Al Gore.

Prior to the 1994 elections, Tennessee was represented in Congress by two Democratic senators and six Democratic members of the House of Representatives; Republicans held the remaining three House seats.[2]

The governor of the state was also a Democrat and both chambers of the state legislature were controlled by the Democratic party. Sasser and Gore were elected in 1988 and 1990, respectively, with solid majorities of more than 65 percent of the votes cast in each election. The Clinton-Gore ticket also carried the state in 1992.

The Frist-Sasser contest proved to be one of the most expensive statewide races in the history of Tennessee politics. Frist spent more than $7 million, including more than $1 million of his own money, on the campaign. Sasser spent just over $5 million. The Thompson-Cooper special election proved to be less costly; each candidate for the open senate seat raised and spent just under $4 million. The NRA provided PVF PAC primary and general election support to both Frist ($9,900) and Thompson ($4,950). In addition, the NRA-ILA conducted independent expenditure efforts for both candidates, spending $177,227 on television, radio, and direct-mail campaigns (Makinson and Goldstein 1996).

Frist and Thompson were successful, winning their elections with 56 percent and 60 percent of the votes cast. The NRA played an important role in each of these races, but not necessarily in financial terms. The NRA PAC contributions to the candidates represented less than 0.5 percent of their total PAC contributions and less than 0.2 percent of their total spending. The independent expenditure campaigns were more helpful in defining the candidates on matters relating to firearms. But the grassroots support from NRA members across the state proved to be the most decisive element in the NRA strategy. In our conversation with Senator Frist, he was quick to point out that the local NRA associations and groups were on board with him much earlier than the NRA-ILA and the PVF in Washington. Although he benefited from the independent expenditure campaign conducted by the NRA-ILA, he stressed the meaningfulness of the votes delivered by NRA members across the state, particularly those who were being cross-pressured by competing organized interest groups. In many ways, these Senate contests were decided by the split in voters who were cross-pressured by Democratic forces, namely unions, and Republican forces, namely the NRA and the Christian Coalition. In Tennessee, union households are often NRA households or Christian Coalition households.

To confirm this perception we talked with Thomas Owens, assistant director for legislation at the AFL-CIO. Owens worked extensively on the Tennessee races in 1994. He concluded that the AFL-CIO-backed candidates, Sasser and Cooper, were done in by a variety of factors, the most crucial of which was the cross-pressuring of the union's membership base by opposing organized interest groups. First, the Tennessee economy was booming in fall 1994; union plants were working three shifts and offering overtime. As a result, union members were not as clearly attracted to the pocketbook issues offered by the Democratic candidates. Second, Owens referred in shorthand fashion to the tenacity of the opposing groups active in the campaigns—"Guns, God, and Gays." He was referring to pro-gun (NRA) forces and pro-God and antigay (Christian Coalition) forces. In the end, Owens concluded: "We got rolled by our own membership; 50 percent of our union members voted Republican in Tennessee in 1994" (Owens 1995). Elsewhere across the country union households defected from the Democratic party in 1994, but not at the level found in Tennessee, with a range from 30 to 45 percent voting Republican, according to AFL-CIO polling.

Although the financial support of the NRA through independent expenditures may have been a necessary condition for electoral success in Tennessee, it was not sufficient to sway vote choices *and* mobilize voters to support their endorsed candidates. The NRA grassroots efforts on election day delivered voters to the polls. There are numerous instances of hotly contested congressional and gubernatorial elections where the grassroots mobilization efforts of the NRA proved decisive (see, e.g., the 1994 congressional race between Speaker of the House Tom Foley and Republican challenger George Nethercutt in Washington and the Louisiana gubernatorial election of Mike Foster in 1995) (Faucheux 1996).

In the Tennessee case and in many other elections, NRA voters, including NRA members and their attentive public, represent a minority of all voters. Nonetheless, they are a cohesive bloc of voters that in many cases is sufficiently large to sway election outcomes. During the 1994 election cycle, a number of polling firms, in conducting statewide voter surveys in 25 states, included a series of items that measured the level of respondents' commitments to a variety of political organizations. One was as follows: "I am going to name a number of organizations, and I want you to tell me if this organization speaks for you (1) all of the time, (2) most of the time, (3) some of the time, or (4) never." Table 9.1 reflects the "all of the time" responses. The National Rifle Association is compared with the Republican and Democratic parties. The table includes the polling firm that conducted each poll, the date of the poll, and the state in which the poll was conducted.

It is significant that in 19 of the 25 states, the percentage of NRA staunch supporters is higher than in each of the partisan categories. These findings are interesting from a variety of perspectives. First, the size of the Republican and Democratic core constituencies—true believers in their party's entire philosophy and issue agenda—is rather small. Only the Democratic parties in Pennsylvania and Tennessee may

TABLE 9.1
Organizational Representation

State	Pollster	Date	GOP	DEM	NRA
AL	ISSR	6/95	5.9%	7.2%	9.6%
AK	P&S	10/94	5.0	5.0	17.0
CA	LRC	7/94	7.0	8.0	6.0
CT	RC	11/94	3.0	2.0	6.0
FL	MD,PMR	5/94	4.0	3.0	8.0
GA	MD,PMR	5/94	5.0	6.0	8.0
ID	MI	5/94	3.0	4.0	13.0
IL	PMR	10/94	8.0	7.0	4.0
IA	MD	9/94	3.0	3.0	2.0
MA	MD,PMR	10/94	7.0	7.0	9.0
MI	MRG	10/94	5.0	5.0	8.0
MN	MD	6/94	6.0	8.0	8.0
MO	MD,PMR	7/94	7.0	5.0	9.0
MT	MI	5/94	4.0	5.0	14.0
NV	P&S	10/94	7.0	5.0	12.0
NJ	LRC	7/94	5.0	3.0	6.0
NY	P&S	10/94	4.0	4.0	6.0
OK	LRC	7/94	4.0	5.0	10.0
OR	MI	5/94	6.0	6.0	8.0
PA	LRC	7/94	6.0	11.0	10.0
SC	MD,PMR	6/94	5.0	4.0	8.0
TN	MD,PMR	9/94	9.0	10.0	13.0
TX	MD,PMR	9/94	5.0	4.0	4.0
VT	DSJW	10/94	5.0	6.0	7.0
VA	MD,PMR	10/94	7.0	7.0	14.0

Source: Hallow and O'Leary (1995:217).
Notes: ISSR=Institute for Social Science Research, Univ. of Alabama; P&S=Penn & Schoen; LRC=Luntz Research Co.; RC=Roper Center; MD=Mason-Dixon; PMR=Political/Media Research, Inc.; MI=Moore Information; MRG=Marketing Research Group; DSJW=Dresner, Sykes, Jordan & Wickers.

claim a core voter base of support of 10 percent or more. Conversely, the NRA garners a core constituency of 10 percent or more in 8 of the 25 states. Obviously, the NRA agenda is dramatically more concise than that of either major political party. Nonetheless, these findings provide sobering evidence of the potential electoral strength of the NRA grass roots. In virtually all of the states presented, the realization of these patterns in the electoral context would result in a decisive voting bloc in all but the most lopsided elections. Finally, regarding the earlier case in Tennessee, the findings highlighted in Table 9.1 identify quite a sizable bloc (13 percent) of NRA supporters in the Volunteer State. These NRA supporters are crucial not only in the elections but in the grassroots mobilization efforts in legislatures across the nation.

NRA Grass Roots: Legislative Consequences

From a grassroots lobbying perspective, "going hunting where the ducks are" often means shopping for the right political forum to wage a successful legislative campaign. For example, if the NRA-ILA is gaining little ground in the U.S. Congress, it may direct its attention to the state legislative level, as it did in 1994 and 1995 with demonstrable successes. At this level, the NRA is often unopposed because the gun control movement and its organizational components, for example, Handgun Control, Inc., are not equipped to fight grassroots battles in a variety of legislative venues.

Since 1993, the NRA has worked to pass "right to carry" legislation in more than a dozen states. As of the end of 1996, 31 states had enacted right-to-carry legislation supported by the NRA. The ILA has also fought successfully to pass preemption legislation that overturned local gun control ordinances in several states. Here again, the power of numbers at the NRA grassroots level is apparent. However, the real impact of the NRA grass roots is most clearly articulated by someone who has felt its wrath. Tom Loftus, former speaker of the Wisconsin assembly, recently wrote a book chronicling his political career (Loftus 1994). His battles with the National Rifle Association warranted an entire chapter in his memoir. Loftus begins his critique of the NRA by highlighting the unique character of the organization and its unchallenged position in the legislature.

> The National Rifle Association is a unique interest group because of the zeal of its members and the mythology of guns in America. For every interest group that wants something from the legislature, there is almost always a countervailing force—usually a competing interest group. This

is not the case with the NRA. The press could exert countervailing pressure, but there has to be a story to report on for a war to be waged. The Speaker has the power, money, loyalty, and press attention to thwart a powerful interest group. But he or she will pay a political price if that group is the NRA. (88)

After discussing the various details of the legislative battles surrounding the NRA and the legislative agenda, Loftus focuses on the grassroots tactics deployed by the NRA against him. "Things changed when the NRA identified me as the anti-gun devil and provided my telephone number to its 80,000 members. Like zombies programmed to call, the NRA true believers dialed my number one after another, and the phone started to ring nonstop. . . . Trying to converse with them was usually out of the question. Their mission was to deliver a message, and they did not want me to paint any gray on their black and white view of gun legislation" (94). While dreading their tenacity, Loftus grudgingly acknowledged the high level of commitment exhibited by NRA supporters. "A lot of interest groups have a big membership list and use newsletters to exhort their members to contact their legislators. The NRA, however, has zealots that really call, and they call every time they are asked. Not big labor, not big business, not environmental groups, not teachers, not trial lawyers, and not even chiropractors have such obedient followers. And if a legislator was at a plant gate, or a parade, there would be the more than occasional comment about guns or a shout, 'No gun control!' " (94–95).

These are the words of a staunch opponent of the NRA. His words are echoed in the halls of Congress and in state legislatures across the nation. Obviously, elected officials who support the grassroots activities of the NRA are much more glowing in their remarks. Nonetheless, there are few, if any, groups on the American political landscape that garner the commentary offered by Loftus and echoed by scores of politicians in every state. This is real grassroots prowess. When one combines the grassroots efforts undertaken by the NRA in the electoral arena with the grassroots lobbying efforts in Congress and in legislatures across the nation, the NRA is unmatched. Although the NRA leadership has at times squandered this valuable political resource by providing aid and comfort to its opponents in the form of patently outrageous remarks against elected officials and government employees, the NRA remains the preeminent grassroots organization in the United States.

Notes

The authors wish to thank Tanya Metaksa, executive director of the NRA Institute for Legislative Action (ILA); Glen Caroline, director of the Grassroots Division, NRA-ILA; Jim Manown, manager of the NRA Web site; Bill Powers in the Public Affairs Office of the NRA; Senator Bill Frist (R-TN); and Thomas Owens, assistant director for legislation, AFL-CIO, for their assistance in the preparation of this chapter.

1. One of the most controversial statements made by NRA leaders appeared in a direct-mail letter signed by Wayne LaPierre following the Oklahoma City bombing. LaPierre referred to federal agents as "jack-booted thugs." He later apologized for the statement after being widely criticized in the press. More recently LaPierre has made similarly controversial claims in direct-mail campaigns: "A small handful of President Clinton's anti-gun government agents continue to intimidate and harass law-abiding citizens. . . . They've launched a new wave of brainwashing propaganda aimed at further destroying our Constitutional freedoms" (Dreyfuss 1996, 47).

2. Harlan Mathews was appointed in January 1993 to serve as the junior senator from Tennessee, replacing the recently elected vice president, Al Gore. He served until the next congressional election cycle. Mathews chose not to run for the seat to which he had been appointed, leaving an open seat special election in 1994.

10

Trying to Stop the Craziness of This Business: Gun Control Groups

Diana Lambert

When I was eighteen years old, I was sent off from my home in a little Mississippi town to a college down the road about thirty miles. My daddy gave me a small pistol for my protection; I had never held a gun before. But my father warned me to be careful with it because, and I'll never forget his words, "these things can blow up in your hand." He was normally a very smart man. It shows you the craziness of this business. I did not question my father; this was just what people did. Anyway I graduated and was living in Memphis; I still had that gun. A friend and her young child came one weekend to stay in my apartment while I was away. Upon my return, I found an irate note from my friend—her four year old son had found that loaded gun under my bed and was waving it around. Luckily nothing happened. Well, I just took that pistol and threw it in the Mississippi River. I thought I was through with guns, but I was wrong. Some years later, my husband and I returned home late at night to find a man burglarizing our house; my husband was killed by this man using a handgun. The craziness of this business never seems to stop.

—Member of Handgun Control, Inc.[1]

Gun control groups made their appearance on the national scene soon after the assassination of President Kennedy. Their common purpose was to secure legislation, at the federal, state and local levels, to either regulate or ban handguns. For most of their existence, the advancement of their goal resembled the labors of Sisyphus; no sooner was a forward step taken in gun control than the powers of repeal and diminution came back with a bitter force. The much-celebrated Gun Control Act of 1968 was eviscerated by the so-called Firearms Owners

172

Protection Act of 1986; the Brady Bill, first introduced in 1987, was finally signed into law seven years later, but only after debilitating amendments were accepted; and less than a year after the assault weapons ban became law, the U.S. House of Representatives came roaring back with passage of an outright repeal.

Yet winds of change in the politics of gun control are becoming evident; indeed, the same 104th Congress that championed assault weapons also embraced the notion that the universe of people who have no right to own guns needs to be widened. A propitious confluence of factors has occurred in the realm of gun control advocacy. Changes in society, changes in the tactics and coalitions of interest groups, and changes in the government have combined in recent years to create an increasingly powerful gun control political force. Gun control advocates no longer scamper about the perimeter of public policy; they are the vanguard of a fundamental change in the way America views the handgun.

Central to these changes has been the escalating street violence in America's cities, which has increased popular support for gun control and led police groups to lobby for gun control in an attempt to limit the firepower of criminals. In addition, changes in strategies and tactics by the NRA have led to a widening split with its former police allies and have led some prominant conservatives to repudiate the organization. Finally, the gun control organizations themselves have changed their tactics and gained new political allies.

Changes in Society: Streets Running Red with Blood

Escalating street violence has changed the politics of gun control; every day the 400 new homicides due to handguns add another cohort of gun control spokespersons and new voices for federal involvement.[2] Popular support for national gun control has been demonstrated in polling figures since the 1930s (Spitzer 1995, 118); but beyond a few modest federal statutes, including the Gun Control Act of 1968,[3] this popular support has never before been translated into political support for strong regulation of firearms at the federal level. The principal obstacle to gun control legislation has been the effective advocacy of interest groups, notably the National Rifle Association (NRA) and to a lesser extent the Committee for the Right to Keep and Bear Arms and Gun Owners of America, which proclaim that the private and individual ownership of firearms is protected by the Second Amendment and that any handgun law is the first step to firearms confiscation.[4]

Yet local governments are beginning to pass gun control legislation despite NRA activity, primarily in response to escalating street vio-lence. Morton Grove, Illinois, put itself on the political map in 1981 when the town by ordinance banned the sale and possession of hand-guns; subsequently, the NRA took Morton Grove to court, claiming the local law violated the Second Amendment of the U.S. Constitution, but the Supreme Court allowed the ordinance to stand.[5] This ordinance "gave the still mostly inchoate gun-control movement encourage-ment—and set off warning lights at NRA headquarters. If Morton Grove could pass such a sweeping bill, both sides realized, so could other towns" (Davidson 1993, 133). And so other towns and states did: gun control efforts increasingly appeared like stars in the evening sky. Among many other examples, Chicago requires all handguns to be registered and certificates of new ownership to be obtained from the police, and Maryland has enacted and reaffirmed by referendum a state law banning Saturday night specials. As gun violence grew, so did efforts to limit access to guns.

At the federal level, efforts to pass gun control legislation to build on the 1968 act have proceeded at a glacial pace; yet after years of struggle the Brady Bill became law in 1993. The president of the Inter-national Association of Chiefs of Police (IACP) attributed the 1994 House passage of a bill to ban assault weapons to a public weary with gun violence. "For five frustrating years, the IACP has been calling for legislation to ban assault weapons. . . . What made the difference this time? The fear of violence and crime, and the shortage of solutions have definitely had an impact" ("President's Message" 1994).

For the first time in history, antigun groups are marshaling the ma-jority support they have always claimed. Michael Beard of the Coali-tion to Stop Gun Violence explained, "The difference today is that young kids are dying, not the street gangs, but innocent children" (Beard 1996). As Handgun Control, Inc., prepared for the 105th Con-gress, its legislative director concluded that the public was now behind its efforts: "People now realize the situation is out of control; parents are dramatically concerned about the safety at schools. It is now a situ-ation that threatens our children" (Handgun Control, Inc. 1996).

Changes in the Interest-Group Environment: The Police Cross the Line

One of the most important changes in the universe of interest groups involved in the gun control debate has been the growing support of police organizations for gun control. Historically, the police and the NRA have enjoyed a close, mutually supportive relationship. Since its founding in the late nineteenth century, the NRA has taught gun safety to generations of hunters and provided the training to scores of policemen on the beat. Internal changes in the NRA, beginning with the so-called Cincinnati Revolt of 1977, undermined the cordial police-NRA-relationship and transformed the NRA into a national lobbying powerhouse with a reduced emphasis on gun safety, hunting, and training into a group whose raison d'être is the rigid opposition to any law or regulation that placed any controls on the ownership, possession, or transportation of firearms (see Sugarmann 1992). The NRA's strident defense of the unregulated, individual "right to bear arms" ultimately resulted in a schism with the police; law enforcement parted company with the NRA after many years of cordial relations and tentatively crossed the line into gun control territory.

The first crack in the NRA-police alliance came with the legislative struggle over the "cop-killer" bullet. Representative Mario Biaggi, Democrat from New York and a 28-year police veteran who had been shot ten times in the line of duty, was asked by the New York Patrolman's Benevolent Association to sponsor legislation to ban armor-piercing bullets. KTW bullets, or "apple greens" for the green coating of Teflon on the tip, were developed in 1970, ironically by a medical coroner and several police friends; it seems that the police were increasingly frustrated in the pursuit of suspected criminals who were able to get away by simply jumping in a car, totally unperturbed by the fusillade of police bullets that pinged off the car's metal frame. Law enforcement wanted a bullet that could penetrate an automobile; it got the apple green. But this powerful bullet turned out to be very dangerous: it went in one side of a car and out the other, creating havoc. In short order, state legislatures banned these ballistics, but that did not stop a 1981 *NBC News* segment on "cop-killer" bullets or the ensuing congressional melee over federal legislation to ban these ballistics.

Michael Beard, director of the National Coalition to Ban Handguns, which later became the Coalition to Stop Gun Violence, contacted the NRA in an effort to reach a mutual agreement to ban these bullets; however, the gun lobby, fresh from its purifying Cincinnati Revolt, was in no mood for compromise: it would oppose a ban on armor-piercing bullets (Davidson 1993, 88). Police organizations supported the bill, however, and after the NRA discovered that its opposition to the legislation was causing serious erosion of its relationship with the police, its lobbyists worked with the Reagan White House to draft a compromise administration bill. In June 1984, Ronald Reagan presented the police with a fait accompli—legislation that banned several but not all armor-piercing bullets. A less than comprehensive bill banning certain specific ammunition, including some types of cop-killer bullets, was ulti-

.ied in August 1985,[6] its legislative journey in the new
hardly noticeable. The NRA was looking ahead to a much
.gnificant legislative struggle, and the gun lobby wanted police

ʃut NRA-police relations were further eroded by the struggle over
ʌe McClure-Volkmer Act in 1986, which weakened the Gun Control
Act of 1968. The Firearms Owners' Protection Act, (S 49 and HR 945),
sponsored by Senator James McClure (R-ID) and Representative Harold Volkmer (R-MO), was intended to eviscerate the regulations put
into place by the modest Gun Control Act of 1968 on the selling, ownership, and possession of all firearms, including handguns. The police,
still very much legislative novices, again faced off with the NRA. In
fall 1985, as law enforcement officers stood at attention in the Capitol,
the Senate passed the McClure-Volkmer Bill. The police have undergone a road-to-Damascus experience: "It was at that point that we realized we had to organize in some fashion, to be able to present ourselves
as a large organized group to the legislators—to offset the tremendous
lobbying capability of the NRA" (Davidson 1993, 98–99).

So police groups began to organize to support gun control.[7] Perhaps
the single most critical step the police took was the October 1985 establishment of an umbrella group to coordinate their legislative efforts:
the Law Enforcement Steering Committee Against S. 49. The steering
committee also provided political cover for the many police officers
and chiefs of police around the country who wished to voice their personal support for gun control, something that had been in the past
professionally dangerous (Davidson 1993, 99). Police associational
magazines began to churn out editorials expressing clear opposition to
McClure-Volkmer: "There's absolutely no good reason to relax the gun
laws already on the books. If anything, they should be strengthened.
S. 49 and HR 945 are irresponsible and reprehensible pieces of legislation" ("McClure/Volkmer" 1986). These same journals also engaged
in grassroots lobbying, printing appeals to law enforcement officers to
contact their members and senators to express opposition to the legislation. A letter signed by ten police organizations was sent to President
Reagan, calling on him to oppose McClure-Volkmer ("McClure/Volk-
mer" 1986). Then disagreement between law enforcement and its erstwhile allies became ugly and personal: an NRA chapter tried to revoke
the NRA membership of the president of the International Association
of Chiefs of Police (IACP), John J. Norton, citing his support for gun
control legislation and his appearance before a House subcommittee
that was critical of the McClure-Volkmer legislation. This incident
prompted a quick rebuttal in the form of a public letter from the IACP

to the NRA and served to magnify the increasing estrangement between the two groups:

> Historically the National Rifle Association has enjoyed a positive relationship with the law enforcement community in this country. . . . Recent events with respect to S. 49, the McClure/Volkmer Act, have focused attention on a very serious difference of opinion between the NRA and law enforcement. . . . [The IACP] opposes the tactics utilized by the NRA to ramrod this legislation through Congress. Your tactics have included taking the liberty of improperly acting as a spokesman for law enforcement in this country. . . . You have distorted the facts to suit your purpose and have attempted to suppress free and open public debate on perhaps the most critical safety issue to come about in recent memory. ("S. 49 Dispute" 1986)

Despite the direct and indirect lobbying activities on the part of the police organizations, the House passed the McClure-Volkmer Bill. "The police were on hand in full force. More than 100 blue-uniformed officers, representing major law enforcement associations, formed an accusatory gauntlet outside the House of Representatives as Congressmen filed in to consider [the McClure-Volkmer Bill]. Later, after checking their own arms, the police filled two sections of the spectators' gallery to watch the debate" (Doerner 1989, 145). The House, under the steady gaze of the police, nevertheless passed the bill, but with an amendment to retain the provision of the Gun Control Act of 1968 that banned the interstate sale of handguns. The Senate subsequently approved the House version, and the McClure-Volkmer Bill became law on May 19, 1986. The Law Enforcement Steering Committee was successful several months later in nursing through Congress a modest modification to McClure-Volkmer to address several very specific police problems; for example, firearms transported across state lines may not be stored in the glove compartment of an automobile. After its failure to stop the McClure-Volkmer Bill, the steering committee was not disbanded but retained with a new mandate: to address possible future legislative problems for the police. Hence the police had achieved a permanent and potentially sophisticated lobbying capability.

The McClure-Volkmer legislation was a significant defeat for law enforcement and other gun control advocates, and it was also the beginning of a critical and long-term rift between the police and the NRA. The split widened during the debate over plastic handguns. The issue of plastic guns arose after the Department of Defense concluded from a commissioned study that disposable machine guns were not possible; gun control advocates got wind that the manufacturers were planning to use that study to examine the feasibility of plastic handguns and alerted the media. In a 1986 series of reports, syndicated columnist Jack Anderson alerted the public to the existence of something called the Glock 17, a foreign plastic gun that allegedly could pass through airport security stations undetected. The Reagan administration was actually ready to propose a bill to ban plastic guns when the NRA in behind-the-scenes negotiations convinced Attorney General Edwin Meese to shelve the bill. "While police groups were growing adept at playing the image game—dubbing armor-piercing bullets 'cop killers' and framing other issues they cared about as either being pro- or anti–law enforcement—they were still no match for the NRA at back room lobbying. The police simply weren't as well connected as the NRA, which now had a decade of experience playing the game of power politics" (Davidson 1993, 107). With the administration effectively muzzled, the gun control groups convinced Senator Howard Metzenbaum in fall 1987 to introduce a bill to ban plastic guns. Predictably, the NRA announced its opposition, arguing that the guns could not evade airport security (the evidence was not conclusive) and that any gun control represented an opening in the floodgates that would result in the ultimate banning and confiscation of all firearms, including long guns. The NRA mobilized its enormous grassroots lobbying operation; Senate leaders delayed floor consideration until 1988. Much like in the cop-killer-bullet scenario, the White House worked out a draft bill with the NRA that banned some plastic and ceramic guns and offered the proposal to the police as a take-it-or-leave-it proposition. The Undetectable Weapons Act was signed into law November 11, 1988, but the debate had widened the split between the NRA and law enforcement.

  Police groups proceeded with their efforts to create a grassroots lobbying campaign, exhorting their members to contact the Congress: "Still we do not have effective federal legislation that protects our citizens from the dangers posed by handguns" ("President's Message" 1991). The International Association of Chiefs of Police in 1988 went on record in support of a waiting period for handgun purchases, and by so doing, the law enforcement establishment entered for the first time into a compact with Handgun Control, In., (HCI) to seek the enactment of the Brady Bill. Although it is clear that HCI has helped the police organize into a lobbying force, law enforcement is reticent about this new relationship; after all, there is a long history of alliance with the NRA (Davidson 1993, 197). HCI heartily embraced this coalition with law enforcement. Upon the enactment of the Brady Bill, in an advertisement in *Police Chief* magazine (January 1994), Sarah Brady professed to the police, "We have finally done it and I do mean WE! Without the strong support of the International Association of Chiefs of Police and the individual police chiefs across the country, the Brady Bill would not be the Brady Law." The coalition was acknowledged at the White House signing ceremony for the Brady Bill, where Jim and Sarah Brady and IACP president Sylvester Daughtry were in attendance.

With the police endorsing a ban on the sale and manufacturing of assault weapons, the IACP "launched a blitz to convince the 75 undecided lawmakers to vote" for the assault ban legislation pending before the House, commenced a prodigious grassroots campaign to convince local police officers to speak out to Congress, and sent its president to testify before congressional committees ("President's Message" 1994). Subsequently, the assault weapons ban became law in 1994; this issue made the law enforcement–NRA estrangement, which had started out as a repairable fissure in 1985, a permanent chasm (see Sugarmann 1992, 201).

Police officials are now regular witnesses at committee hearings and are called for counsel by both congressional parties and the White House. The police, which prior to 1986 had allowed others to carry their water and had been betrayed by them, now are demanding a seat at the table of public policy, and the policy they seek is gun control. Gun control is now a law enforcement issue; gun control is now a crime issue.

The shift of police organizations from allies of the NRA to supporters of gun control has helped transform the debate on gun control from one centering on individual liberties (the right to bear arms) to one of crime control. It has also helped to erase the image that support for gun control comes only from liberals. The potential for police organizations to mobilize public support for gun control initiatives is clear. Yet it was not inevitable that the police would become part of the gun control coalition—the changed tactics of the NRA are largely responsible.

Changes in Group Tactics:
With Enemies Like the NRA, Who Needs Friends?

Today's National Rifle Association bears little resemblance to the original organization, founded in 1871 in Manhattan for the purpose of hunter safety and firearms training. The NRA today is a potent political force with one agenda: unfettered individual ownership, possession, and transportation of all firearms. The current NRA policy of absolutely no compromise with the "gun grabbers" can be traced to the 1977 Cincinnati Revolt. It was then that the old guard, which supported the notion of a rifle club and an outdoors association, was over-thrown and in its place was installed a new breed of hard-liners who transformed the NRA into a powerful lobby with an unabashed agenda of no gun control. Over the years, this unyielding policy that brooks no compromise on gun control has led to a decline of membership, although the NRA will not admit this directly. Membership peaked in 1995 at 3.5 million, but the NRA now claims 3 million. The NRA reduced its Washington staff of 400 by over 30 in September 1996; although the gun lobby will not confirm that money problems are behind this reduction, the NRA did admit a need to focus on grassroots programs.

The uncompromising demeanor exhibited by the NRA since 1977 has created in the public's mind the specter of extremism, as aptly demonstrated by one NRA official who argued before Congress that released felons should not be denied the right to own and possess firearms—any resulting loss of safety for the public at large is simply "a price we pay for freedom" (Edel 1995, 114). Extremism on the part of the NRA benefits gun control advocates, who in comparison practice the politics of compromise: HCI, for example, supports keeping firearms out of the hands of only dangerous people, and the Coalition to Ban Firearms Violence supports banning only certain "bad" guns (cop-killer bullets, assault weapons, Saturday night specials, plastic guns, etc.); neither group advocates the banning of long guns (rifles and shotguns) used by sportsmen.

In February 1982, the NRA announced its position of opposition to the banning of cop-killer bullets, and the public caught its first view of the NRA on the road to extremism. The open and angry criticism of police during the debate over the McClure-Volkmer Bill in 1986 engendered public opprobrium by singling out various law enforcement officers who were denounced for their pro–gun control positions (Davidson 1993, 100–106). While the debate on McClure-Volkmer continued, the issue of plastic guns made its appearance; written in the minds of the public was an increasingly frightening and extreme NRA.

Another episode, ratcheting up public wariness toward the NRA, came in the 102nd Congress when Senator Dennis DeConcini (R-AZ), darling of the NRA, asked the gun lobby to talk to him about assault weapons. President Bush had taken a first step in 1989 by banning the importation of assault weapons, but now the domestic manufacturing of these firearms needed to be addressed. Law enforcement officials approached DeConcini to ask him to join with Senator Metzenbuam in sponsoring legislation to ban the domestic production of assault weapons. DeConcini, light-years from Metzenbaum on any measure, demurred but decided to deal directly with his friends at the NRA to develop a draft proposal they both could support. Despite the outstanding NRA credentials of DeConcini, a "100 percenter" in the NRA rating game on important votes, the senator was sent packing—no deal. A familiar ritual unfolded: DeConcini introduced his bill to ban sales of domestic and foreign assault weapons, allowing present owners to keep their firearms, and the NRA unleashed a furious campaign against its erstwhile ally. Ultimately, DeConcini's bill was voted down by the House even though the day before the vote a deranged man armed with the infamous Glock 17 (of plastic gun fame) killed 22 people in Killeen, Texas.

Early in the 102nd Congress (1991–1992), the NRA replaced its chief lobbyist, Warren Cassidy. The selection of Wayne LaPierre signaled that now the policy became not only to oppose all gun control laws but to work for the repeal of any on the books.

"To the public, the NRA [is] an increasingly reactionary, extreme and dangerous organization" (Sugarmann 1992, 222). The gun lobby had fought against bans on cop-killer bullets that rip police bulletproof vests apart, plastic guns that do not register on airport security detectors, and assault weapons that kill masses of innocent people with one pull of the trigger. Many legislative friends in the U.S. Congress and in state legislatures are finding the NRA's take-no-prisoners attitude increasingly uncomfortable, the rift with police increasingly worrisome, and the divergence from public opinion increasingly unacceptable.

Changes in Political Elites:
No Liberal and No Pinko-Commie Here

The March 30, 1981, attempted assassination of President Ronald Reagan and the crippling of his press secretary, James Brady, were national tragedies created by John Hinckley Jr., a disturbed young man obsessed with Jodie Foster. Hinckley bought a .22 caliber revolver from a Dallas pawnshop for $29 and set out for Washington to perform an act to impress the actress. Initially the assassination attempt pumped money and members into gun control groups, and this alone was a significant alteration in the political landscape. More critical, however, to the long-term antigun effort was the successful recruitment of Sarah Brady, wife of well-known victim James Brady, by Handgun Control, Inc. Indeed, immediately after the shooting, gun control groups had approached Sarah Brady, but she demurred due to familial demands, including caring for her two-year-old son and her handicapped husband. Also, James Brady stayed on in title as press secretary at the

White House, and his wife felt it best not to take on an issue clearly at odds with the position of the president (Davidson 1993, 171–173).

As recounted by Sarah Brady, she felt stunned in 1986 when the gun control debate was heating up and there was a real possibility that the Senate would pass the McClure-Volkmer Bill to weaken gun control. "That's when I called HCI back up and said, 'Hey, I'm ready to get involved now' " (Davidson 1993, 174). Sarah Brady joined the board of HCI in October 1985, and almost immediately HCI's membership and resources grew again; she became cochair in 1986. The Brady name was soon affixed to the legislation promoted by HCI for a number of years; this proposal combined the idea of a cooling-off period to allow potential killers to reconsider and a background check by local police to ascertain that purchasers were not proscribed by law from owning a gun (felony criminals, fugitives from justice, etc.). The Brady Bill now became the mantra for many gun control advocates.

With the linking of Sarah Brady to Handgun Control, Inc., and the gun control movement, the defenders of private handgun possession and ownership could no longer brand gun control efforts as liberal. Sarah Brady was raised in Alexandria, Virginia, by her FBI agent father and a conservative Republican family; prior to the crippling of her husband, she had worked for the National Republican Committee. Initially the NRA, at a loss to deny the Bradys' conservative bearings, did try to portray Sarah Brady as the stooge of the gun grabbers, but this effort was short-lived. Sarah and Jim Brady possessed indisputable conservative credentials, and the addition of the Bradys to the gun control forces began the transformation of the gun control issue. Simply put, gun control was no longer a liberal issue.

Handgun Control, Inc., with the celebrity status and conservative credentials of the Bradys, quickly became the leading antigun interest group. When Ronald Reagan in 1991 announced his support for the Brady Bill in a very forceful article in the *New York Times*, all lingering vestiges of the liberal label were dispelled. As so appropriately characterized by Representative Ed Feighan (D-OH), "If he ain't cover, then there's no such thing" (Davidson 1993, 249). Conservative blessings continued for gun control when President George Bush by executive order banned the importation of assault weapons and registered his rifles in Washington, D.C., as required by local law, remarking that it was an unremarkable event.

By the beginning of the 1990s, clearly a rift had developed between the NRA and various conservative political leaders; the NRA regretted this but nevertheless dismissed the matter: "We're not a conservative organization. We're a pro-gun organization" (Davidson 1993, 178). Symbolically, the NRA suffered a major blow when former president

George Bush, in response to an NRA fundraising letter referring to federal law enforcement officers as jack-booted government thugs, tore up his lifetime NRA membership card.

Changes in Group Tactics:
Gun Control Groups Undergo Self-Help

The gun control interest-group landscape is dominated by two organizations, Handgun Control, Inc., and the Coalition to Stop Gun Violence (CSGV).[8] HCI, a citizen membership group, is clearly the premier gun control organization; the chairwomanship of Sarah Brady and the co-operation with the law enforcement community has brought it members, money, and media. It has intentionally shed a radical image, gained early in its development, by instituting changes in its strategy so as to accommodate the political reality that the public wants gun control, not gun banning; and in so doing, HCI successfully contributed to and even orchestrated several important gun control laws in the 1980s and 1990s.

The beginnings of HCI are traced to the random murder of a young man who was unloading sporting gear from his car. Nick Shields, shot three times in the back, was a victim of the so-called 1974 Zebra killings in San Francisco. His father, Nelson "Pete" Shields, a DuPont executive in Delaware, took a leave of absence to prod the government in Washington to tackle this gun violence problem; he joined forces with a skeletal outfit known as the National Council to Control Handguns, founded that very year by Dr. Mark Borinsky, himself the victim of gun violence, and Ed Welles, a former CIA employee. This one-year sabbatical soon turned into a lifetime of work.[9] In 1975 Shields retired from DuPont to devote his time to the National Council to Control Handguns; he soon became its chairman.

Despite the name of this nascent interest group, its early goal as articulated by Shields and others was an outright banning of handguns. The public supported controls on guns rather than their prohibition, however, and the group found itself effectively marginalized in the political process. In 1981 Shields changed the name to Handgun Control, Inc., and changed its agenda to modest and incremental controls, focusing on one legislative proposal at a time (Sugarmann 1992, 257). These alterations hardly produced any immediate or dramatic differences in political strength. In 1981, NRA chief Harlon Carter, when asked about antigun groups, responded, "There is no gun-control movement worthy of mention. There are a few isolated situations, but no large movement of people" (Davidson 1993, 169). This rather bleak picture changed dramatically after the assassination attempt on President Reagan—contributions and members began to flow to HCI and other gun control groups, and accordingly political strength began to build.

Basically, HCI's goal became keeping guns out of the wrong hands. The Gun Control Act of 1968, as the Federal Firearms Act of 1938, which it replaced and repealed, prohibited felons and fugitives from justice from owning and possessing firearms, but to make that law work the local police needed a waiting period for time to run a background check. As noted in an HCI pamphlet, "We represent a broad coalition . . . who want to prevent handgun violence . . . and pass federal legislation to keep handguns out of the wrong hands." HCI in the 1980s adopted the seven-day waiting-period proposal as its fundamental legislative mission; as one HCI lobbyist remarked, "If we cannot agree to keep guns away from criminals, then there is no hope for a gun control policy" (Handgun Control, Inc. 1996).

Legislation to ban certain people from ownership has proven easier for the Congress to enact than measures to ban certain guns. Even the 1986 McClure-Volkmer Act, which in many ways gutted the 1968 Gun Control Act, added mental incompetents to the list of persons banned from owning guns. Speaking at the 1996 Democratic National Convention in Chicago, Sarah Brady really asked for only one additional statute—to prohibit those convicted of a misdemeanor involving family abuse from owning a gun. The 104th Congress responded in September 1996 by including a provision in the FY 1997 Omnibus Consolidated Appropriations Act that prohibits gun ownership or possession for those convicted, either by judge or a jury, for domestic violence, including spousal or child abuse.

By seeking incremental gun control laws, HCI has erased a perception of political ineptitude and shaken its loser image. The strategy is working: federal law now includes the Brady Act and a ban on cop-killer bullets, plastic guns, and assault weapons. The strategy even produced in the generally hostile 104th Congress an extension of the list of groups of people who are prohibited from owning guns, in this case the domestic violence perpetrators.

The next legislative step in the incremental regulation of handguns is under consideration. "Brady II," a bill drafted by HCI and introduced in the 103rd Congress by Senator Howard Metzenbaum (D-OH) and Representative Charles Schumer (D-NY), stands as the group's comprehensive policy; it was not sponsored in the 104th Congress but it will be reintroduced in a future session. This legislative proposal includes the licensing of purchasers, the registration of purchases, the registration of all transfers after initial purchase, limits on multiple purchases, banning of Saturday night specials, and mandatory manu-facturer safety device installation on handguns. HCI may choose to promote one aspect of Brady II or the expansion of the Brady Act to include a waiting period—irrespective of instant-check capability—so as to provide cooling-off time for those not necessarily criminal but under emotional stress.[10]

In addition to adjusting its strategic goals, HCI is developing a so-phisticated advocacy organization that in many ways attempts to mimic its adversary. The functions of this organization are threefold. First, a professional, experienced, and growing staff is dedicated to direct lobbying at both the federal and state levels; this capability is perhaps the easiest to master. Establishing a grassroots organization similar to that of the NRA is a long and arduous process. With a mem-bership base of 400,000, a mailing list of 1 million, and an annual bud-get of $7 million, HCI activities are somewhat constrained and its mailings somewhat leaner than those of the NRA. Indeed, the NRA is estimated to have ten times the money and membership (Spitzer 1995, 116).

Lacking the NRA's tremendous budget and membership list, HCI has managed, nevertheless, to put in place an energetic, if not yet pro-digious, grassroots effort that works closely but informally with state and local organizations in networking and coalition-building (HCI has no formal local chapters); for example, when the 104th Congress was elected and existing gun control laws were threatened, HCI joined in coalition with over 120 organizations nationwide, including the Coali-tion to Stop Gun Violence, to promote the goals of the Campaign to Protect Sane Gun Laws. HCI also duplicates NRA grassroots-building propaganda that has been particularly effective. For example, the NRA produced a film in the late 1980s entitled *It Can't Happen Here*, which portrays the alleged abuses of the Bureau of Alcohol, Tobacco, and Firearms (ATF), the federal agency charged with the enforcement of federal gun control laws; it was in this film that the expression "jack-booted thugs" was originally coined by Representative John Dingell (D-MI) to refer to allegedly overzealous ATF agents. This film was widely popular among gun enthusiasts, who used it as evidence that the gun grabbers were intent on violating the rights of the American people. Several years later, HCI produced its own film, *Five American Guns*, to chronicle stories of gun misuse and abuse; the premier of this film took place at the National Press Club in Washington in 1994 with an appropriate audience of members of Congress who no longer feared the NRA, and other luminaries. The grassroots work, original and copied, is finally paying handsome dividends; one HCI staffer noted, "Members used to say to me, 'Look, I support your position but

I cannot support your bill—my constituents would massacre me.' I don't hear this anymore—our grassroots efforts are starting to pay off" (Handgun Control, Inc. 1996). Michael Beard of CSGV observed, however, that both his group and HCI started out as national groups and tried subsequently to create a grassroots base. This order of progression served as a major weakness for many years as the national organization tried to backfill with a grassroots foundation (Beard 1996).

Last, HCI is developing a campaign-contribution component to meet the NRA head on in the electoral arena. The NRA has developed a reputation for inflicting punishment on those with the temerity to oppose the gun lobby; to vote against the NRA has been likened to electoral suicide. Although a causal relation is unclear, the NRA does command a prodigious PAC operation; the gun lobby created its Political Victory Fund in 1976 to defeat antigun office seekers and to elect pro-gun candidates. HCI has made tentative incursions into electoral politics in a similar effort to reward friends and punish enemies, to warn legislators that their political lives are on the line with votes on gun control issues. Due to obvious financial constraints, HCI must select its campaigns carefully and at present cannot compete with the NRA in numbers of campaigns targeted. For the 1992 election cycle, for example, the NRA's campaign spending amounted to $535,000 in direct contributions to House members; this compared with a meager HCI offering of $12,000 (Congressional Quarterly 1995, 277). Nevertheless, the NRA is not happy with "the changing battlefield suggested by HCI's willingness to pour money into the electoral arena. This would clearly spell trouble ahead" (Davidson 1993, 235).

The CSGV was founded in the same year as HCI. The Board of the Church and Society of the Methodist Church established the National Council to Ban Handguns (NCBH) to bring together religious groups for the initial purpose of supporting a bill to ban handguns that had been introduced in Congress by D.C. delegate Walter Fauntroy. This coalition now comprises nearly 50 civic, religious, professional, and business organizations. Originally the National Council to Control Handguns (NCCH) was a member of the NCBH. However, this arrangement did not long endure; NCCH soon pulled out and renamed itself Handgun Control, Inc. For reasons having more to do with personalities than anything else, HCI and the NCBH, which renamed itself in 1990 as the Coalition to Stop Gun Violence (CSGV) to reflect its support for the banning of handguns and assault rifles, really failed to cooperate or seek alliances in their common goals; for much of 20 years, these two gun control groups walked parallel paths. However, the two organizations, sensing a historical opportunity to create a parity between antigun and pro-gun forces, now work together in a range of activities; for example, in September 1996, the CSGV conducted a two-day conference for grassroots activists "to come together to share strategies and learn how to organize their communities effectively to reduce gun violence." HCI was a valued participant.

Whereas this cooperation has been beneficial for the gun control movement and has surely contributed to the changing politics of gun control, HCI, with its $7 million annual budget and its well-known chairwoman, is clearly the lead player; CSGV continues as a stable but modest operation with a stated objective markedly different from HCI: "the orderly elimination" of all handguns and assault weapons in the United States. "CSGV seeks to ban handguns and assault weapons from importation, manufacture, sale and transfer by the general American public, with reasonable exceptions made for police, military, security personnel, gun clubs where guns are secured on club premises, gun dealers trading in antique and collectible firearms kept and sold in inoperable condition. Hunting weapons would be unaffected by these bans."[11]

The CSGV sees its role as one of public education and grassroots organization. With only seven full-time staff, the coalition prefers not to engage in direct lobbying but advises its member groups on when to go to Congress and state legislatures, whom to approach, and how to get the message across. CSGV funnels the research results of the Violence Policy Center to its member groups, counseling them on how best to use this information in public education and in the creation of a grassroots network that can affect the policy process.

The CSGV views the "wrong hands" philosophy of HCI as basically flawed and continues in its efforts to ban "wrong guns." Gun-elimination advocates argue that criminals will not obey gun control laws; and the failure of these "wrong hands" gun control laws, like the Brady Bill, to stop crime will be trumpeted by the NRA as a failure of gun control. As Michael Beard, director of the CSGV, noted, "The Brady Bill is a nice, innocuous piece of legislation. To us it is a minor step forward" (Davidson 1993, 194). The coalition wants to slowly narrow the range of guns available from both ends of the gun spectrum—from Saturday night specials to assault weapons. Recognizing that a total ban is not feasible at this time, the CSGV is prepared to chip away at the range of guns available. Whereas HCI states that certain people are the problem, CSGV maintains that guns are wrong—certain guns are inherently bad; certain guns are only for killing people. In the near future, CSGV plans to work for a prohibition on guns kept in the home—all guns would be locked up in gun clubs—and the registration of guns. In the more distant future, the CSGV envisions a society when a child can ask his father, "What's a handgun?" (Beard 1996).

Changes in Government: The Bully Pulpit

In marked contrast to White House policy under recent administrations, the election of Bill Clinton in 1992 created a political opportunity to pass gun control legislation. Gun control advocates endured many years without a voice in the White House; President Lyndon Johnson was a strong supporter of gun control, but no gun control zeal was displayed by Presidents Nixon, Ford, or Carter. When President Ronald Reagan was elected, the NRA and other gun supporters thought they had achieved nirvana. Indeed, despite the assassination attempt in 1981, Reagan remained a strong opponent of any gun control efforts. President Bush, an NRA member who banned the importation of certain assault weapons, was a somewhat ambiguous chief executive. But with the election of Bill Clinton, the presidential dynamics of gun control changed dramatically.

The three assassinations in the 1960s predictably led to a public outcry for governmental action; the NRA, representing the pro-gun American constituency, argued for increased penalties and more prisons; the antigun faction, only beginning to be organized, demanded controls on guns. The Congress, reacting to both constituencies and spurred on by President Johnson, responded with the Omnibus Crime Control and Safe Streets Act and the Gun Control Act of 1968, a bill that Johnson noted fell short of his goal—the national registration of all guns and licensing of everyone who owned a gun—because his preferred provisions had been thwarted "by a powerful gun lobby" (Edel 1995, 103).

With the presidency passing into Republican hands, gun control advocates entered a wasteland; despite the introduction of various gun control initiatives in Congress, some even by senior members of the majority Democratic party, such as House Judiciary Chairman Peter Rodino (D-NY), the absence of White House support proved to be an insurmountable obstacle. Yet after the assassination attempt of Governor George Wallace in 1972, even President Nixon stated, "I have always felt that there should be a Federal law for the control of handguns . . . Saturday night specials" (Edel 1995, 106). Indeed, Nixon was reiterating planks in the 1968 and 1972 GOP presidential platforms that called for some control on "cheap, readily available handguns." But gun control advocates were soon disappointed; the president did not send any proposals to Congress. The same cycle of events occurred in 1973, when the venerable and senior senator from Mississippi, John Stennis, was shot in Washington, D.C., as he walked toward his home. Again the president indicated support for gun control, "I have never hunted in my life. I have no interest in guns. . . . I am not interested in the National Rifle Association. . . . I have asked the Attorney General to give us a legislative formula that can get through Congress" (Edel 1995, 106). But after this promising statement, only silence emanated from the White House; no proposals made their way to Congress.

The tenure of President Gerald Ford proved unfertile for gun control efforts as well, and this despite two attempts made on the life of the president himself by persons wielding handguns. "I am not going to recommend the registration of owners of guns, or handguns" (Edel 1995, 106). Much like his predecessor, Ford was restating the GOP platform, which in 1976 had dropped any reference to gun control efforts and instead embraced the notion of sanctions: more prisons, mandatory and harsher punishments, and additional police.

With the election of President Jimmy Carter, gun control advocates were cautiously optimistic; indeed, the Democratic platform called for both approaches to gun violence—gun control and stronger criminal laws—and the candidate Carter had often espoused strong gun control. "I favor registration of handguns, a ban on the sale of cheap handguns, reasonable licensing provisions including a waiting period, and a prohibition of ownership by anyone convicted of a crime involving a gun, and by those not mentally competent" (Orasin 1981, 97–98). With a 1978 administration proposal tasking the Bureau of Alcohol, Tobacco, and Firearms to issue regulations mandating the individual identification of every new firearm by manufacturer, model, and caliber and requiring periodic reports of all purchases and sales by dealers, President Carter initially appeared to be the medicine the gun controllers needed. However, under withering attack by both the NRA and its Republican allies in Congress, Carter essentially abandoned support for his own proposal. The Carter White House turned its back while the House of Representatives voted down this proposal with only 80 defenders recorded; this roll call occurred only one day after the tenth anniversary of the assassination of Robert Kennedy. In response to reporters' questions, Carter stated, "I think to pursue [gun control] aggressively in the Congress would be a mistake" (Orasin 1981, 100). Gun control advocates felt betrayed; indeed, Handgun Control, Inc., accused President Carter of violating his own campaign promises to work for tougher gun control laws. What began as a promising administration ended in estrangement between gun controllers and President Carter.

The 1980 Democratic platform, which called for tough handgun control including the banning of Saturday night specials, rang hollow; but the election of Republican Ronald Reagan was a bitter pill for gun control supporters. Reagan was a card-carrying member of the NRA and a vocal opponent of gun control laws, insisting they were simply unenforceable; Reagan, like other gun enthusiasts, maintained that the answer to gun violence was tougher mandatory punishment. Early into his term, Reagan directed the creation of a task force within the Department of Justice to study the crime issue, expecting a confirmation of his views; the report, with its unwanted recommendations that gun control be strengthened, was quickly shelved. The pro-gun groups within Congress and without sensed a singular opportunity to weaken and even repeal the modest Gun Control Act of 1968; President Reagan stoked this zeal in 1983 with his personal appearance and address before a national meeting of the NRA. While gun control groups hunkered down, the NRA set its sights on the disestablishment of the ATF, the despised agency that enforced the weak gun control laws. This campaign included the production of the highly controversial film *It Can't Happen Here.*

Although Congress ultimately did not agree with the administration proposal to eliminate the ATF by dividing its duties between the Secret Service and the Bureau of Customs, the Reagan years were fruitful ones for the pro-gun advocates, culminating in the 1986 enactment of the Firearms Owners' Protection Act, commonly known as the McClure-Volkmer Act. Although the McClure-Volkmer Act did not repeal the Gun Control Act of 1968, experts are in agreement that the 1986 statute weakened the already modest gun control law (Davidson 1993, 79). When asked on many occasions how he could support a diminution of gun control law in light of his own attempted assassination experience, President Reagan retreated to the standard pro-gun argument that the violence of guns can be controlled only by tougher, mandatory criminal penalties.

The forces of gun control, however, were not entirely bereft of any legislative accomplishments during the Reagan years. The McClure-Volkmer Act ultimately, after a protracted congressional battle, did not amend the prohibition on the interstate sale of handguns, and for this reason the gun control groups claimed a Pyrrhic victory. In 1984 Reagan signed into law a bill increasing the sentence of anyone convicted of a crime in which was used a "handgun loaded with armor piercing ammunition"; and in 1986, another law was enacted to ban the production and importation of all armor-piercing bullets.

Days before the inauguration of President George Bush, a man walked into a Stockton, California, school and killed 5 children and wounded 29 others using an AK-47 Chinese-made semiassault weapon; this massacre created an image for the average American that street gang warfare could not. Although Bush stated, "I'm not about to suggest that a semi-automatic hunting rifle be banned," he could not ignore the clamor for action; even Senator Robert Byrd, Democratic gun owner from West Virginia and chairman of Senate Appropriations, said assault weapons were for "mass murderers, cop killers, kid killers and drug dealers" (Edel 1995, 128). In March 1989 the president ordered a review of the importation of assault weapons: "And you're hearing this from one who prides himself on being a sportsman, and have been a hunter all my life. And at the conclusion of this study and after careful consideration, we will permanently ban any imports that don't measure to these standards [of appropriate sporting purposes]. I am going to stand up for the police officers in this country" (Edel 1995, 50). In April President Bush instituted a ban on the importation of 29 semiautomatic assault weapons; this action blocked over 100,000 weapons on order (Davidson 1993, 207). Already viewed suspiciously by gun enthusiasts due to an offhand comment that gun registration was no "big deal," made after he registered his hunting rifles with the District of Columbia as required by local law, Bush was promptly attacked by the NRA and other pro-gun groups, which were hardening in their opposition to any controls, however modest, on firearms. Neither did Bush reap any goodwill from gun control advocates who viewed this action as incredibly weak, since domestic manufacturers of assault weapons could easily take care of any consumer demand. Watching from the sidelines, the skittish Congress was anxious not to be drawn into this no-win situation. "The 101st Congress ended with a familiar ritual. Gun control advocates retreated to lick their wounds and point fingers. Congress heaved a collective sigh of relief, having for the most party avoided the issue. And the NRA having turned defeat into victory celebrated" (Sugarmann 1992, 214).

The dynamics of the politics of gun control were dramatically changed when former president Ronald Reagan, speaking before the George Washington Medical Center in Washington on the tenth anniversary of his attempted assassination, endorsed the Brady Bill. The next day, on March 29, 1991, the *New York Times* carried an op-ed article by Reagan in which he again repudiated his stand of eight years in the White House by simply stating that he supported enactment of the Brady Bill, currently pending before the 102nd Congress. "And it's just plain common sense that there be a waiting period to allow local law enforcement officials to conduct background checks on those who wish to purchase handguns. . . . I support the Brady Bill and I urge Congress to enact it without further delay." Indeed, the Brady Bill, first introduced under that moniker in 1987,[12] had faced stiff opposition from the NRA and its supporters; the gun control groups were not sanguine about its enactment. That equation had now been altered in ways unimagined. The Great Communicator, the essential conservative, the revered former president, had placed his imprimatur on the Brady Bill and its concept that all prospective handgun buyers must face a waiting period. President Bush, approached by his mentor and former chief executive, also changed his position: if Congress would pass an acceptable comprehensive crime bill including habeas corpus reform and expansion of crimes punishable by death, and if that bill contained the Brady Bill, then he would sign the legislation. This conditional support plus a virulent campaign by the NRA, including direct and grassroots lobbying and prodigious campaign contributions targeted at defeating any candidate who supported gun control, doomed both initiatives—the 102nd adjourned sine die while the conference report on the Comprehensive Crime Bill, together with the Brady provisions, awaited final chamber action.

Gun control, indebted to the turnabout position of President Reagan and the subsequent failure of the 102nd Congress to take any action, became an issue of the presidential campaign of 1992. As in many previous elections, both parties had platform planks regarding gun violence. These planks were predictable: the GOP opposed gun control and embraced increased, mandatory penalties; the Democrats likewise espoused tough penalties for those who used guns in the commission of a crime and even promoted guns used for sporting and hunting purposes—but also firmly expressed support for the Brady Bill and the banning of all assault weapons. Upon election, President Clinton continued the campaign of his party for gun control, repeatedly exhorting Congress to pass the Brady Bill; and in November 1993 after an intense struggle, Congress sent the president this legislation to require a five-day waiting period for the purchase of a handgun so that law enforcement officials could make a criminal background check. Although the legislative passage in many ways weakened the original intent of the Brady Bill, notably by jettisoning the notion of a cooling-off period, the Brady Bill was hailed by gun control advocates as a major milestone and as the most important gun control law since the Gun Control Act of 1968. The NRA, supporting Harley Staggers's (D-WV) substitute bill, which called for the development of a national instant-check system, shrugged off the enactment, claiming that once a state has developed an instant-check system, the Brady Act would no longer be applicable, and in any event, Brady would sunset in five years.[13] In the following year, the Clinton administration, against the railings of the NRA and its congressional champions, succeeded in enacting a ban on the manufacture, sale, or possession of 19 assault weapons.[14]

When the 104th Congress swept into office in 1995, Speaker Newt Gingrich (R-GA) and his army of GOP freshmen felt an obligation to the NRA for their newly anointed majority status; indeed, the NRA was widely perceived to have been instrumental in the defeat of scores of gun control–supporting Democrats. The Clinton administration was helpless as the House in March 1995 passed a bill to repeal the year-old assault weapons ban; but the bill went no further—the president had promised a veto, Senate Democrats promised a filibuster, and GOP presidential candidate Bob Dole did not want to defend a repeal of the assault weapons ban during his campaign.

Presidents can create political opportunities for gun control or gun owner groups, and Clinton welcomed the opportunity to campaign for and trumpet his support for the Brady Bill. Of course, party control of the presidency changes periodically, and it is likely that any new Republican president would be less supportive of gun control efforts. Yet it is striking that Dole let the repeal of the assault weapons ban die in the Senate, an action that may have helped cost him the official endorsement of the NRA. With the public generally supportive of gun control, the NRA widely perceived as an extremist organization, and police groups joining with gun control organizations to lobby for restrictions, it will be difficult for any presidential candidate to champion a repeal of existing regulations.

Conclusion

No stronger evidence is needed to convincingly demonstrate that the dynamics of gun control politics have been dramatically and perhaps irrevocably altered than the appearances of Mike Robbins, a retired Chicago policeman shot in the line of duty a remarkable 11 times, and Sarah Brady as prime-time speakers at the 1996 Democratic National Convention. When Jim and Sarah Brady slowly walked together across the platform on that Monday night in Chicago, they represented a union of all the various forces that had been agonizingly advancing gun control laws throughout the nation over the previous 30 years. The Democratic party had since the 1960s included in its platform a plank supporting gun control, but until the presidency of Bill Clinton, its only other elected president had been less than faithful to that promise. The first term of President Bill Clinton fulfilled that plank with the Brady Act and the ban on assault weapons. In 1996 the Democratic party and its president conspicuously and fully embraced the concept that gun violence cannot be stopped with only mandatory punishments and more prisons; the mayhem of handguns demands strengthened regulation of gun possession and ownership and, in some cases, an outright gun ban. The president joined hands with gun control advocates, no longer radical or marginalized, and the law enforcement community; he shared his bully pulpit with Sarah Brady, who pleaded for laws "to keep guns out of the hands of criminals and out of the hands of children," and Mike Robbins, who asked for those who support gun control to no longer remain silent.

The trilateral alliance of gun control advocates, the Democratic party, and law enforcement has been forged; its foundations are strong and its convictions are clear. The alliance, many years in the making, is not a union of convenience; its growing political power will determine how this country responds to the scourge of gun violence.

Notes

1. From an author interview with an anonymous member of Handgun Control, Inc., September 12, 1996.

2. In 1993, firearms caused 39,595 deaths, of which 18,571 were homicides and 18,940 were suicides; handguns account for one-third of the total firearms in the United States but two-thirds of firearms crime and 80 percent of firearms homicide. See the home page of the Coalition to Stop Gun Violence at http://www.gunfree.inter.net/csgv.

3. The Gun Control Act of 1968 (PL 90–618) extended to long guns the restrictions applied to handguns contained in the Omnibus Crime Control and Safe Streets Act of 1968 (PL 90–351). However, for purposes of this chapter, all firearms provisions enacted in 1968 will be referred to as the Gun Control Act of 1968.

4. Recently established in 1993, the American Firearms Association attempts to walk a middle ground between the pro-gun and antigun groups; the AFA is a "non-profit nationwide gun-owners and sportsmen's organization dedicated to safeguarding and promoting the shooting sports while seeking to reconcile the Second Amendment and gun owners rights with fair and reasonable gun control legislation." See its home page at http://www.firearms.org/afa.

5. The Supreme Court has only rarely spoken on the meaning of the Second Amendment, and then in obscure terms. See Halbrook (1984) and Cramer (1994).

6. The FBI identified eight armor-piercing bullets not banned by this law; see Sugarmann (1992, 187).

7. There has been little academic research on the attitudes of police rank and file and police officers on handgun control; further, the results have been ambivalent. See, for example, Siwik and Blount (1984).

8. Each of these gun control advocacy groups has a counterpart educational, research organization that is forbidden by its tax-exempt status to conduct either direct or grassroots lobbying activities. HCI's counterpart is the Center to Prevent Handgun Violence; CSGV is aligned with the Educational Fund to End Handgun Violence and the Violence Policy Center. (The NRA maintains a Web site that lists the antigun groups along with their executive staff and affiliations: http://www.access.degex.net/~pst/antigun.html.)

9. Shields died January 25, 1993, after 18 years as Chairman of HCI; upon his death Sarah Brady took over the helm. See his obituary in the *New York Times*, January 27, 1993.

10. The law enforcement establishment has expressed support for such a cooling-off period. See "Legislative Alert" (1994).

11. See its home page at http://www.gunfree.inter.net/csgv.

12. The notion of a waiting period for the purchase of handguns had been around since 1968, when the Gun Control Act was signed. In 1976, for example, the House Judiciary Committee had reported a major handgun control bill that banned the manufacturing of all handguns not of a sporting type and required a prior police clearance for all handgun purchases.

13. In 1989, Attorney General Richard Thornburgh issued a report stating that a minimum of ten years would be required to develop and establish a national computerized system to check criminal records.

14. PL 103–322 also specifically exempted 670 semiautomatic weapons and allowed gun owners to keep guns already legally owned.

11

Public Opinion and Gun Control: Appearance and Transparence in Support and Opposition

David R. Harding Jr.

It's the least Congress can do. And it certainly appears to be what the American people want.

> —Representative Constance A. Morella (R-MD),
> speaking of the ban on assault weapons
> proposed in the 1994 crime bill then under
> consideration (*New York Times*, August 6, 1994,
> sec. 1, 9)

When it comes to regulating access to firearms, even the least that Congress can do is too much for some of the American people. Furthermore, though Representative Constance Morella's certainty belies the point, there is some controversy over just what the American people actually do want. How much gun control is too much? Which aspects of firearms and their use should control focus upon: ownership, sale, possession, criminal use? Which weapons should be regulated: handguns, assault weapons, all guns? Should the goal be the management of gun ownership or outright bans? If bans, should they be universal or should they be applied only to certain types of people? Public opinion surveys and polls have asked questions about most of these policy options.

Determining which of these possibilities is "what the people want" is not simple, for seldom do the American people speak with a single voice. Often, some Americans support one policy while others oppose it, and even when most are on one side of an issue, there are subtle themes and variations in exactly what they want. On most policy matters, a narrow majority or plurality support a policy. This is not the case with many gun control proposals, which are favored by large majorities and throughout most segments of the American populace. As support for many moderate forms of gun control has increased since the mid-1980s, the gap between control advocates and opponents has widened, at least as gauged by the rhetoric surrounding the issue. Although symbolism and the rhetoric of fear and hate are not a new factor in American gun politics, moves to equate gun control with a hidden government agenda aimed at crippling popular sovereignty resonate with some Americans and are closely tied to changes in other attitudes toward the institutions and officers of the federal government. Taken together, these changes are indicators of a period of instability in American firearms politics and gun control policy.

"It Certainly Appears to Be . . .": Interpreting Opinion Polls

Proponents and opponents of gun control frequently assert very different interpretations of what policies the public supports. Such divergent claims are possible because the interpretation of public opinion polls remains "more an art than a science" (Asher 1992, 121). If these polls are appraised in a relatively unsophisticated or deliberately obfuscating manner, it can seem that a significant number of Americans hold ambivalent or contradictory opinions on gun control. It is fairly easy to find examples of polls indicating that majorities both support gun control and believe in a constitutionally protected right to bear arms (Mauser and Kopel 1992, n. 2). What are we to make of such apparently conflicting beliefs?

The problem of interpretation of poll results is exacerbated by the difficulty of designing unbiased, straightforward questions. For example, when questions mention specific weapons or link gun control to crime, support for gun control is usually quite high. Consider the wording of four questions regarding assault weapons bans in Table 11.1.[1] At first glance it appears that support for bans on assault weapons dropped about 20 percentage points in less than two and a half years. However, a closer examination of the symbols invoked within the body of the questions should lead the reader to question such a conclusion. The major differences are in the use of the words "crime," "ban," and "AK-47." The earliest question in the series, the one that establishes the initially high levels of support, not only calls up the bogeyman of crime but also mentions the AK-47, arguably the most infamous of the general class of assault weapons. At the other end of the spectrum is the April 1996 question, which mentions neither crime

TABLE 11.1

Changing Support or Changing Symbols: Bans on Assault Weapons

Wording of the question	Date	% in Favor
Please tell me whether you would generally favor or oppose each of the following proposals which some people have made to reduce crime... a ban on the manufacture, sale and possession of semi-automatic assault guns, such as the AK-47.	December 1993	77
Please tell me whether you would generally favor or oppose each of the following proposals which some people have made to reduce crime... a ban on the manufacture, sale and possession of certain semi-automatic guns, known as assault rifles.	August 1994 April 1995	71 68
Suppose that on election day this year you could vote on key issues as well as candidates. Please tell me whether you would vote for or against each one of the following propositions... a law which would make it illegal to sell, or possess, semi-automatic guns known as assault rifles.	April 1996	57

Sources: 1993 & 1994, Gallup 1994; 1995 & 1996, Gallup 1996.

nor the AK-47. It also refers to the measure that elicits the least support. Without questions with similar wording, it is impossible to tell whether popular support for a ban an assault weapons has gone up, gone down, or stayed the same.

Questions sometimes mention specific weapons or link gun control to crime because the public has often not thought much about the issue of gun control. Yet it is possible to criticize such questions because such wording may strongly influence the results—the public is generally in favor of almost anything that might reduce the rate of violent crime, for example, and some of these questions appear to be quite argumentative.

Other types of questions do not provide cues for individuals, but these may pose different problems. For example, one question regularly used by the Gallup organization is "In general, do you feel that the laws governing the sale of firearms should be made more strict, less strict, or kept as they are now?" Some scholars have charged that because most Americans are quite unaware of the current state of gun control laws, it is impossible to determine just what they want when they say they want more strict or less strict laws (Crocker 1982; Kleck 1991; Mauser and Kopel 1992). Rising to the defense of the question, Robert Spitzer argues the long-term visibility of the issue should "increase confidence that American opinion on this subject is as well informed as that regarding any policy issue" (1995, n. 71). Answers to the strictness question, however, are not so readily interpreted as Spitzer would have it. Spitzer insists that "the political and policy mandate of a citizenry that prefers stronger controls than currently exist is perfectly clear to officeholders and decisionmakers," yet he never states just what that mandate might be (1995, n. 71). Clearly, however, he rejects the notion that it is simply "that many people want 'something' to be done about gun violence" (Kleck 1991, 362).

This entire debate serves mainly to underscore the central message regarding the nature of appearance and reality in the discussion of public opinion on any matter, much less one so filled with vituperation and ferocity. Minimally, when using public opinion polls to measure public opinion, the full wording of the question must be considered, paying special attention to the use of symbols and loaded terms. Unfortunately, given the grounding of the debate in the Second Amendment and the control of crime, avoiding symbolism altogether is impossible.

Opposition to Gun Control: All or Nothing

The controversy over how much is too much is not isolated to gun control policy. The degree of government intervention called for in any public policy is one of the central questions to be resolved in the process of politics. Striking a balance between the government's need to maintain order and the individual liberties expressly or implicitly guaranteed in the Constitution can be difficult when, for many, even the most minimal intervention is too much. Three reasons underlie the all-or-nothing nature of the battle: the indivisible nature of a right, the implacability of gun control advocates, and the balance of power between citizen and government.

Sanctification of Gun Ownership

At the center of the debate over gun control is the controversy over the very existence of the constitutional guarantee upon which many of the objections to gun control are founded. Among constitutional scholars and jurists, this debate often takes the form of a disagreement over the nature of the right protected in the Second Amendment: does it confer that right upon individuals or upon the collective?[2] Whatever the truth of the matter, a belief in the right of individuals to own firearms persists in public discourse and in the minds of a large proportion of average Americans.

The use of the Second Amendment to frame the gun control debate is of special importance because it casts the debate in absolute terms. Rights occupy a very special place in American political culture. They are spoken of reverentially; the specific rights and liberties seem almost to constitute a pantheon for our nation's secular religion: the law. If the liturgy of this faith is litigation, its most sincere form of prayer is certainly what one scholar has called "rights talk" (Glendon 1991). Rights talk as a general phenomenon is simply the tendency on the part of Americans to elevate any especially prized activity to the status of a right in order to convince others, and perhaps themselves, that the freedom to perform that act is both inalienable and inviolable.

This view of gun ownership is well summarized by Wayne LaPierre, executive vice president of the National Rifle Association. Gun ownership is "a birthright confirmed for us by the Constitution. It was ours the moment we were born beneath these heavens" (*New York Times* [hereafter NYT], September 11, 1994, sec. 6, 66). Many Americans share this view, although the precise level of that support is difficult to determine. In the late 1970s, as measured in a poll sponsored by the NRA, almost nine of every ten Americans subscribed to that notion (Wright 1981). In a Gallup poll in 1993, a few months after the tragedy at the Branch Davidian compound in Waco, Texas, 46 percent of those surveyed agreed that "strict gun control laws violate the Constitution" (Gallup 1993, 52). Moreover, the right to bear arms extends, for a sizable minority of Americans, well beyond simply arming oneself. For example, a 1995 Gallup poll asked the question, "Based on what you know about the Constitution, do you think Americans have the right to purchase and store large quantities of weapons or don't you think the Constitution should be interpreted that way?" Gallup found that 24 percent of Americans believed the Constitution guaranteed a right to accumulate such personal arsenals (Gallup 1995).

The importance of the status of gun ownership as a right, at least in popular opinion if not necessarily in the law, cannot be understated. Such talk leads, as Glendon (1991) notes, to the impoverishment of political discourse, making it more contentious and decreasing the likelihood of any meaningful exchange or peaceful compromise between the two sides. Though scholars may see such battles as a consequence of conflicting rights, those involved in the fray have a different view. For them, the antithesis of a right is not another right, it is a wrong.

Never Compromise with an Uncompromising Enemy

Even were the status of right to be denied to the keeping and bearing of arms, opponents of gun control would still be loath to compromise with an opponent who they fear is out not simply to control guns but to ban them entirely. This anxiety comes in two basic forms: "give 'em an inch and they'll take a mile" and "citizen soldier versus Big Brother."

To compromise even slightly on gun control, so the first of these arguments goes, is to begin the long slide toward total firearms prohibition. Whereas some refer to this as the "slippery slope" (Kleck 1991, 9), that phrase does not capture the underlying logic of the position. The real fear is not simply of stumbling into complete prohibition but of being constantly pulled toward it by an implacable foe who hides his ultimate goal behind a series of half-measures. This fear may have some basis in fact. In examining public opinion among the general populace, Kleck has shown that *"most* supporters of [gun registration and permit laws] also favor a total ban on private gun possession" (1991, 9; emphasis in original]. Gun control opponents have no difficulty finding examples of this logic in statements made by prominent politicians and gun control advocates. The NRA, in its informational pamphlet on the politics of semiautomatic "assault" weapons, quotes the *Washington Post* on the topic of the assault weapons ban as "symbolic" legislation whose sole virtue is as "a stepping stone to broader gun control" (NRA 1996c).

It is the other version of this fear that may prove to be of greater consequence to the future of American gun politics. Many within the anticontrol movement have a deep-seated fear of government and of the motives behind any move to restrict access to firearms. Consider the words of NRA executive vice president Wayne LaPierre:

> I don't think any government is terribly benign or benevolent as long as they have the power to do what they want. Benign by its definition means that you leave things alone. We've had the government jumping into houses because they got a tip from some lowlife and killing people and ruining their lives looking for drugs. Now I'm sorry, it's the wrong address. This is a benign government? . . . The agenda of this government is to increase the size of government and to put more and more of our lives under the control of government bureaucrats. (*NYT,* September 11, 1994, sec. 6, 66)

Interestingly, a fair number of those serving in or seeking to serve in that government share similar points of view.

- Representative John D. Dingell (D-MI)—"If I were to select a jack-booted group of fascists who are perhaps as large a danger to American society as I could pick today, I would pick A.T.F. [the Bureau of Alcohol, Tobacco , and Firearms]" (from the NRA documentary film *It Can Happen Here*; quoted in *NYT*, May 8, 1995, A17).
- Mark Killian, Speaker of the Arizona House of Representatives— "If you downgrade the Second Constitutional Amendment and its gun protection provisions, then next it's the Fifth Amendment and then the First and on and on. Protecting them is what the N.R.A. is all about" (*NYT*, May 21, 1995, sec. 1, 1).

This sort of rhetoric has at times even entered into the presidential race. Republican presidential candidate Pat Buchanan, at a candidate forum sponsored by the Gun Owners of New Hampshire, conjured up images of the American Revolutionary War, drawing a comparison between an oppressive British colonial government intent on crushing all opposition and the American government of today. In speaking of the Second Amendment, he proclaimed, "That right ain't about shooting ducks. That right is about a man's right to defend his wife, his family, his freedom and his country" (*NYT*, January 15, 1996, A12).

America's mythology concerning the motivation of the founders and the nobility of the Revolutionary soldier, as well as the legends surrounding the rugged, self-sufficient heroes of the frontier era, lend power to such rhetoric.[3] Apparently, it is a feeling that resonates with a significant minority of Americans.

Responding to a question regarding the "incident in Waco," 21 percent of Americans polled in April 1995, two years after that event and immediately after the Oklahoma City bombing, said that the "people at the Branch Davidian compound should have been left alone to live as they pleased." Seventy-three percent felt the government's action was appropriate (Gallup 1995). At the same time, Gallup also asked respondents if they thought "ordinary citizens should be allowed to arm and organize themselves in order to resist the powers of the federal government." Overall, 19 percent agreed. However, among those aged 18 to 29, almost one third (31 percent) agreed compared to 20 percent among those aged 30 to 49 and a mere 9 percent among those 50 and older. The South (20 percent) and West (29 percent) were also home to larger numbers of supporters. As could well be imagined, attitudes toward gun control were strongly related to attitudes on this question as well. Among those respondents who favored stricter gun laws, only 13 percent agreed that ordinary citizens had the right of armed resistance; among those who felt gun laws should remain the same or be made less strict, 28 percent supported that right.

In an earlier poll, about six months after the Waco standoff came to its fiery end, Gallup asked three questions regarding these matters (1993, 52). Respondents to the first of these, related to the incrementalist approach to gun control and the ultimate goal of control advocates, show that notions of gun control leading to a ban on all weapons are not simply the paranoid beliefs of a few gun activists. Fully 50 percent of Americans believe that "gun control measures will eventually lead to stricter laws which will take guns away from all citizens." Among professed gun owners, the proportion in agreement was even higher, 59 percent. Fear of a shift in the balance of power between citizen and government is also widespread throughout the general populace. A slight majority of 52 percent agreed with the statement, "Stricter laws [on the buying and owning of guns] would give too much power to the government over average citizens." Among gun owners, the number in agreement jumped to two-thirds (66%). In this same survey, roughly 46 percent overall and 61 percent of gun owners felt that "strict gun control laws" were unconstitutional.

Fear of a state monopoly on power, disagreements over constitutionality, and hidden government agendas all suggest a problem more fundamental than simple intransigence over a single matter of public policy. They suggest a building crisis of legitimacy, a lack of support for the system as a whole, and a failure to agree on the basic rules of the game. In discussing what he calls "the Feds under our beds," James Bovard reminds us that almost four of every ten Americans believe "the Federal Government has become so large and powerful it poses an immediate threat to the rights and freedoms of ordinary citizens" (*NYT*, September 6, 1995, A25). It is one thing to disagree with a party or administration over the proper role of government in our lives—such disagreements are at the heart of politics. It is quite another to feel threatened by the institutions of government itself. Fears of that sort are at the heart of the breakdown of politics.

Support for Gun Control: A Matter of Degree

The data cited above paint a picture of a sizable minority that fears a loss not only of firearms but of sovereignty as a result of gun control legislation, but a clear majority of Americans favor many specific gun control proposals. An incredible array of regulations has been proposed over the years, from universal bans on all civilian ownership of firearms to mandatory safety training before purchase. Kleck (1991, 323–333) outlines five major categories of control: the type of activity to be regulated (including manufacture, importation, sale, purchase, possession, and use); the type of firearm affected (e.g., handguns, automatics, semiautomatics); the class of persons affected (e.g., criminals, minors, gun dealers); the level of restrictiveness (e.g., "shall issue" or permissive permit laws, such as those supported by the NRA, which guarantee a permit except to those falling in a prohibited class, versus discretionary or restrictive licensing, which requires an applicant to prove a need for a permit); and in our federal system, the level of government that has enacted and that will enforce the law (municipalities, states, or the federal government). Like the federal prohibition on the manufacture and sale of alcohol, federal gun bans are met with disapproval by most Americans. However, proposals to manage access through licenses or age restrictions or even bans at a local level are far less noxious.

Gun Bans: Restricting Access

Within the plethora of gun control proposals, gun bans stand out as the most restrictive and the most broadly applicable across categories of persons. Although gun bans may be targeted at a specific type of weapon or at all firearms or may outlaw a broad or a narrow range of activities, the very word "ban" seems to set this type of gun control apart from other methods. Typically, unless the proposed ban is very limited in its effect or the question used to measure support is heavily loaded with symbolic language, support for bans lags far behind support for other types of controls. Virtually all nonban types of controls, including permits, registration laws, and mandatory waiting periods, are usually favored by large majorities, often over three-quarters of all Americans. Table 11.2 presents information regarding support for various gun ban proposals and Table 11.3 for nonban proposals.

Gun bans that are not specifically targeted at a narrow class of persons or weapons are extremely unpopular; other types of bans garner much more support. Furthermore, though it is difficult to compare levels of support over time due to differences in questions, there seems to be a general trend toward increased support for bans on certain types of weapons. In the mid- to late 1980s, bans on the sale or possession of firearms in general were favored by roughly one-quarter of Americans. However, restricting the ban to *handgun* sale or possession produces an increase in the level of support, to the range of 35 to 40 percent. Bans on the possession of handguns in limited areas (high-crime areas,

TABLE 11.2
Restricting Access to Firearms: Attitudes Toward Firearm Bans

Control Measure	Special Aspects of the Measure			Date	Source	% in Favor
	Activity[a]	Gun[b]	Gov't[c]			
General Bans						
Private citizens surrender all guns to government	O			1976	NORC	<17[d]
Ban sales of all guns	S			1985	Roper	22
Illegal for civilians to own guns	O			1989	Time/CNN	29
Handgun Bans						
Buy back, destroy, handguns mandatory	O	H		1978	Caddell	26
Ban further manufacture, sales, of handguns	M,S	H		1978	Caddell	32
Ban private possession of handguns	O	H		1993	Gallup	39
Ban sales of handguns	S	H		1994	NYT/CBS	46
Ban handgun possession in high-crime areas	O	H		1975	Harris	<47
Local ban on sale, possession, of handgun in R's own community	S,O	H	L	1986	Gallup	47
Ban further manufacture, sale of nonsporting handguns	M,S	HS		1978	Caddell	48
Federal ban on interstate sales of handguns	S	H	F	1986	Gallup	67
Ban further manufacture, sale, of small, cheap handguns	M,S	HS		1978	Caddell	70
Ban manufacture, sale, of cheap handguns	M,S	HS		1993	Gallup	72
Federal ban on manufacture, sale, possession, of Saturday night specials	M,S,O	HS	F	1989	Gallup	71

Continued Next Page

Sources: 1976–1990, Kleck 1991, Table 9.2; 1993–1996, Gallup (1993, 1994, 1995, 1996); 1994 NYT/CBS—New York Times (January 23, 1994, sec. 1, 1).

TABLE 11.2—*continued*

Control Measure	Special Aspects of the Measure			Date	Source	% in Favor
	Activity[a]	Gun[b]	Gov't[c]			
Assault Weapons Bans						
Federal ban on manufacture, sale, possession, of semi-automatic assault guns such as the AK-47	M,S,O	SA	F	1990	CSUR	69
A proposal to reduce crime: ban on manufacture, sale, possession, of semiautomatic assault guns such as the AK-47	M,S,O CR	SA		1993	Gallup	77
A proposal to reduce crime: ban on manufacture, sale, possession, of semi automatic guns known as assault rifles	M,S,O CR	SA		1994	Gallup	71
				1995	Gallup	68
Ban on sale, possession, of semiautomatic guns known as assault rifles	S,O	SA		1996	Gallup	57
Other Bans						
Federal ban on manufacture, sale, possession, of plastic guns	M,S,O	O	F	1989	Gallup	75

[a]Type of activity regulated. M = manufacture; S = sale; O = ownership; P = purchase; U = use, C = carrying; CR = criminal use.
[b]Type of firearm regulated. H = handgun; HS = specific type of handgun; R = rifle; S = shotgun; SA = semi-automatic or "assault" weapon; O = other.
[c]Level of government imposing/enforcing regulation. F = Federal; L = local.
[d]Value shown is the maximum possible percentage, derived from 100% minus percentage opposing, as reported in source.

TABLE 11.3

Managing Access to Firearms: Attitudes Toward Nonban Control Measures

Type of Control	Special Aspects Activity[a]	Gun[b]	Person[c]	Date	Source	% in Favor
Permit Laws						
Police permit required to buy ammunition	P	AM		1965	Gallup	<56[d]
Required permit to purchase a rifle	P	R		1975	Harris	<69[d]
Require police permit to purchase a gun	P			1993	NORC	81
Required license to own a handgun	O	H		1978	Caddell	74
Require a permit to carry a gun outside home	C			1988	Gallup	84
Registration						
Register all shotguns owned	O	S		1989b	Time/CNN	65[e]
Register all rifles owned	O	R		1989b	Time/CNN	68[e]
Register all guns owned	O			1989	Time/CNN	73
Register all handguns owned	O	H		1993	Gallup	81
Register all gun owners	O			1940	Gallup	74
Register all semiautomatic weapons owned	O	SA		1989b	Time/CNN	77[e]
Register all gun purchases	P			1990	Harris	79
Register all handgun owners	O	H		1938	Gallup	84
Register all handgun purchases	P	H		1978	Caddell	84
Safety training						
Require mandatory safety	P			1989b	Time/CNN	82[e]
A proposal to reduce gun violence: require safety classes to qualify to own a gun	P, CR			1993	Gallup	89
Mandatory penalty laws						
Mandatory minimum 1 year jail term, carrying gun without a license	C			1981	Gallup	62
Require mandatory prison sentence for persons using a gun in a crime	CR		CR	1978	Caddell	83

Continued next page

Sources: 1938–1990, Kleck 1991, Table 9.2; 1993–1996 Gallup (1993, 1994, 1995, 1996); 1993 NORC General Social Survey.

TABLE 11.3—*continued*

Type of Control	Special Aspects			Date	Source	% in Favor
	Activity[a]	Gun[b]	Person[c]			
Waiting periods						
A proposal to reduce gun violence: the Brady Bill, 5-day waiting period, all gun purchases, to allow criminal record check	P, CR		CR	1993	Gallup	87
21-day waiting period to allow criminal record check, handgun purchases	P	H	CR	1981	Gallup	91
14-day waiting period, any gun purchase	P			1989	Time/CNN	89
7-day waiting period, handgun purchases	P	H		1988	Gallup	91
Restrictions on special persons						
Completely forbid use of guns by those <18	U		M	1967	Gallup	<68[d]
A proposal to reduce crime:prohibit purchase of guns by those <18	P, CR		M	1993	Gallup	88
				1994	Gallup	88
A proposal to reduce gun violence: prohibit purchase and ownership of guns by those with criminal history	P,O CR		CR	1993	Gallup	87
Other measures						
Buy back, destroy handguns, voluntary	O	H		1978	Caddell	33
Illegal to have loaded weapons in home	U			1965	Gallup	<47[d]
A proposal to reduce gun violence: high federal sales tax to raise cost of ammunition for handguns >50%	P,CR			1993	Gallup	55
A proposal to reduce gun violence: limit purchases to one per month	P,CR			1993	Gallup	69

[a]Type of activity regulated. M = manufacture; S = sale; O = ownership; P = purchase; U = use, C = carrying; CR = criminal/violent use.
[b]Type of firearm regulated. H = handgun; HS = specific type of handgun; R = rifle; S = shotgun; SA = semiautomatic or "assault" weapon; AM = ammunition.
[c]Type of person regulated. HC = high-crime areas; M = minors; CR = criminals.
[d]Value shown is the maximum possible percentage, derived from 100% minus percentage opposing, as reported in source.
[e]Computed as simple average of separate percentages for gun owners and nonowners.

the respondent's own community) also receive just under 50 percent support.

Support is much higher when the targeted weapons are not simply handguns but are "criminal" handguns: small, cheap Saturday night specials. According to measures taken at three time points across a span of 15 years, almost three-quarters of all Americans support some type of ban on such weapons. As already mentioned in connection with the problem of question wording, these levels of support are similar to those found for bans on assault weapons, but only when the question asked connects assault weapons with crime and violence either directly or through guilt by association with the AK-47. When assault weapons are not associated with violence, support drops to less than 60 percent, a sizable but not overwhelming majority of citizens.

Nonban Proposals: Managing and Monitoring Access

Many types of nonban control measures are supported by an overwhelming majority of citizens, as shown in Table 11.3. Requiring permits in order to purchase, own, or carry various classes of firearms receives the support of two-thirds to three-quarters of Americans. Registration laws across a variety of weapons are typically supported by well over two-thirds of those surveyed. Of the major categories of nonban controls proposed, waiting periods tend to receive the highest levels of support. From the 5-day waiting period associated with the Brady Bill to earlier proposals for a 21-day waiting period, support for this type of control comes as close to unanimity as one is likely to see in American politics; about 90 percent of all Americans support these measures. The only other class of controls that reaches similar levels is restrictions on purchases targeted at very narrow categories of persons, such as youth under the age of 18 or persons with a criminal history, which also receive support from about 90 percent of Americans.

Measures that go beyond simply managing access, which would entail actual restrictions for the average citizen, are among the least favored of the nonban proposals. Permit laws, gun registration, and waiting periods, it must be remembered, are essentially ways to monitor ownership. Though such measures may be used to limit access, for example, through the use of restrictive permit laws that allow the regulating authority to deny permits to those who cannot establish a need to carry a handgun, this distinction is not typically made in the survey questions being asked. Thus a respondent may not feel that these controls would limit his or her access to firearms.

Two of the measures included in Table 11.3 would explicitly do so. The first of these is a limit on the number of guns that could be purchased in a one-month period, a proposal received favorably by 69 percent of those questioned in a 1993 Gallup poll. This level of support, although still a large majority, is substantially lower than the almost 90 percent in favor of the other measures asked about in the same Gallup survey. Similarly, a proposal to place a very restrictive tax on handgun ammunition in order to raise its cost by at least 50 percent was supported by only 55 percent of respondents in that survey. This latter figure is especially surprising given that the question associates such a tax with a reduction in gun violence and given that the tax would be targeted at handguns, two factors that are associated with higher levels of support. Taken together, these results suggest that a majority of Americans would limit access to certain types of weapons and that an overwhelming majority support regulating access through permits and waiting periods.

Kleck argues that some of the variation in support for different types of measures is related to the "short-term dollar cost" of the proposal (1991, 370). He cites, for example, low levels of support for gun buyback programs, which would cost taxpayer dollars. This thesis might help explain the low level of support for an ammunition tax, at least in part. There is, however, some evidence that cost may not be the culprit. Writing in 1991, Gary Kleck attributes high levels of support for mandatory safety training before a gun purchase to its relatively low cost, because such a measure would not require such training for those who already own a gun. Since that time, Gallup has asked a question concerning more costly mandatory safety classes "to qualify to own a gun" (1993). Admittedly, the comparability of the two questions is jeopardized somewhat by the term "gun violence" in the latter, but the fact that 89 percent support this measure suggests that cost may not be a major concern. Furthermore, because support for voluntary buy-back programs is slightly lower than that found for outright bans during the same time frame, a difference of 6 percent could be largely explained by sampling error. The cost factor cannot be totally rejected, however, without finding some other way of explaining the extremely low levels of support for voluntary buy-back programs.

One of the major implications of the cost argument is that Americans do not care enough about gun control to spend their money on it, a view that lends support to the notion that gun control is a low-salience issue for most Americans (Bordua 1983; Crocker 1982; Kleck 1991). This lack of salience is associated with instability in the level of support for gun control and, ultimately, with the perceived failure of pro-control measures to meet with much success in the legislative arena. In the next section I discuss the salience of gun control.

Measuring and Weighing Support: Intensity, Salience, and Influence

One of the basic problems associated with democratic forms of government is the translation of public opinion into public policy. In addition to the matter of determining *how many* people support any given policy, there is the issue of how much weight to place on the voice of any individual. Elections may enshrine the notion of "one person, one vote" and thus of political equality in determining public policy, but the realities of the American policymaking process seem, at least in part, deliberately designed to foil such parity (Schattschneider 1960). With the possible exception of the referendum and ballot initiative, the indirect character of policymaking virtually guarantees that the voices of some will carry more weight than the voices of others.

In fact, in its early years, public opinion polling was seen by some as a technological fix for the problems of indirect democracy, capable of producing the equivalent of a referendum and therefore of bringing about real political equality in the making of public policy. Archibald Crossley, along with George Gallup, Elmo Roper, and others, saw it as "the long-sought key to 'Government *by* the people'" and a way to overcome the power of special interests (Converse 1987, 122). In short, they saw polling as a way to translate public opinion into public policy without distorting the inherent equality of all voices.

There are a number of problems with such a view. Even direct policymaking in the form of ballot initiatives is not immune to the effects of differences, often associated with class, that shape the costs and thus the likelihood of voting. David Magleby, in discussing ballot-proposition campaigns, implicitly recognizes these differences in distinguishing between effective and ineffective voter participation—effective participation requires that the voter be aware and informed (1989). To cast a vote without being either is to give voice to nonsense, the electoral equivalent of a nonattitude (Converse 1970).[4] The severity of this problem is far worse in public opinion polls, where the cost of expressing one's opinion is almost completely borne by the polling organization. Of course, reputable pollsters do attempt to avoid soliciting nonattitudes, but identifying meaningless responses is a notoriously difficult task (Asher 1992, 21–37).

Moreover, even if one were able to recognize and eliminate all such responses, there is an additional factor involved—the link between the cost of expressing an opinion and the intensity of that opinion. "In general, the willingness of individuals to bear the cost of publicly asserting their views is closely tied to the intensity with which they hold those views" (Ginsberg 1989, 275). This relationship and its consequences for enhancing the relative influence of intense minorities is one that was confronted by the founders, most notably James Madison, long before the advent of modern public opinion polling (Dahl 1956). Furthermore, the distribution of public opinion typically found by pollsters also differs from that found in more costly modes of expression in that the proportion of those holding relatively extreme opinions tends to decrease when measured using polls (Clausen, Converse, and Miller 1965). The upshot of polling, then, is to hide differences in the intensity and extremity of opinions.

The American electoral system makes no allowances for weighting votes by interest, intensity, or informedness. However, given the relationship between them and the costs associated with the act of casting a ballot, there is a de facto weighting scheme already in place even in that most egalitarian of arenas, the voting booth. When one looks beyond that booth to the legislative chamber, the significance of the relationship between salience, intensity, and assessing public preferences becomes even greater.

Legislators, too, are familiar with the relationship among the cost of expressing an opinion, the intensity of that opinion, and the value assigned to that opinion by its holder. The question for them, as it is for anyone trying to assess the link between public opinion and public policy, is if or how these considerations should come into play. What is a legislator to make of a campaign by the "National Rifle Association generating three million telegrams in seventy-two hours and blanketing Capitol Hill with so many phone calls that members cannot make outgoing calls" (Smith 1988, 240; cited in Cigler and Loomis 1995, 395)? If the telegrams come as form letters provided by an interest group and merely signed by a constituent, they may simply become part of the tally for that group. If the phone calls are patched through to the member's office by telemarketers who have contacted constituents and offered them a free phone call to Washington, they will serve as a measure of the strength of the NRA and its resources, which is not to say they are an indicator of public sentiment.

Several analysts have concluded that as far as the issue of gun control goes, most Americans "do not think about it much, care about it very deeply, or have firm stable opinions on it" (Kleck 1991, 364; see also Crocker 1982). This allows well-organized, intensely motivated minorities to thwart the marginally concerned majority. Two types of evidence are typically used to support these conclusions.

On the one hand are answers to open-ended questions asking respondents to identify the most important problem facing the country or the steps that should be taken to reduce crime. For example, Kleck reports that only 11 percent of Americans mentioned gun control as a step to reduce crime and only 1 percent listed the availability of guns as the factor most responsible for high crime rates. From this, he concludes there is "very little 'will of the people' to be thwarted" (1991, 365). Yet this evidence is not conclusive: a person may care deeply about gun control, think about it all the time, and hold stable opinions on it and still not consider it to be the most important step in reducing crime. Even among those who favor stronger gun control, it may be that criminals or social conditions are seen as the proximate and most important factor in high crime rates, not the guns used to commit those crimes.[5]

Another type of evidence used to support the assertion that most voters do not care about the issue of gun control is based on a longitudinal examination of support for control measures in which analyses of the stability and volatility of attitudes are used to gauge the depth of feeling or salience of an issue. Kleck, for example, argues that the volatility of aggregate opinion on some specific measures is indicative of the low salience of the issue for most Americans (1991, 367). In support of this claim, he offers measures of support for three specific proposals: purchase permits, handgun bans, and handgun registration, chosen for the invariability in the wording of the questions over several decades. These data, with updates for several ensuing years, are presented in Table 11.4.

These data make it clear that public support is, in the aggregate, fairly stable over periods of intermediate lengths but quite prone to sudden dips or rises over the short term. This, however, does not constitute evidence of the volatility required to justify claims of low levels of salience. Salience, it must be remembered, is a characteristic associated with an attitude held by a single individual. Instability in the attitude of a single individual over time, as measured in a panel study, has been linked to low salience of the issue involved and to nonattitudes in surveys (Converse 1970; Achen 1975; Schuman and Presser 1981). Furthermore, as Spitzer has pointed out, the level of volatility evident in these aggregate data is typical for many issues and does not in itself indicate that mass opinion with respect to gun control is particularly changeable.

There is another message to be drawn from these longitudinal data. As was already made clear from the discussion of support for various types of control, there is widespread support for at least some proposals to regulate access to firearms. To this we can now add the assertion that majorities of Americans have expressed that support for several decades. Moreover, it appears that support has been increasing for at least two types of control proposals since the mid-1980s. Public opinion regarding purchase permits hovered within three points of 72 per-

TABLE 11.4
Stability and Volatility in Aggregate Support for Three Control Proposals

Year	Purchase Permits[a] % in Favor	Ban Handgun Possession Source	Ban Handgun Possession % in Favor	Handgun Registration Source	Handgun Registration % in Favor
1938				Gallup	84[b]
1959	75	Gallup	60[b]		
1963	79				
1965	73	Gallup	49		
1965	70				
1966	67				
1967	72				
1971	72				
1972	72				
1972	70				
1973	73				
1974	75				
1975	74	Gallup	41	CBS	78
1975		Harris	37	Harris	77
1975				Harris	77
1976	72				
1977	72				
1978		Caddell	31	Caddell	74
1978				Harris	80
1979		Gallup	31	Harris	78
1980	69	Gallup	38	Harris	67
1981		Gallup	39		
1981		Gallup	41		
1982	73	Gallup	45	Gallup	66
1984	70				
1985	72			Gallup	70
1987	72	Gallup	42		
1988	74	Gallup	37		
1989	78			Harris	78
1990	79	Gallup	41	Gallup	81
1991	81	Gallup	43	Gallup	80
1993	81	Gallup	42	Gallup	81
1993		Gallup	39		

Sources: 1938–1990 (except as noted), Kleck 1991, Table 9.1; all GSS values calculated by author from 1972–1993 General Social Surveys (NORC); Gallup 1938, 1990–1993, Gallup 1994.

[a]Gun purchase permit values for 1959–1972 (first of the 1972 entries) are from Gallup polls. All other values for this measure are taken from NORC General Social Surveys.

[b]The wording of these early questions varies significantly from that used in later surveys.

cent for roughly two decades until 1989, when it climbed to the vicinity of 80 percent. Data on handgun registration are not as consistently available, but the number of supporters, which had dropped to roughly two-thirds of all Americans in the early 1980s, has risen once again to include about 80 percent of those surveyed.

Why, then, the failure to enact these proposals into law? One possibility is that legislators are convinced that those who oppose gun control are much more likely than those who favor it to vote on the issue in an election (Mauser and Kopel 1992, 85–86; Kleck 1991, 364–365). Perhaps a better way to look at the whole question is to consider what has been done, rather than what has not. Three major pieces of federal legislation have been passed since 1986: the Law Enforcement Officers Protection Act of 1986, which affected the sale, manufacture, and importation of cop-killer bullets; the Brady Handgun Violence Protection Act of 1993, which established a five-day waiting period on handgun transfers and mandated the creation of a national instant criminal background check; and finally a provision in the hotly debated Omnibus Violent Crime Control and Prevention Act of 1994, more popularly referred to as the Crime Bill, which included a ban on certain firearms defined as having "assault-weapon" characteristics (Kruschke 1995). The timing of these events coincides roughly with the upswing in support for gun control observed in Table 11.4. Whereas the timing of these changes does not constitute proof of an opinion-policy linkage in and of itself, it does go a long way in silencing those who see an unusual disjunction of opinion and policy in the matter of gun control (Spitzer 1995; Mauser and Kopel 1992; Kleck 1991). When public support for gun control increases, the passage of gun control legislation becomes more likely.

The Breadth of Support for Gun Control

Of course, making public policy in the United States is more than simple majoritarian politics, as the whole issue of intensity and influence implies. Whether one calls the system pluralism, pressure group politics, or a "special interest democracy" (Wooten 1985; quoted in Spitzer 1995, 122), aggregations of individuals, formally in interest groups and informally or even unknowingly in demographic groups, play a large role in the process. To consider the extent of support requires more than determining what proportion of the total population favors gun control; one must also consider the spread of that opinion throughout the population, its permeation into the nooks and crannies of American culture.

The data chosen to investigate the breadth of support for gun control are from a frequently asked question regarding purchase permits that was included in the National Opinion Research Center (NORC) General Social Survey for several decades: "Would you favor or oppose a law which would require a person to obtain a police permit before he or she could buy a gun?" This measure has several useful qualities for the purpose at hand. The question has been asked for many years in the same format as part of an established academic poll; it is hoped that the latter renders many of the criticisms of Mauser and Kopel (1992), generally aimed at media polls, irrelevant. Kleck regards the specific type of control asked about in the question as "moderate, neither extremely restrictive nor trivial, and it covers all guns (1991, 372).[6] Perhaps the most important quality is the change in support for permit laws from the early 1980s to the early 1990s, as noted in Table 11.4. With this in mind, it is possible to consider not only the breadth of support itself but also the breadth of change in that support.

Levels of support for purchase permits across the categories of ten major demographic variables and five attitudinal measures are reported in Table 11.5.[7] Values for each of the two periods were calculated by combining all responses from the two surveys in each period (1980 and 1982, 1991 and 1993), thus smoothing out short-term fluctuations.

The general conclusion from these data is that (1) support for purchase permits is widespread throughout virtually all segments of American society and (2) the shift toward greater support in the period beginning in the early 1980s was comprehensive. Broad majorities of Americans support purchase permits regardless of race, income, education, or place of residence. In fact, the gap between blacks and whites, young and old, rich and poor had all but disappeared by the early 1990s.

The pattern seen across the categories of sex, education, and place of residence is more typical.[8] Increases in support of about 10 percent occurred in all these categories, thus preserving the differences found across categories. The 10 percent shift was also found among hunters, the least supportive category of persons reported on in the analysis. Yet even among this group, a majority of 56 percent expressed support for gun purchase permits by the early 1990s.

The theme is continued among the attitudinal groupings. Ideological self-placement remains weakly correlated with approval, but even among conservatives support levels run over 75 percent. Fear of crime and violence, as indicated by a positive response to a question on fear of walking in one's own neighborhood, also remains weakly correlated with approval. Those who express such a fear are slightly more likely

TABLE 11.5
Composition of Support for Gun Control: Purchase Permits

Respondent Characteristic	Percent in Favor of Purchase Permit Law (1980&1982)	Level of Association	Percent in Favor of Purchase Permit Law (1991&1993)	Level of Association
Total	72.0		82.3	
Sex				
Male	66.0	-.117[a]	74.3	.183[a]
Female	76.5		88.4	
Race				
White	70.7	.080[a]	81.7	n.s.
Black	82.1		82.7	
Age				
Under 25	75.3	-.042[a]	81.1	n.s.
25-39	74.7		81.7	
40-64	67.9		83.5	
65 or over	72.3		81.4	
Household Income				
Under $10,000	74.8	-.025[a]	81.3	n.s.
$10,000-19,999	72.0		79.6	
$20,000-24,999	70.4		85.4	
$25,000 or more	71.8		83.4	
Education (years of formal schooling completed)				
0-7	68.4	.041[a]	83.8	.073[a]
8	71.6		70.1	
9-11	69.7		79.3	
12	72.4		80.5	
1-3 years of college	74.7		83.2	
4 years of college	74.7		85.3	
>4 years of college	78.0		89.2	
Region at age 16				
New England	90.7	.172[b]	91.7	.113[b]
Middle Atlantic	84.7		85.9	
East North Central	73.4		82.4	
West North Central	70.7		84.4	
South Atlantic	67.7		80.1	
East South Central	67.1		80.0	
West South Central	64.4		71.5	
Mountain	55.4		81.7	
Pacific	71.1		83.0	

Continued Next Page

Source: National Opinion Research Center, combined 1973 through 1993 General Social Surveys. Analysis of the 1980–1982 data (with the exception of Region at 16, Residential type at 16, Robbed in the Past Year, Violence, and Defense), reported in Kleck 1991, Table 9.3. All other analysis conducted by the author.

TABLE 11.5—*Continued*.

Respondent Characteristic	Percent in Favor of Purchase Permit Law (1980&1982)	Level of Association	Percent in Favor of Purchase Permit Law (1991&1993)	Level of Association
Residential Type at age 16				
Farm	62.6	.156[b]	72.6	.141[b]
Country, nonfarm	65.6		77.7	
Town < 50,000	72.5		83.6	
City 50,000-250,000	76.7		83.0	
Suburb of big city	80.2		86.9	
City > 250,000	82.7		89.7	
Region of interview				
New England	93.0	.132[b]	91.7	.152[b]
Middle Atlantic	85.9		83.9	
East North Central	73.8		81.9	
West North Central	74.3		87.3	
South Atlantic	64.4		81.5	
East South Central	68.1		79.7	
West South Central	59.6		64.7	
Mountain	42.4		84.9	
Pacific	73.0		83.7	
Population of place of residence				
Under 5,000	61.1	.132[a]	75.1	.100[a]
5,000-49,000	74.7		82.3	
50,000-249,000	72.8		84.8	
250,000-999,999	78.6		86.2	
1 million or larger	84.5		89.2	
Hunter				
Yes	47.5	.254[a]	56.0	.291[a]
No	77.3		87.0	
Political views				
Liberal	76.6	-.088[a]	88.9	-.105[a]
Moderate	73.8		82.1	
Conservative	66.0		77.9	
Afraid to walk in area				
Yes	76.3	.089[a]	86.5	.097
No	68.3		79.1	
Robbed in past year				
Yes	70.0	n.s.	79.5	n.s.
No	72.8		82.4	
Violence: Approve of a man punching another				
Yes	68.1	.075[b]	79.6	.070[b]
No	75.4		85.2	
Defense: Approve of hitting stranger who has broken into house				
Yes	69.9	.044[b]	81.1	n.s.
No	75.2		85.8	

[a]Kendall's Tau-b, p<.05. [b]Contingency Coefficient, chi square significant at p<.05.

to favor permit laws. However, having a recent history of victimization, as indicated by having been robbed in the previous year, is not associated with differences in levels of support for purchase permits.[9] Tolerance for violence, as measured by approval for the striking of one man by another under any circumstances, remains weakly associated with gun control attitudes; those who are more tolerant of violence are slightly less in favor of purchase permits. Those who approve of violence for self-defense are also slightly less likely to support purchase permits, but this difference is not statistically significant.

Given that they are the group most directly affected by gun control laws, gun owners have often been found to differ from non–gun owners in their support for those laws. The extent of that difference, however, is much debated and depends heavily on the type of gun ownership and the type of control in question. With regard to the matter of purchase permits, Kleck reports differences of 25 to 30 percent depending on the type of ownership (1991, Table 9.3). A Gallup poll conducted in 1993 showed 67 percent of all Americans and 47 percent of all gun owners in favor of stricter laws on the sale of firearms, a difference of 20 percent (Gallup 1993). In the same survey, a question on the sale of handguns revealed similar differences between the general population, with 72 percent in favor of stricter laws, and gun owners, with only 55 percent in favor. The latter figure, however, masked a sizable split in the gun-owning community between handgun owners (50 percent in favor of stricter laws) and those who owned only long guns (66 percent in favor).[10] The differences between those who owned only long guns and the general population disappeared in connection with a question on the registration of handguns; 81 percent was in favor in both of those groups, whereas only 65 percent of handgun owners favored such a law. On questions concerning a seven-day waiting period, Spitzer reports only a 1 percent difference between gun owners and the population as a whole (1995, 121).

A detailed analysis of the General Social Survey data, reported in Table 11.6, shows that there have been important changes in support for purchase permits and that the size of those changes varies with the type of firearm ownership. The overall 10 percent increase in support for purchase permits has come about in large part because of relatively major changes in support among the gun-owning segment of American society. The biggest change has come among those households where both handguns and long guns are present; support went from less than 48.1 percent in 1981–1982 to 64.4 percent in 1991–1993. Similar increases may be observed in handgun-only households, where support increased by over 12 percentage points, and among respondents who personally owned only a handgun, where support went up al-

TABLE 11.6
Gun Ownership and Support for Purchase Permit Laws

Type of Ownership	Percent in Favor (1980&1982)	N	Percent in Favor (1991&1993)	N
No guns in household	83.4	1738	89.9	1177
Handgun only in household	71.3	237	83.7	129
Long-gun only in household	65.6	715	73.9	353
Both in household	48.1	484	64.4	323
R personally owns a gun, any type	54.5	882	65.7	543
R personally owns only a handgun	67.3	159	81.9	83
R personally owns only a long-gun	59.2	385	65.9	223
R owns a gun, both types in household [a]	43.2	338	59.9	237

Source: National Opinion Research Center, 1973–1993 Combined General Social Surveys.
[a]Due to the way in which the series of questions was asked, it is impossible to determine the type of personal ownership in households containing both handguns and long-guns.

most 15 points. The slowest rate of change came in households with long guns only, where support increased by about 8 points, and especially among those who personally owned only long guns, where support was up by less than 7 percentage points.

It seems trivial to say that gun ownership has an impact on attitudes toward gun control; yet the statement hides as much as it reveals. The type of gun, or guns, owned is likely to be an indicator of a deeper orientation to firearms and the gun culture (Hofstader 1970; Lizotte, Bordua, and White 1981; Kleck 1991). Being a male; growing up in the South, the Rocky Mountains, or the Midwest; living in a less urban area; and even one's attitudes toward violence are all important predictors of gun ownership and type of gun ownership (Kleck 1991). Some of the relationships are obvious—handgun owners are more likely to oppose control proposals targeted at handguns, for example.

When it comes to a nonspecific, moderate measure such as purchase permits, handgun ownership is not the critical determinant. Of the two general types of ownership, it would seem that long-gun ownership is more likely to be associated with anticontrol attitudes. Long-gun ownership, by itself or in conjunction with handgun ownership, is also very likely to be associated with membership in the gun culture; handgun ownership, by itself, is more typically motivated by fear of victimization (Kleck 1991). In a 1993 survey, 41 percent of all handgun owners (compared to 29 percent of all gun owners and only 7 percent of those who owned only long guns) reported that they had bought a gun *just* for protection against crime (Gallup 1993).

Nothing to Fear but Fear Itself

As long as there is confusion over how to weight the voices of opponents and proponents, how to reconcile the wishes of a relatively undemanding majority with those of an insistent minority, change in gun control policy will come slowly. There is no doubt that many control proposals receive majority support, but the focus has been and will remain on opponents of gun control, who must attempt to make up for their lack of numbers by pursuing their claims with tenacity and expressing their opinions with ferocity. But there are signs of weakness: important divisions among opponents signal that many do not believe the "rights talk" so often at the heart of anticontrol arguments.

Handgun owners buy their guns out of a fear of crime; yet handguns are often seen as, if not a cause of crime, at least one of its primary concomitants. Handgun control is one of the more popular types of control not only among the general populace but among gun owners as well, many of whom are not handgun owners. Most long-gun owners, the carriers of the rural gun culture, do not seem to mind handgun control. This is perhaps due to their feelings about crime and safety. Those who own only long guns are more likely than handgun owners to see the problem of gun violence as worsening, at 82 percent and 75 percent, respectively (Gallup 1993, 50). Handgun owners see safety in their guns: 66 percent of handgun owners say they would feel less safe if possession by those other than the police were made illegal, compared to 55 percent of long-gun owners. Four out of five handgun owners report that having a gun in the house makes them feel more safe, compared to only two in three for those who own only long guns (Gallup 1993, 50–51).

Yet when it comes to more general proposals, such as purchase permits for any weapon, those who own only handguns are not at all unlike the non-gun-owning segment of the population. Long-gun owners, in contrast, not only lag far behind other segments of society in their support for purchase permits but have as a group been far more resistant to change than those who own only handguns.

So in the end, the future of gun control comes down to fear, but not in any simple way. The pattern of attitudes found among gun owners, the group in society most likely to be opposed to gun control, suggests that these are not people who fear the loss of all guns or who are unwilling to compromise on a fundamental right, though many are certainly willing to express those fears or insist on their belief in that right if it furthers their goal. Instead, these are attitudes of people who fear the loss of *their* guns. Although many say they are afraid of being pulled down a slippery slope, a fair number are willing to take the first step as long as they themselves can make the journey armed.

Notes

1. Throughout this chapter, I have endeavored to follow, as closely as possible, the source being quoted in my choice of such labels as "assault weapon" or "assault rifle" versus "semiautomatic weapon." As Kleck points out, even the term "assault weapon" is a loaded one with no definitive technical meaning (1991, 361).

2. See O'Connor and Barron , Chapter 4 in this volume.

3. For a general discussion of the role of the gun in American culture, see Kennett and Anderson (1975) and Kleck (1991).

4. There is some evidence that many voters do try to avoid ineffective participation. Magleby (1984) reports a drop-off of as much as 25 percent on ballot propositions.

5. For example, in a *New York Times*–CBS poll conducted in January 1994, 46 percent of those holding an opinion reported that they would favor a ban on the sale of handguns even though only 34 percent thought that gun control laws would reduce violent crime (*NYT*, January 23 1994, sec. 1, 1). At best (i.e., if all those who believed gun control would reduce violent crime also were in favor of the handgun ban), at least 12 percent of respondents professing to have an opinion on the issue were in favor of the gun ban but did not think it would have an effect on crime. Put another way, more than one in four of those in favor of the ban did not believe it would reduce violent crime.

6. Kleck's use of the same data, albeit only for the earlier period, also recommends its use here, in large part to test his assertions that neither the level nor patterns of support have changed in recent decades (1991, 372).

7. It is not my intention to establish any causal connection between these attitudes or characteristics and opinion on gun control or to fully model the complex web of relationships among these variables. Such an effort lies well beyond the scope of this chapter. I recognize, for example, that being male and being a hunter are related, and thus the bivariate relationship between either of these characteristics and attitudes toward gun control may change if the other variable was accounted for at the same time. This does not render the simple bivariate relationships useless or meaningless, for the same reasons as those cited in the text for examining group differences in the first place. Group membership matters in American politics. It is important to understand the cleavages that divide us and the shared interests that unite us in this most basic form.

8. The high level of support among those persons with the least amount of formal education is quite unexpected. A check on race and education reveals that an unusually large percentage of respondents in this category were members of a non–African American minority group, a segment of the population that shows overwhelming support for gun permit laws (91.8%). However, con-

trolling for race does almost nothing to contradict the finding that those in this education category show unexpectedly high levels of support for purchase permit laws—82.6 percent of whites in this category support purchase permits.

9. Finding differences based on a recent history of victimization might be a difficult matter given that there are two logical responses to that event. On the face of it, there seems little reason to expect a pattern given that the victim might turn against guns in the hope of preventing crime or turn to guns in the hope of providing self-defense.

10. The source reported support levels among "handgun owners," who may or may not own long guns as well.

12

The Electoral Politics of Gun Ownership

Ted G. Jelen

The issues surrounding gun control and firearms regulation in the United States pose a fascinating problem for theories of representation, public opinion, and democracy. Gun control appears to be an issue in which the translation of public opinion into public policy is very indirect and subject to substantial distortion. It is clear that in the regulation of firearms, "minorities rule" (Dahl 1956).

For much of the twentieth century, and indeed for much of American history, there has been substantial public support for firearms regulation (Spitzer 1995; Erskine 1972; Wills 1987). Virtually whenever it has been possible to measure public sentiment on the issue of gun control, large majorities of Americans appear to favor limited access to firearms, the registration of firearms, and the complete prohibition of certain classes of weapons that are considered particularly lethal (Spitzer 1995). Gun control would appear to be an "easy" issue (Carmines and Stimson 1980) in which issue attitudes are easily translated into political behavior. Further, there are clear partisan differences on the gun control issue. Spitzer (1995) reports that since 1968, Republican party platforms have consistently supported the "right to bear arms," and Democratic platforms have supported firearm regulation with equal consistency. Whereas candidates for different offices undoubtedly exhibit diverse levels of support for their parties' platforms, voters have, for the last generation or so, had a cognitive shortcut available to them. Since the Johnson administration, the Democrats have been the gun control party, and the Republicans have been the party of gun control opponents. Thus applying issue positions to vote choices should be unusually easy for voters with respect to gun control.

However, despite a large popular majority that favors gun regulation and despite the fact that the Supreme Court has never overturned a federal or state gun control statute on Second Amendment grounds (Spitzer 1995, 38–42), government regulation of firearms has typically been ineffective and intermittent. Guns of many types remain widely available in the United States.

How has gun control policy resisted the will of a large, stable majority of the public? Two general answers have been suggested. First, it has been argued that organized interest groups that oppose the regulation of firearms, the most well-known of which is the National Rifle Association, have effectively removed gun control from the agenda of electoral politics and have succeeded in thwarting the will of the majority by exercising influence in nonelectoral (typically legislative) arenas (see Langbein and Lotwis 1986; Spitzer 1995; Hrebenar and Scott 1990). The NRA, it is suggested, has come to dominate government policymaking in this area by the use of lobbying, campaign contributions, and other elite-level tactics to weaken the connection between public opinion and public policy.

Conversely, other analysts (Mundo 1992) have suggested that the most important tactic used by the NRA and other organized groups that oppose gun control is precisely the mobilization of public opinion. Gun control has been regarded as an instance in which an intense minority is willing to commit political resources to a particular issue and can thus overcome the preferences of a large, but relatively apathetic, majority (see Dahl 1961 and Banfield 1961 for general accounts of this argument). Gun control opponents, who are most likely to own guns themselves, may be more likely to vote on the basis of this issue and to commit time, energy, and money to nonelectoral political activity as well. Elected officials may therefore be most attentive to the "issue publics" whose preferences on the gun control issue are the strongest and whose activity is most likely to have consequences for the outcome of elections.

The purpose of this chapter is to examine the "electoral connection" to the issue of gun control and to compare the political attitudes and behaviors of gun owners and nonowners. How do gun owners and opponents of gun control differ from the rest of the population? Are gun owners distinctive with respect to their partisanship or voting behavior? Finally, does an analysis of the relationship between gun ownership and electoral behavior shed any light on the noncorrespondence between public opinion and public policy on the issue of firearms regulation?

Data and Method

Despite the long-standing salience of firearms in American politics,[1] relatively few national surveys have devoted much attention to this issue. Because of the limited survey data on this topic, data for this study are drawn from only two sources. The main source is the General Social Survey (GSS; 1972–1993), which has contained a number of questions about gun control attitudes and gun ownership during virtually the entire period of its use. These data are supplemented with the Voter News Service (VNS) exit polls in 1994, a subpresidential election year when the NRA was widely credited for helping produce the first GOP majority in the House in a generation.

The principal independent variable in this study is gun ownership. In the GSS, this is ascertained by asking respondents, "Do you happen to have in your home (IF HOUSE: or garage) any guns or revolvers?" The GSS also supplements this item by asking about ownership of specific types of guns (shotgun, pistol, rifle) and whether any firearms in the home belong to the respondent. The GSS contains a gun control item, which reads,"Would you favor or oppose a law which would require a person to obtain a police permit before he or she could buy a gun?"

In the VNS exit polls, the measurement of the independent variable is somewhat less elaborate. For the VNS national exit poll and for 17 of the state polls, respondents are asked to "check all that apply." Included in the list are "currently married," currently employed," "victim of a crime last year," and "gun owner," among others. This is the only item relating to firearms in the 1994 national exit poll and in all state exit polls except New Jersey (discussed later on).

The GSS data are divided into five time periods: 1972–1976 (the Nixon-Ford administrations), 1977–1980 (the Carter administration), 1981–1984 (Ronald Reagan's first term), 1985–1988 (Reagan's second term), and 1989–1993 (the Bush administration and first several months of the Clinton administration).[2] For most purposes, the gun-ownership item is used as the independent variable in analyses involving the GSS in order to maximize comparability with the VNS exit polls. Of course, not all gun owners oppose gun control, but in the GSS, the bivariate relationship (gamma) between the gun-ownership item and attitudes toward gun registration range from .58 to .51 in these time periods.

The New Jersey exit poll contains items asking respondents whether they favor or oppose a ban on assault weapons, and respondents were allowed to check off an item asking whether they considered themselves "National Rifle Association supporters." In New Jersey, the gun-owner item exhibited a relationship (gamma) of .68 with the assault weapons ban item, and .88 with the NRA-support item. Similarly, an item on the Wisconsin state poll asking whether the respondent favors a ban on handguns is also strongly related to gun ownership (gamma = .66). Thus gun ownership is not identical to political attitudes about firearms but is strongly related to such attitudes. In general, it seems likely that the use of the gun-owner item where necessary is a methodologically conservative strategy in that gun ownership is a fairly weak surrogate for more directly attitudinal measures. Most likely, the relationships reported in the rest of this chapter are weaker than they would be if more direct measures were available.

The Sources of Gun Ownership and Gun Control Attitudes

As might be expected for an "easy" issue such as gun control (Converse and Markus 1979), attitudes toward gun control, as well as the frequency of gun ownership, are quite stable (Spitzer 1995; Erksine 1972). Table 12.1 simply reports the frequency with which GSS respondents reported having firearms in the household, as well as attitudes

TABLE 12.1
Gun Ownership and Support for Gun Control, by Electoral Era

	Own Gun	Support Police Permit
1972-1976	47.2	74.3
1977-1980	49.3	71.9
1981-1984	44.8	73.4
1985-1988	42.9	73.8
1989-1993	42.9	81.0

Source: National Opinion Research Center's General Social Surveys.

toward gun control. As these data indicate, the proportion of respondents indicating gun ownership varies within a relatively narrow range from 49 to 42 percent with a slight downward trend over time. Similarly, support for the registration of firearms is quite high and varies between 72 and 81 percent across the span of the GSS with a slight tendency toward greater support. Further, these patterns appear insensitive to at least some variations in the political environment. One might anticipate that support for gun control would increase in 1977 (in response to two assassination attempts on President Ford) or in 1982 (the first GSS to be taken after the assassination attempt on President Reagan and the permanent injury to James Brady). However, examining the trends in gun control support reveals that such predicted increases do not occur.[3]

It is perhaps noteworthy that in the New Jersey exit poll, about 75 percent of respondents expressed support for a ban on assault weapons. Thus despite quite different question wordings, a comparison between the GSS and the New Jersey exit poll suggests that there may exist *generalized* attitudes toward government control of firearms, with approximately three-fourths of the population expressing such support.

A moderately complex multivariate analysis (not shown) suggests that across the time periods covered in this survey, demographic variables dominate statistical models in which gun ownership is the dependent variable.[4] For all time periods, the strongest predictor of gun ownership is rural residence (see Kennet and Anderson 1975; Lizotte and Bourda 1981). Other consistent predictors of gun ownership include gender (Marks and Stokes 1976; Lizotte and Bordua 1980; Wright, Rossi, and Daly 1983), race, and region at age 16 (Young 1986). Although some previous research (O'Connor and Lizotte 1978) has suggested that current residence in the South has a significant effect on gun ownership, my analysis suggests that this effect attains statistical significance only during the earliest period considered here (see also Young 1986).

By contrast, the effects of attitudinal variables toward crime are generally weak and inconsistent. Attitudes toward the leniency of the courts on crime (which appear to represent a more general liberal-conservative orientation) have significant effects on gun ownership in all periods except the second Reagan term; the effects of fear of crime in one's neighborhood attain statistical significance only during the Bush administration (see Lizotte, Bordua, and White 1981 and Young 1985 for contrasting analyses of the effects of fear of crime on gun ownership).

The models explaining attitudes toward control are much simpler.

Over the five political eras considered here, the strongest predictor of attitudes toward gun control is gun ownership. Other variables having consistently significant effects on gun control attitudes include gender and rural residence. Attitudes toward the courts have significant effects on these attitudes only during the Carter and second Reagan administrations, and fear of crime becomes significant during the Nixon-Ford and second Reagan periods.

Thus these analyses suggest that the independent variables considered in this study have roots that are primarily cultural and demographic rather than political. Men, respondents raised in the South, and rural residents are most likely to own guns, and gun owners are most likely to oppose gun registration. The effects of such situational variables as fear of crime, although occasionally reaching statistical significance, are quite inconsistent over time.[5]

The Salience of Gun Control as an Electoral Issue

As noted, it is often suggested that the issue of gun control is a classic instance of an intense, committed minority prevailing over a largely indifferent majority. That is, gun control opponents constitute an "issue public" with an unusually strong interest in the gun control issue. Arguably, such people can often prevail in political decision-making because gun control opponents are more likely to base voting decisions on this issue and may be more likely to commit time, energy, and money to nonelectoral forms of political participation.

Three state exit polls permit a partial test of this hypothesis. In a number of state polls, voters were asked to select (from a list) the one or two issues that mattered most in their votes for U.S. senator or governor. In New Jersey, Michigan, and Pennsylvania, gun control was included on the list of possible important issues. In New Jersey and Michigan, voters could select gun control as the first or second most important issue in their votes for U.S. senator; Pennsylvania respondents were able to select gun control as an important issue with respect to votes for both U.S. senator and governor.

As Table 12.2 shows, gun control was significantly more important to gun owners in all three states and, in the case of New Jersey, to opponents of an assault weapons ban and supporters of the National Rifle Association. Although gun control was salient to only about 10 percent of the voters in each state, such respondents were disproportionately likely to own guns. Gamma coefficients, which are not constrained by the skewed marginal distributions of the salience variable, are reported to provide a sense of the magnitude of the relationships

TABLE 12.2

Importance of Gun Control as Electoral Issue by Gun Ownership and Attitudes Toward Gun Control, 1994

	Own Gun	Ban Assault Weapons	NRA Support
New Jersey			
Importance gun control (U.S. Senate) [10%]	.11*** (.42)	.08** (.27)	.10** (.39)
Pennsylvania			
Importance gun control (U.S. Senate) [9%]	.16*** (.51)		
Importance gun control (governor) [9%]	.18*** (.54)		
Michigan			
Importance gun control (U.S. Senate) [9%]	.11** (.35)		

Source: Voter News Service 1994 State Exit Polls.
***significant at .001. **significant at .01.
Notes: Entries are product-moment correlations. Figures in parentheses are gamma coefficients. All tables on which gammas are based significant at .01 (chi-square). Figures in brackets are percentages of state electorates indicating gun control as first or second most important issue.

between the importance of gun control as an electoral issue and gun ownership. Although analysis of the GSS suggests that as a group, gun owners are no more likely to vote than nonowners (at least in presidential elections), the analysis of the 1994 exit polls suggests that gun owners are more likely to cast votes on the basis of the gun control issue than nonowners. Thus these data provide impressive support for the "intense minority" hypothesis.

Gun Ownership, Gun Control, and
Partisan Behavior: An Overview

Of course, the main focus of this study is on the electoral consequences of gun ownership and attitudes toward gun control. To what extent does gun ownership, or gun control attitudes, affect partisan self-images and electoral behavior? This question is addressed in a preliminary way in Table 12.3, which contains the correlations between gun ownership and support for gun registration according to party identi-

TABLE 12.3
Gun Ownership and Support for Gun Permits by Partisanship and Presidential Voting, by Electoral Era.

Party Identification

	1972-76	1977-80	1981-84	1985-88	1989-93
Own Gun	.05*	.06**	.09**	.06**	.07**
Support gun registration	.05**	.06**	.09**	.05**	.07**

Presidental Vote (Major Party)

	1968	1972	1976	1980	1984	1988	1992
Own Gun	.13**	.11**	.07**	.13**	.12**	.12**	.14**
Support gun registration	.12**	.09**	.04	.12**	.11**	.11**	.14**

Third Party/Independent Candidate Vote

	Wallace (1968)	Anderson (1980)	Perot (1992)
Own Gun	.08**	-.07**	.05*
Support Gun registration	.10**	-.07**	.02

Source: National Opinion Research Center's General Social Surveys.
Note: Entries are product-moment correlations.
*significant at .05. **significant at .01.

fication and presidential vote for the period covered by the General
Social Surveys. As the data in Table 12.3 show, both gun ownership
and attitudes toward gun control have relatively small, but consistent
and highly significant, relationships with party identification. Moreover, these relationships retain their statistical significance after the im-
position of multivariate controls described previously.[6]

Further, both independent variables are moderately, and significantly, related to presidential vote choice in each of the presidential
elections during the period in which the GSS was conducted. The relationship between the choice of either major party candidate and the
gun variables does not change much between each respondent's (re-
called) vote in 1968 and 1992, with the exception of 1976. Apparently,
Jimmy Carter's identification with white southerners limited the partisan effects of gun issues during that year. However, despite Bill Clinton's efforts to emphasize his southern roots and his efforts to identify
with an aspect of southern culture in which the sporting use of guns is
quite common,[7] Clinton was still considerably less popular with gun
owners and opponents of gun control than George Bush, who was a
lifetime member of the NRA at the time of the election.[8]

Table 12.3 also contains the relationship between gun variables and
votes for highly visible third-party or independent candidates in 1968,
1980, and 1992. Perhaps not surprisingly, George Wallace did significantly better among gun owners and opponents of gun registration
(both relationships retain their significance when controls for region of
residence are imposed) than among the rest of the electorate, and John
Anderson was significantly less popular among these groups. Ross
Perot drew slightly more support among gun owners than nonowners,
but Perot's support was not affected by respondent attitudes toward
gun control.

Several analysts (Young 1986; Lizotte and Bordua 1980; Lizotte, Bordua, and White 1981; O'Connor and Lizotte 1978) have suggested that
gun ownership may in fact have two rationales: Guns may be used for
sporting purposes, such as hunting, marksmanship competition, and
so on or may also be used for protection against crime. The partisan
implications of this distinction are explored in Table 12.4. The data in
this table strongly suggest that it is "sporting" gun owners who account for the relationship between gun variables and party identification. Rural gun owners, as well as rural opponents of gun registration,
are significantly more Republican than the rest of the sample, as are
owners of "long guns" (rifles and shotguns) for virtually the entire
period under investigation. Moreover, respondents who hunt (or
whose spouses hunt) exhibit small but significant tendencies toward
Republican identification beginning in 1981. By contrast, the effects of

TABLE 12.4

Partisan Impact of Aspects of Gun Ownership, by Electoral Era

Party Identification

	1972-76	1977-80	1981-84	1985-88	1989-93
Own pistol	-.01	.03	.03	.02	.05**
Own shotgun	.06**	.03	.06**	.06**	.07**
Own rifle	.07**	.07**	.12**	.08**	.07**
Gun owner * Fear Neighborhood	.006	.005	-.000	.006	.002
Gun owner* rural	.10**	.08**	.10**	.08**	.06**
Support gun regis*rural	.08**	.07**	.11**	.08**	.08*
R Hunts		.03	.05**	.05**	.06**

Source: National Opinion Research Center's General Social Surveys.
Note: Entries are product-moment correlations.
*significant at .05. **significant at .10.

owning a pistol (arguably a more urban weapon, possibly better suited to deterring violent criminals) attain statistical significance only during the most recent period, and the consequences of the interaction between fear of crime and gun ownership and party identification are not statistically distinguishable from zero during any of the time periods considered here. During the most recent period, respondents who were more fearful of crime were more likely to own guns than were other respondents. However, fearful gun owners were no more likely to identify as Republicans than the rest of the population. Thus the partisan effects of gun ownership appear to reflect the influence of a rural, hunting subculture that has southern roots.[9] This result is somewhat surprising, because it is the urban gun owners who are generally depicted as more adamant in their support of unlimited gun ownership.

Gun Ownership and Presidential Voting

It is possible to gain additional insight into the political consequences of gun ownership by taking a more detailed look at recent presidential elections. Table 12.5 compares the effects of gun ownership on the 1992

TABLE 12.5
1992–1996 Presidential Vote by Gun Ownership

1992 (General Social Survey, 1993)

	Clinton	Bush	Perot	All	N
Gun owner	35.0	42.0	23.0	43.1	317
Non-owner	52.0	34.9	13.1	56.9	419

1992 (General Social Survey, 1993: Major Party Candidates)

	Clinton	Bush	All	N
Gun owner	45.5	54.5	40.1	244
Non-owner	59.9	40.1	59.9	364

r = -.14**

1992 (Based on 1994 Exit Polls)

	Clinton	Bush	Perot	All	N
Gun owner	25.9	52.4	21.7	44.2	1247
Non-owner	52.2	38.9	8.8	55.8	1571

1992 (Based on 1994 Exit Polls: Major Party Candidates)

	Clinton	Bush	All	N
Gun owner	33.0	67.0	40.5	976
Non-owner	57.3	42.7	59.5	1432

r = -.23**

1996 (Based on published exit polls)

	Clinton	Dole	Perot	All
Gun owner	38	51	10	37
Non-owner	54	37	7	63

Sources: Computed from 1993 NORC General Social Survey. Computed from 1994 Voter News Service Exit Poll, National General Election Exit Poll. Published results of 1996 Voter News Service Exit Poll, National General Election Exit Poll, from www.allpolitics.com.
**significant at .01.

presidential vote using the 1993 GSS[10] with those obtained by asking respondents in the 1994 exit polls to recall their 1992 presidential vote (see Andersen 1979 for an account of the accuracy of voting-recall data).

As the data in Table 12.5 indicate, gun ownership made a substantial difference in vote choice in the 1992 presidential election. According to the 1993 GSS, Clinton did 17 percent better among nonowners than among gun owners. Bush, by contrast, received a plurality of the votes of gun owners and had a 7 percent advantage with gun owners as opposed to nonowners. Similarly, Perot performed 10 percent better among gun owners. When attention is confined to the major party candidates, there is a difference of about 15 percent in the vote of gun owners and nonowners.

The comparison between the 1993 GSS and the 1994 exit poll is perhaps most revealing. Many analysts (Campbell 1960; Wolfinger, Rosenstone, and McIntosh 1981; Campbell 1987; Cover 1985; and Born 1990) have addressed what might be termed the "two electorates" hypothesis. Briefly, the argument is that the composition of the active electorate is much different in presidential elections than in midterm elections. Presidential electorates are considerably larger and contain relatively large numbers of voters whose partisan ties are rather weak and whose interest in politics is rather casual. By contrast, midterm electorates are generally smaller and are held to be composed of committed, highly motivated voters. To the extent that gun owners are regarded as highly mobilized (perhaps by the activities of the National Rifle Association), one might expect owners to be disproportionately influential in years in which the presidency is not contested.

It is difficult to estimate the proportion of the voting electorate that owns guns for either the GSS or the VNS exit polls.[11] Nevertheless, the comparison between the two surveys is quite illuminating. Among non–gun owners, Clinton's percentage is virtually identical for the two surveys. Despite the fact that the 1994 voting electorate was much smaller and considerably more Republican than in 1992, both surveys show that Clinton received a bare majority among respondents who did not own guns. Again among nonowners, Bush gained about 4 percent in 1994, and Perot lost about 4 percent in this smaller, more partisan voting electorate. Thus among nonowners, the two voting electorates of 1992 and 1994 do not appear to differ. However, among gun owners, the estimate of Clinton's vote declines about 9 percent in the 1994 electorate, Bush gains about 10 percent, and Perot's percentage remains virtually unchanged. When attention is confined to the two major party candidates, Clinton's share of the active electorate declines by 2.6 percent among nonowners and by over 13 percent among gun owners.

Thus in this simple, bivariate comparison, gun ownership appears to account for nearly the entire difference in the 1992 presidential vote between the presidential and midterm electorates. Although this conclusion is not definitive (the VNS exit polls make extensive multivariate analysis difficult), the comparison does provide some qualified support for the "two electorates" hypothesis: gun owners appear to have a greater impact on the outcome of an election during nonpresidential years.

Table 12.5 also contains the results of a published exit poll for VNS for 1996.[12] According to the 1996 exit poll, Clinton's percentages among gun owners and nonowners are roughly comparable to the GSS estimates for 1992 for all candidates; Clinton runs 2 to 3 percent better among both groups than he did in 1992. Dole fares slightly better than Bush among non–gun owners and much better (about 9 percent) among gun owners. Most of Dole's gains (relative to Bush in 1992) appear to have come at the expense of Perot, who loses about half of his support among both groups between 1992 and 1996.

To what extent do differences between gun owners and nonowners in presidential voting reflect differences in partisan identification, and to what extent can these differences be attributed to candidate-centered distinctions? In other words, are the effects of gun ownership limited to affecting basic partisan orientations, or can gun ownership (and resulting attitudes toward gun control) act as a "wedge issue" that exposes the contradictions of a party coalition? These questions are addressed in Table 12.6, which examines the effects of gun ownership on presidential voting over time across different partisan self-identifications.

Among Republicans, gun ownership appears to have, at most, a negligible effect on presidential voting. Differences between Republican gun owners and nonowners approach statistical significance only in 1972 and 1984, and even in these years, the difference in party loyalty is only 3 percent. Gun ownership makes an identification with the Republican party more likely but does not appear to affect the voting loyalty of Republican identifiers at the presidential level.

By contrast, the effects of gun ownership on the presidential votes of Democrats are strong and significant in four of the six elections considered here. In all elections except 1976 and 1992 (the only elections during this period in which the Democratic candidate won), Democratic gun owners are approximately 10 percent less loyal to their party's nominee than are nonowners. It is perhaps noteworthy that the Democratic candidates who did not experience a "gun gap" (Carter

TABLE 12.6
Gun Ownership by Presidential Vote, by Party Identification

1972 (percent Democratic)

	Democrat	Independent	Republican
Gun owner	59.1	28.8	3.2
Non-owner	68.7**	40.1**	6.2*

1976 (percent Democratic)

	Democrat	Independent*	Republican
Gun owner	85.6	50.8	14.4
Non-owner	87.4	59.1	14.7

1980 (percent Democratic)

	Democrat**	Independent**	Republican
Gun owner	80.4 (81.9)	35.3 (39.1)	10.6 (10.9)
Non-owner	83.4 (88.2)	46.9 (54.7)	11.2 (11.6)

1984 (percent Democratic)

	Democrat**	Independent**	Republican*
Gun owner	70.6	25.6	2.1
Non-owner	80.8	38.5	5.1

1988 (percent Democratic)

	Democrat**	Independent**	Republican
Gun owner	68.1	23.4	4.8
Non-owner	79.5	38.7	4.7

1992 (percent Democratic)

	Democrat	Independent**	Republican
Gun owner	81.1 (91.7)	26.5 (46.4)	5.9 (6.9)
Non-owner	85.6 (92.8)	45.9 (59.3)	8.3 (9.3)

Source: NORC, General Social Surveys.
Notes: Entries in parentheses are percentage democratic votes among votes cast for major party candidates.
*difference between owners and non-owners significant at .05.
**difference between owners and non-owners significant at .01.

and Clinton) were southerners. However, Democratic presidential candidates McGovern, Carter (in 1980), Mondale, and Dukakis all fared significantly worse among Democratic gun owners than among nonowners. Similarly, gun ownership has a strong and significant effect on the presidential voting of independents. Support for the Democratic presidential nominee among independents is 8 to 19 percent stronger among non–gun owners than among respondents who own guns. Moreover, in virtually every comparison within the category of independents, the differences between gun owners and nonowners is highly significant statistically.[13]

Thus, the short-term effects of gun ownership on presidential vote choice vary across partisan identifications. Analyses presented earlier suggest that gun ownership is positively related to a Republican identification. However, among Republican partisans, the effects of gun ownership on vote choice are generally insignificant and inconsequential. Conversely, gun ownership is an important short-term force affecting the vote choices of Democrats and independents.

Gun Ownership and Subpresidential Voting

Of course, the presidency is not the only office in which policy toward gun issues is made. Indeed, the interests of gun owners and gun control opponents are more likely to be affected by the actions of Congress and the acts of state governments than by presidential initiatives.[14] The GSS does not contain data on voting for lower offices, but it is possible to estimate the effects of gun ownership on subpresidential voting in the 1994 exit polls.

Table 12.7 shows the effects of gun ownership on vote choice for U.S. senator, U.S. representative, and governor for 1994. As was the case in the earlier examination of presidential voting, the effects of gun ownership on voting for these offices is strong and significant. Among non–gun owners, Democratic candidates for all three offices (in the aggregate) received a slight majority even among the heavily Republican electorate of 1994 (see Wilcox 1995). However, gun owners gave huge majorities (between 69 and 77 percent) to Republican candidates.

Do these differences simply reflect partisan differences between gun owners or nonowners, or was gun ownership a short-term force, supplementing the effects of party identification in 1994? This question is addressed in Table 12.8, which simply repeats the analyses in Table 12.7 while imposing controls for respondent partisanship. The pattern shown in this table closely resembles that which characterized the effects of gun ownership on presidential voting. Again, the effects of gun

TABLE 12.7
Gun Ownership by Subpresidential Vote, 1994

U.S. Senate

	Democrat	Republican	All	N
Gun owner	30.8	69.2	44.2	773
Non-owner	53.4	46.6	54.8	975

r = -.22**

U.S. House of Representatives

	Democrat	Republican	All	N
Gun owner	30.0	70.0	44.8	1253
Non-owner	52.7	47.3	55.2	1541

r= -.23**

Governor

	Democrat	Republican	All	N
Gun owner	23.5	76.5	42.6	642
Non-owner	50.3	49.7	57.4	864

r = -.27**

Source: Computed from 1994 Voter News Service, National General Election Exit Poll.
**significant at .01.

ownership on vote choice among Republicans are small and typically insignificant. Only in voting for governor does this small difference (just over 5 percent) attain statistical significance at the level of .05. However, gun ownership does divide Democratic identifiers (by between 10 and 16 percent) and independents (by 14 to 16 percent). Thus at both the presidential and subpresidential levels, gun ownership may represent a wedge issue for Democrats (and an important short-term force for independents) but does not have an important effect on the votes of Republican partisans.

State-by-state analysis of individual races for senator or governor (using state exit polls) generally support this pattern. There appears to be no systematic variation in exceptions to this pattern, and those exceptions that do exist appear to result from circumstances unique to particular states. For example, gun ownership was significantly related

TABLE 12.8

Gun Ownership by Subpresidential Vote, by Partisan Identification, 1994.

U.S. Senate (percent Democratic)

	Democrat**	Independent**	Republican
Gun owner	76.9	28.4	9.3
Non-owner	86.3	46.4	10.4

U.S. House of Representatives (percent Democratic)

	Democrat**	Independent**	Republican
Gun owner	78.1	31.0	6.2
Non-owner	91.9	46.1	5.9

Governor (percent Democratic)

	Democrat**	Independent**	Republican*
Gun owner	62.5	22.5	6.4
Non-owner	78.6	48.4	11.7

Source: Computed from 1994 Voter News Service Exit Poll, National General Election Exit Poll.
*difference between owners and non-owners within category of party identification significant at 05.
**difference between owners and non-owners with category of party identification significant at 01.

to the vote for U.S. senator among Virginia Republicans in 1994. This result appears to be attributable to Oliver North's strong identification with the gun control issue and the presence of former Republican J. Marshall Coleman, who ran for the U.S. Senate as an independent. Many Republicans who did not own firearms voted for Coleman; a somewhat smaller number voted for Democrat Charles Robb.

The Effects on Context and Culture

At the individual level, the analyses presented to this point have suggested that the political effects of firearms issues may occur within particular subcultures. Gun ownership is significantly related to being raised in the South, and rural gun owners, hunters, and owners of long guns are all more significantly Republican than are other owners of firearms. However, it remains to be determined whether and how gun owners affect the political environments they inhabit. Does gun ownership alter the social and political context within which partisan activities are conducted?

There are at least three possible relationships between gun ownership and political environments. First, the political effects of gun ownership may simply be additive. That is, gun ownership (or nonownership) may affect the interests of particular individuals but may not have systematic effects beyond that. Gun owners may be politically influential in jurisdictions in which they are numerous but may not affect the views of those around them.

Second, gun owners may exert a contextual effect on the political environments they inhabit by affecting or dominating political discourse within a particular state or region. That is, gun owners (who already have been shown to hold more intense preferences on the issue of gun control) may feel relatively uninhibited about expressing their preferences in public or private social interactions if gun ownership is common within a particular state, region, or locality. Conversely, nonowners, or supporters of gun control, may feel outnumbered and may avert the risk of social isolation by remaining silent on the gun control issue (see Neolle-Neumann 1993 for a detailed account of this phenomenon).

Finally, a highly visible public presence on the part of gun owners or gun control opponents may occasion countermobilization among the supporters of gun control. That is, the frequent public assertion of opposition to gun control may increase the salience of the issue for supporters of gun control and might magnify the relationship between nonownership and Democratic identification. Put another way, in areas in which gun owners are numerous, nonowners might identify more frequently as Democrats than they otherwise might.

In order to test these possibilities, Table 12.9 contains the results of a cross-level regression in which individual party identification is the dependent variable and individual and state-level gun ownership are independent predictors. Individual gun ownership is simply the dummy checkoff item in the national exit polls, and state-level gun ownership is measured by taking the statewide mean for the gun-owner item.

To account for a (necessarily) high level of multicollinearity between the gun-ownership variables at different levels of observation, a "centering" procedure is employed, which involves recomputing the variables in the equation by comparing them to certain expected values. For example, individual-level gun ownership is recomputed by calculating the difference between an individual respondent's ownership status and the statewide mean. State-level gun ownership is computed by taking the difference between the statewide mean and the overall

TABLE 12.9
Regression of Individual and State-Level Gun Ownership on Party Identification, 1994

	b	beta	t-score
State	1.68	.11	7.64***
Individual	-.69	-.16	-11.05***
Constant	2.14		141.21***
N = 4877, R² = 0.04			

Source: Computed from 1994 Voter News Service, National General Election Exit Poll.

mean for the entire national sample. Similarly, the dependent variable (party identification) is centered by taking the difference between each respondent's score in this variable and a statewide expected value. The latter is, in turn, calculated by multiplying the statewide mean on the gun control item by the unstandardized slope from the regression of partisanship on gun ownership for each state. (For explanations of this procedure, see Boyd and Iversen 1979; Iversen 1991; and Tate 1984. For illustrations, see Wald, Owen, and Hill 1988; Jelen 1992; Cook, Jelen, and Wilcox 1993; and Jelen, O'Donnell, and Wilcox 1993.)

The results reported in Table 12.9 offer clear support for the counter-mobilization hypothesis. Although the predictive power of the model is not impressive, the coefficients associated with both individual and state-level gun ownership are of moderate magnitude and statistically significant. For present purposes, what is most important is that the effects of gun ownership at different levels of observation have opposite signs. The effects of individual-level gun ownership are strong and negative, indicating that (as expected) gun ownership is associated with identification with the Republican party. However, the effects of state-level gun ownership are somewhat weaker but are significant and positive. This means that non–gun owners who live in states in which gun ownership is relatively common are significantly more likely to identify as Democrats than nonowners in states in which gun ownership is unusual.[15] This finding suggests that gun control may be a polarizing issue, which occasions more frequent (and perhaps stronger) identification with the appropriate political party in areas in which the interests of gun owners are highly salient.[16] Although it seems unlikely that issues relating to the regulation of firearms would dominate the political discourse in most U.S. political jurisdictions, the presence or absence of large numbers of gun owners may make an appreciable difference in the partisan composition of a particular constituency. Moreover, the individual-level coefficient has a slightly larger value, suggesting (again) that the effects of gun ownership on partisanship are stronger for gun owners. However, the magnitude and direction of the state-level coefficient suggests that the net partisan effect of gun ownership may be relatively limited.

Conclusion

The findings of this chapter must be interpreted with caution, since the data on which they are based contain a number of significant limitations. Nevertheless, the results reported here provide some insight into the politics of gun control.

First, the net effect of gun control on aggregate partisan identification is rather limited. This study has confirmed a piece of conventional wisdom in that gun owners, although likely a minority, hold relatively intense preferences on issues of gun control and are more likely to base voting decisions on this issue. However, at least with respect to general partisan orientations, the socializing effects of gun ownership are offset to some extent by countermobilization among citizens who do not own guns in states in which gun ownership is quite common. Although the political effects of gun ownership appear to be strongest within particular subcultures, such effects are not uniform throughout particular jurisdictions. Where gun ownership is relatively common, ownership appears to produce Republican identifiers; nonownership appears to have an effect on the recruitment of Democrats.

Second, the effects of gun ownership on voting behavior across different groups of partisans may provide some insight into the weak translation of public opinion into public policy. As noted earlier, gun owners attach somewhat more electoral importance to the issue of gun control than do nonowners. Further, among Republican identifiers, there are generally no important differences in the voting behavior of gun owners and nonowners. Although circumstances obviously might vary across states or electoral districts, these two findings might well present many Republican candidates with a dominant strategy. That is, if Republican nonowners do not exact electoral reprisals against anti–gun control candidates, Republican candidates can appease an intense minority issue public within their ranks, and attempt to attract the votes of independents and Democrats. Thus, Republican candidates may have a strong incentive to take anti–gun control positions and may assume little, if any, corresponding risk. The fact that the party has had an image as the pro–Second Amendment party for over a generation might make the attraction of votes from Democrats and independents even easier.

By contrast, the issue of gun control may pose something of a strategic dilemma for Democratic candidates. Among Democrats and independents, gun control does appear to exert short-term influences over particular vote choices over and above the effects of party identification. Democratic candidates often lose the votes of Democratic and independent gun owners in particular elections. Any position a Democrat might take risks alienating some important constituency: either the majority of non-gun-owning (and often pro–gun control) Democrats and independents, or an intense, attentive gun-owning minority within these categories. Thus Democratic candidates may have an incentive to downplay or qualify their support for firearms regulation or to make distinctions between different types of weapons or different uses to which firearms might be put. If one assumes that there is at least an approximate correspondence between positions taken by candidates and their actions once elected, the electoral dynamics of the gun control issue may well pit a unified, antiregulation Republican party against a divided, ambivalent Democratic party. This degree of party consensus may in turn allow the Republic position to prevail even when Republicans are a minority within national or state legislatures.

This last point is admittedly based on very little direct evidence and must be regarded as a suggestion for future research rather than a firm conclusion. However, it does seem clear that gun owners in the United States are a politically distinctive constituency and that the issue of gun control has an important long-term and short-term impact on the outcome of American elections.

Notes

1. For example, see the extended discussion of gun control in the American West during the "frontier" period of the mid- to late nineteenth century in Wills (1987).

2. For many purposes, the analyses that follow were rerun for individual years. Except where noted, there were no substantively important differences between years within any of the political eras described here.

3. Spitzer (1995) notes that gun control appears to have become a partisan issue in around 1968. However, Erskine (1972) notes that support for gun control has been quite stable since in mid-1930s with no apparent increase in sup-

port in the wake of the assassinations of John Kennedy, Robert Kennedy, or Martin Luther King.

4. For all multivariate models using GSS data, the full range of independent variables includes southern residence, raised in the South, gender, race, age, urban-rural residence, education, respondents' attitude toward the leniency of courts toward crime, and fear of crime. Gun ownership is included in models in which attitude toward gun control is the dependent variable, and gun ownership and attitude toward gun control are included in models explaining variation in party identification.

5. These analyses are available upon request from the author.

6. Analysis of more recent General Social Surveys (1994 and 1996) shows that the correlation between gun ownership and party identification has increased to .12 in both of these years and that this difference with earlier years is modest but statistically significant. Thus the possibility exists that the partisan effects of gun ownership and gun control attitudes are undergoing an increase during the most recent historical period.

7. For example, Clinton is periodically photographed in hunting garb while visibly holding a shotgun or the bounty of a recent duck-hunting expedition.

8. Bush later renounced his membership in protest of NRA attacks on BATF agents.

9. Imposing controls for region results in too few cases for analysis.

10. The marginal distributions on presidential vote for the 1993 GSS bear a striking similarity to the actual election returns.

11. In the case of the GSS, there are two possible independent variables. One might use the item in which respondents are asked whether there are guns in the household (the variable used here) or the follow-up item, in which respondents are asked whether any guns in the household belong to them personally. It is difficult to determine which of these questions is most comparable to the "gun owner" checkoff item in the VNS exit polls. Moreover, the choice makes an enormous difference in estimating the marginal distributions of gun ownership (the former typically yields an estimate of over 40%; the personal-ownership item accounts for just over 20% of any given GSS sample).

In the case of the VNS exit polls, the checkoff nature of the gun-owner item makes it difficult to distinguish between respondents who would report not owning guns and missing data. Again, depending on the stringency of the filter one employs in assigning respondents to the "missing data" category, the estimate of the proportion of the electorate owning guns ranges from 24 percent to 44 percent with predictable variations by state.

Perhaps surprisingly, neither the choice of independent variable in the GSS nor the assignment of missing data in the 1994 exit polls makes an appreciable difference in estimates of the relationships between gun ownership and political attitudes and behavior.

12. The exit poll data were not available at the time of this writing.

13. The only exception to this generalization is the two-party (Clinton-Bush) comparison in 1992, in which Perot voters were excluded. Statistically, this is

attributable to the relatively small number of independents voting for either major party candidate that year, which substantively can be attributed to Perot's excellent showing among independents in 1992.

14. The importance of Congress relative to the president becomes particularly apparent when it is noted that it is typically congressional *inaction* that is the most important aspect of federal policy toward firearms. If Congress fails to act, the president's formal veto powers are of little consequence.

15. The coefficients in the model are virtually unaffected by controls for respondent gender or education.

16. If the effects of individual gun ownership were simply additive, the state-level coefficient would be small and perhaps insignificant. If gun owners were successfully able to socialize their friends and neighbors, both coefficients would be negative.

References

Abramowitz, Michael. 1995. "Early Roundup Allegations Were Ignored by ATF Officials." *Washington Post*, July 22.

Abramowitz, Michael, and John Mintz. 1995. "Militia Members Say They Spread Word on Roundup." *Washington Post*, July 21.

Achen, Christopher H. 1975. "Mass Political Attitudes and the Survey Response." *American Political Science Review* 69:1218–1231.

Adams, Greg D. 1997. "Abortion: Evidence of Issue Evolution." *American Journal of Political Science* 41:718–737.

"After Long Debate, Gun Control Measures Pass Bar Conference," 1993. *Recorder*, October 12.

Anderson, Jack. 1996. *Inside the NRA: Armed and Dangerous: An Expose*. Beverly Hills, CA: Dove Books.

Andersen, Kristi. 1979. *The Creation of a Democratic Majority, 1928–1936*. Chicago: University of Chicago Press.

Asher, Herbert. 1992. *Polling and the Public*. Washington, DC: CQ Press.

Asseo, Laurie. 1997. "Court Nixes Part of Brady Gun Control Law." WashingtonPost.com, June 27.

Babcock, Charles R. 1978. "Firearms Rule Draws a Fusillade." *Washington Post*, May 17.

Bailey, Eric, Peter M. Warren, and Dexter Filkins. 1996. "O.C. GOP: Setting Sights on the State." *Los Angeles Times*, July 7.

Baker, Donald P. 1995. "Virginia Considers Easing Concealed Weapons Law." *Washington Post*, January 26.

Banfield, Edward C. 1961. *The Unheavenly City*. New York: Free Press.

Bankston, William B., and Carol Y. Thompson. 1989. "Carrying Firearms for Protection: A Causal Model." *Sociological Inquiry* 59:75–87.

Bankston, William B., Carol Y. Thompson, Quentin A.L. Jenkins, and Craig J. Forsyth. 1990. "The Influence of Fear of Crime, Gender and Southern Culture on Carrying Firearms for Protection." *Sociological Quarterly* 31:287–305.

Barber, Mary Beth. 1994. "The Race for Controller." *California Journal* 25 (August):28–33.

Barnes, Robert, and Amy Goldstein. 1988. "Senate Passes Gun Bill Despite NRA Flak." *Washington Post*, April 10.

Baumgartner, Frank R., and Bryan D. Jones. 1993. *Agendas and Instability in American Politics*. Chicago: University of Chicago Press.

Beard, Michael. 1996. Interview with author. September 24.

Behr, Peter. 1981. "Bureau of Firearms at the Treasury Dept. May Face Extinction." *Washington Post*, February 14.

Bernstein, Dan. 1996. "Lungren Hopes Middle Road Leads to Governor's Office." *Sacramento Bee*, March 1.

Biskupic, Joan. 1989. "Handgun-Control Advocates Keep on Shooting Blanks." *Congressional Quarterly Weekly Report* 47 (December 2):3312–3314.

Block, A. G. 1994. "The Roberti Legacy." *California Journal 25* (November):9–11.

Bock, James. 1988. "Handgun Law Referendum to Go Down to the Wire." *Baltimore Sun*, November 7.

Bordua, David J. 1983. "Adversary Polling and the Construction of Social Meaning." *Law & Policy Quarterly* 5:345–366.

Borland, John. 1995. "The Arming of California." *California Journal* 26 (10):36–41.

———. 1996. "Fade from Brown." *California Journal* 27 (4):8–13.

Born, Richard. 1990. "Surge and Decline: Negative Voting and the Midterm Loss Phenomenon: A Simultaneous Choice Analysis." *American Journal of Political Science* 34:615–645.

Boyd, Laurence H., and Gudmund Iversen. 1979. *Contextual Analysis: Concepts and Statistical Techniques*. Belmont, CA: Wadsworth.

Branscombe, Nyla R., and Susan Owen. 1991. "Influence of Gun Ownership on Social Inferences About Women and Men." *Journal of Applied Social Psychology* 21:1567–1589.

Brazil, Eric. 1982. "Did Rural Gun Owners Defeat Bradley? A Mixed Bag of Messages from Those Ballot Propositions." *California Journal* 13 (12):442–444.

Bureau of Alcohol, Tobacco, and Firearms (BATF). Department of the Treasury. 1996. Mission Statement. http://www.ustreas.gov/treasury/bureaus/atf/atf.html.

Bursor, Scott. 1996. "Toward a Functional Framework for Interpreting the Second Amendment." *Texas Law Review* 74:1125–1151.

California Police Chiefs Association. 1995. "Confronting the American Tragedy: The Need to Better Regulate Firearms." Position Paper.

Campbell, Angus. 1960. "Surge and Decline: A Study of Electoral Change." *Public Opinion Quarterly* 24:397–418.

Campbell, James E. 1987. "The Revised Theory of Surge and Decline." *American Journal of Political Science* 31:965–979.

Carline, Glen. 1996. Interview with author, May 21.

Carmines, Edward G., and Stimson, James A. 1980. "The Two Faces of Issue Voting." *American Political Science Review* 74:78–91.

———. 1989. *Issue Evolution: Race and the Transformation of American Politics*. Princeton, NJ: Princeton University.

Chavez, Ken. 1993. "Wilson Says He's Open to Gun Curbs." *Sacramento Bee*, December 11.

Chou, Timothy. 1993. "On the Firing Line; Female Gun Ownership Up in Violent Times." *Los Angeles Times*, March 1.

Christensen, Terry, and Larry N. Gerston. 1984. *Politics in the Golden State: The California Connection.* Boston: Little, Brown.

Cigler, Allan J., and Burdett A. Loomis. 1995. *Interest Group Politics,* 4th ed. Washington, DC: CQ Press.

Claiborne, William. 1997. "Militant Insurgents Lose Out in Fierce NRA Power Struggle." *Washington Post,* May 6.

Clarke, James W. 1982. *American Assassins: The Darker Side of Politics.* Princeton, NJ: Princeton University Press.

Clausen, Aage R., Philip E. Converse, and Warren E. Miller. 1965. "Electoral Myth and Reality: The 1964 Election." *American Political Science Review* 59:321–332.

Clayton, Janet. 1986. "Bradley Alters Stand, Opposes Gun Control." *Los Angeles Times,* January 6.

Cobb, Roger W., and Charles D. Elder. 1972. *Participation in American Politics: The Dynamics of Agenda-Building.* Boston: Allyn and Bacon.

Cohen, Richard. 1995. "Whoppers of the NRA." *Washington Post,* May 18.

Congressional Globe. 1865. 39th Cong. 1st session.

Congressional Quarterly. 1995. *Congressional Quarterly 1994 Alamanac.* Washington DC: CQ Press.

Converse, Jean. 1987. *Survey Research in the United States: Roots and Emergence 1890–1960.* Berkeley: University of California Press

Converse, Phillip E. 1970. "Attitudes and Nonattitudes: Continuation of a Dialogue." In Edwin Tufte, ed., *The Quantitative Analysis of Social Problems.* Reading, MA: Addison-Wesley.

Converse, Philip E., and Gregory B. Markus. 1979. "'Plus ca Change . . . ' The New CPS Election Study Panel." *American Political Science Review* 73:2–49.

Cook, Elizabeth Adell, Ted G. Jelen, and Clyde Wilcox. 1993. "Catholicism and Abortion Attitudes in the American States: A Contextual Analysis." *Journal for the Scientific Study of Religion* 32:223–230.

Cook, Philip J. 1981. "The Effect of Gun Availability on Violent Crime Patterns." *Annals of the American Academy of Political and Social Science* 455:63–79.

Cottrol, Robert J. 1992. "Second Amendment." in Kermit L. Hall, ed., *The Oxford Companion to the Supreme Court of the United States.* New York: Oxford University Press.

Cottrol, Robert J., ed. 1994. *Gun Control and the Constitution: Sources and Explanations on the Second Amendment.* New York: Garland.

Cottrol, Robert J., and Raymond T. Diamond. 1991. "The Second Amendment: Toward an Afro-Americanist Reconsideration." *Georgia Law Journal* 80:301–378.

Cover, Albert D. 1985. "Surge and Decline in Congressional Elections." *Western Political Quarterly* 38:606–619.

Cramer, Clayton E. 1994. *For the Defense of Themselves and the State: The Original Intent and Judicial Interpretation of the Right to Keep and Bear Arms.* Westport, CT: Praeger.

———. 1995. "The Racist Roots of Gun Control." *Kansas Journal of Law and Public Policy* 4:17–40.

Crocker, Royce. 1982. "Attitudes Toward Gun Control: A Survey." In Harry L. Hogan, ed., *Federal Regulation of Firearms*, Washington, DC: U.S. Government Printing Office.

Dahl, Robert A. 1956. *A Preface to Democratic Theory*. Chicago: University of Chicago Press.

———. 1961. *Who Governs?* New Haven, CT: Yale University Press.

Davidson, Osha Gray. 1993. *Under Fire: The NRA & the Battle for Gun Control*. New York: Henry Holt.

Dean, Paul. 1996. "Permission to Pack," *Los Angeles Times*, January 4.

"Decision '94/Special Guide to California's Elections; US Senate; The Democrat: Dianne Feinstein." 1994. *Los Angeles Times*, October 30.

Department of the Treasury. 1993. *Report of the Department of the Treasury on the Bureau of Alcohol, Tobacco, and Firearms Investigation of Vernon Wayne Howell*. Washington, DC: U.S. Government Printing Office.

Dewar, Helen. 1981. "Treasury's Firearms Bureau Is Targeted for Elimination." *Washington Post*, September 19.

DiCamillo, Mark, and Mervin Field. 1994. "Fear of Becoming a Crime Victim Increasing." *Field Poll*, Release no. 1699.

Doerner, William R. 1989. "Defeat for a Thin Blue Line." In Robert Emmet Long, ed., *Gun Control*, New York: H. W. Wilson.

Downs, Anthony. 1967. *Inside Bureaucracy*. Boston: Little, Brown.

Dred Scott v. *Sanford*. 1856. 60 U.S. 393.

Dreyfuss, Robert. 1996. "Good Morning, Gun Lobby." *Mother Jones*. July-August:38–47, 73.

"Drink and Pack Heat." 1996. *Washington Post*, February 15.

Edel, Wilbur. 1995. *Gun Control: Threat to Liberty or Defense Against Anarchy?* Westport, CT: Praeger.

EDK Associates, Inc. 1996. "Passion and Policy: As Facts Replace Feelings in the Handgun Debate, More Voters Support Efforts to Reduce Access to Handguns." NY: EDK.

Elazar, Daniel J. 1966. *American Federalism: A View from the States*. New York: Crowell.

Erskine, Hazel. 1972. "The Polls: Gun Control." *Public Opinion Quarterly* 36:455–469.

Farley, Pete. 1981. "NRA Aims at U.S. Agency." *Washington Post*, July 23.

Farmer v. *Higgins*. 1982. 907 F. 2d 1041, 11th Circuit.

Faucheux, Ron. 1996. "Only in Louisiana?" *Campaigns and Elections*. December-January:36–39,42.

"FBI Stops Checking Fingerprints for State." 1996. *Roanoke Times*, July 1.

Ferrell, David, and Nora Zamichow. 1996. "L.A. Bans Manufacture, Sale of Cheap Guns." *Los Angeles Times*, September 5.

Field Institute. 1994. "A Digest of California Public Opinion on the Fear of Crime and Accessibility of Guns." San Francisco: Field Institute.

Finn, Peter. 1996. "FBI Stops Checking Virginia Gun Applicants." *Washington Post*, July 12.

Forsyth, Robert. 1989. *Assault Weapons in California: A Case Study in Issue Management and the Media*. Sacramento: California State Senate, December.

Foster, Carol D., Mark A. Siegel, and Nancy R. Jacobs, eds. 1993. *Gun Control: Restricting Rights or Protecting People?* Wylie, TX: Information Plus.

Fountain, John W. 1995a. "Fairfax Streamlines Permit Process for Carrying Concealed Weapons." *Washington Post*, July 8.

———. 1995b. "Rush for Permit to Carry Concealed Gun Ebbs in Northern Virginia." *Washington Post*, July 16.

———. 1996. "N. Va. Gun Rush Short-Lived." *Washington Post*, April 29.

Freeman, Jeff. 1996. Telephone interview with author, July 10.

Fresno Rifle and Pistol Club v. *Van de Kamp*. 1992. 965 F. 2d 723, 9th Circuit.

Gailey, Phil. 1981. "White House Planning to Kill Firearms Enforcement Unit." *New York Times*, September 19.

Gallup. 1993. Gallup Poll, December 17–21.

Gallup. 1994. Gallup Poll, August 15–16.

Gallup. 1995. Gallup Poll, April 23–24.

Gallup. 1996. Gallup Poll, April 25–28.

General Accounting Office (GAO). 1991. *BATF Management Improvements Needed to Handle Increasing Responsibilities*. Washington, DC: Government Printing Office.

———. 1996a. *Federal Firearms Licensees*. Washington, DC: Government Printing Office.

———. 1996b. *Use of Force: ATF Policy, Training and Review Process Are Comparable to DEA's and FBI's*. Washington, DC: Government Printing Office.

Ginsberg, Benjamin. 1989. "How Polling Transforms Public Opinion." In M. Margolis and G. Mauser, eds. *Manipulating Public Opinion*. Pacific Grove, CA: Brooks/Cole.

Glendon, Mary Ann. 1991. *Rights Talk: The Impoverishment of Political Discourse*. New York: Free Press.

Goode, Virgil. 1996. Interview with author. July 23.

Gordon, Kierstan. 1996. "Gun Repeal Bill Fails to Clear Committee." *Fairfax Journal*, February 9.

Gormley, William T. 1986. "Regulatory Issue Networks in a Federal System." *Polity* 18:595–620.

Greenblatt, Alan. 1996. "Repeal of Assault Weapons Ban Unlikely to Go Beyond House." *Congressional Quarterly Weekly Report* 54 (March 23):803.

Griffith, H. Morgan. 1996. Interview with author, July 15.

"Gun Friends Shoot Down Treasury Numbers Plan." 1978. *Washington Post*, May 27.

"Gun Toting Rules May Be Loosened." 1995. *Roanoke Times and World News*, January 26.

Gunnison, Robert. 1990a. "California Poll Finds Support for Waiting Period for Guns." *San Francisco Chronicle*, February 14.

———. 1990b. "New Controls on All Guns Approved by State Senate." *San Francisco Chronicle*, February 9.

———. 1996. "State Gun Sales Drop by a Third." *San Francisco Chronicle*, February 8.

Halbrook, Steven P. 1982. "The Fourteenth Amendment and the Right to Keep and Bear Arms: The Intent of the Framers." In the Subcommittee on the Constitution of the Senate Committee on the Judiciary, *The Right to Keep and Bear Arms*. 97th Cong., 2d sess., S. Doc. S522–3.

———. 1984. *That Every Man Be Armed: The Evaluation of a Constitutional Right*. Albuquerque: University of New Mexico Press.

———. 1994. "The Fourteenth Amendment and the Right to Keep and Bear Arms." In Robert J. Cottrol, ed., *Gun Control and the Constitution: Sources and Explanations on the Second Amendment*. New York: Garland.

Hall, Richard L., and Frank W. Wayman. 1990. "Buying Time: Monied Interests and the Mobilization of Bias in Congressional Committees." *American Political Science Review* 84:797–820.

Hallow, Ralph Z., and Bradley S. O'Leary. 1995. *Presidential Follies: Those Who Would Be President and Those Who Should Think Again*. Boerne, TX: Boru Publishers.

Hangun Control, Inc. 1996. Interview with author, September 25.

Hardy, Michael. 1995. "Allen Defends New Gun Law." *Richmond Times-Dispatch*, December 28.

Hartnett, Daniel M. 1990. "Bombing and Arson Investigations Enhanced by Advances in ATF Labs." *Police Chief*, April.

Hayden-Snider, Betty. 1996. "Gun Toters on the Rise." *Roanoke Times*, July 21.

Helfand, Duke. 1996. "Two-Pronged Attack on Guns Launched." *Los Angeles Times*, April 3.

Hennigan, Dennis A. 1991. "Arms, Anarchy, and the Second Amendment." *Valparaiso University Law Review* 26:107–129.

Herbertson, Carolyn. 1996. "The California Wellness Foundation: Prescribing Health . . . or Havoc?" *Gun Owners* 14:3.

Hershey, Robert D., Jr. 1985. "Vigor Wins New Life for Firearms Agency." *New York Times*, December 23.

Herz, Andrew D. 1995. "Gun Crazy: Constitutional False Consciousness and Dereliction of Dialogic Responsibility." *Boston University Law Review* 75:57–153.

Hirschman, Albert O. 1970. *Exit, Voice, and Loyalty: Response to Decline in Firms, Organizations, and States*. Cambridge: Harvard University Press.

Hofstader, Richard. 1970. "America as a Gun Culture." In Lee Nisbet, ed., *The Gun Control Debate: You Decide*. Buffalo: Prometheus.

Hrebenar, Ronald J., and Ruth K. Scott. 1990. *Interest Group Politics in America*. 2nd ed. Englewood Cliffs, NJ: Prentice-Hall.

Hsu, Spencer. 1995. "Virginia Assembly Votes to Ease Firearms Law." *Washington Post*, February 23.

Idelson, Holly. 1993. "Gun Rights and Restrictions: The Territory Reconfigured." *Congressional Quarterly Weekly Report* 51 (April 24):1021–1026.

———. 1994. "In Surprising Turnaround, House OKs Weapons Ban." *Congressional Quarterly Weekly Report* 52 (May 7):1119–1123.

Ingram, Carl. 1985. "Restricted Ownership of Assault-Type Guns OK'd by Assembly Unit." *Los Angeles Times*, April 9.

———. 1989a. "Governor's Reversal Seen as Major Boost for Ban on Assault Weapons." *Los Angeles Times*, April 4.

———. 1989b. "Normal Political Patterns Melt in the Heat of Gun Control Conflict." *Los Angeles Times*, March 27.

———. 1989c. "Panel Votes Compromise on Assault Weapons Ban." *Los Angeles Times*, May 16.

———. 1989d. "State Senate Votes to Ban Assault Guns; Deukmejian Pledges to Sign Bill If Sports Arms Aren't Included." *Los Angeles Times*, March 10.

———. 1990a. "Bill on Long-Gun Wait Sent to Governor." *Los Angeles Times*, February 16.

———. 1990b. "Firearm Safety Bill Vetoed by Deukmejian." *Los Angeles Times*, May 12.

———. 1990c. "Governor Signs Bill for Delay in Buying Guns." *Los Angeles Times*, March 4.

———. 1990d. "Gun Control Activists Face a Harder Fight." *Los Angeles Times*, January 18.

———. 1990e. "Handgun Safety Bill Passes Senate." *Los Angeles Times*, April 27.

———. 1990f. "Senate OKs 15-Day Wait on Purchase of All Guns." *Los Angeles Times*, February 9.

———. 1991. "Wilson Stand on Gun Issues Will Be Put to the Test." *Los Angeles Times*, September 23.

———. 1994. "State Gun Sales Set Record." *Los Angeles Times*, January 7.

———. 1996a. "Gun Sales in State Drop Record 31% in 1995." *Los Angeles Times*, February 8.

———. 1996b. "Senate Committee Defeats Bill to Ease Concealed Weapon Rules." *Los Angeles Times*, July 3.

Ingram, Carl, and Jerry Gillam. 1989. "Assault Weapon Ban Approved by Assembly; Bill Squeezes Through with Bare Minimum and Is Returned to Senate; Next Step Is Uncertain." *Los Angeles Times*, April 18.

Iversen, Gudmund R. 1991. *Contextual Analysis.* Newbury Park, CA: Sage.

Jacobs, Nancy R., Carol D. Foster, and Mark A. Siegel, eds. 1995. *Gun Control: Restricting Rights or Protecting People?* Wylie, TX: Information Plus.

Japenga, Ann. 1984. "Gun Crazy." *San Francisco Chronicle*, April 3.

Jeffe, Sherry. 1989. "How the NRA Got Shot Down in California." *Los Angeles Times*, July 30.

———. 1992. "California: The Not-So-Golden State Legislature." In Eugene W. Hickok Jr., ed., *The Reform of State Legislatures and the Changing Character of Representation.* Lanham, MD: Commonwealth Foundation/University Press of America.

Jelen, Ted G. 1992. "Political Christianity: A Contextual Analysis." *American Journal of Political Science* 36:692–714.

Jelen, Ted G., John O'Donnell, and Clyde Wilcox. 1993. "A Contextual Analysis of Catholicism and Abortion Attitudes in Western Europe." *Sociology of Religion* 54: 375–383.

Jenkins, Kent, Jr. 1994. "Virginia Judge Revokes North Permit for Concealed Weapon." *Washington Post*, August 6.

Johnson, Clarence. 1996. "S.F. Board of Supervisors Bans 'Junk Gun' Sales." *San Francisco Chronicle*, June 25.

Johnson, John. 1993. "LAPD Calls Tickets for Guns Exchange a Success." *Los Angeles Times*, December 29.

"Judge's Handgun Rule Off Base, State Says." 1995. *Roanoke Times and World News*, October 14.

Kates, Don B., Jr. 1983. "Handgun Prohibition and the Original Meaning of the Second Amendment." *Michigan Law Review* 82:204–273.

Kates, Don B., Jr., ed. 1984. *Firearms and Violence: Issues of Public Policy*. Cambridge, MA: Ballinger/Pacific Institute for Public Policy Research.

Keller, Bill. 1982. "NRA, Liquor Industry Seek to Save BATF." *Congressional Quarterly Weekly Report*, April 3.

Kennett, Lee, and James Anderson. 1975. *The Gun in America: The Origins of a National Dilemma*. Westport, CT: Greenwood Press.

King, Wayne. 1988. "A Bureau That Battled Bootleggers Is Tough Target for Budget Cutters." *New York Times*, February 1.

Kingdon, John. 1995. *Agendas, Alternatives, and Public Policies*. 2nd ed. New York: HarperCollins College.

Kleck, Gary. 1991. *Point Blank: Guns and Violence in America*. New York: Aldine de Gruyter.

Kopel, David B. 1994. "Ignorance Plus Demagoguery = Gun Control." *California Policy Review* 5 (2):23–36.

Kopel, David B., ed. 1995. *Guns: Who Should Have Them?* Amherst, NY: Prometheus Books.

Korwin, Alan. 1995. *Gun Laws of America*. Phoenix, AZ: Bloomfield Press.

Kruschke, Earl R. 1995. *Gun Control: A Reference Handbook*. Santa Barbara, CA: ABC-CLIO.

Kurtz, Howard. 1986. "Arms Bureau Contradicts Ad by NRA." *Washington Post*, March 10.

Labaw, Patricia. 1981. *Advanced Questionnaire Design*. Cambridge, MA: Abt Books.

Lancaster, John. 1988a. "Maryland Gun Law Opponents Try to Enlist Blacks." *Washington Post*, September 5.

———. 1988b. "Attacking Maryland's Gun Law." *Washington Post*, October 16.

———. 1988c. "Maryland Gun Law Supporters Lack Firepower." *Washington Post*, October 22.

———. 1988d. "'We've Had Enough Violence' Cited in First Big NRA Defeat." *Washington Post*, November 10.

Lancaster, John, and Richard Morin. 1988. "Gap Closing in Maryland Gun Control Fight." *Washington Post*, October 27.

Langbein, Laura I. 1993. "PACs, Lobbies, and Political Conflict: The Case of Gun Control." *Public Choice* 77(3):551–572.

Langbein, Laura I., and Mark A. Lotwis. 1986. "The Political Efficacy of Lobbying and Money: Gun Control in the U.S. House, 1986." *Legislative Studies Quarterly* 15:413–440.

Lardner, George, Jr. 1995. "Official Blames Weaver for Initiating Tragedy at Ruby Ridge." *Washington Post*, September 8.

Larson, Erik. 1994. *Lethal Passage*. New York: Crown.

League of California Cities. 1996. Legislative Bulletin no. 24–1996.

Leddy, Edward F. 1987. *Magnum Force Lobby: The National Rifle Association Fights Gun Control*. Lanham, MD: University Press of America.

"Legislative Alert." 1994. *Police Chief* 61 (January).

Leovy, Jill. 1983. "Funds Go to Battle Epidemic of Violence." *Los Angeles Times*, December 30.

Levinson, Sanford. 1989. "The Embarassing Second Amendment." *Yale Law Review* 99:637–644.

Lewis v. *United States*. 1980. 445 U.S. 55.

Lindesmith, Alfred R. 1965. *The Addict and the Law*. Bloomington: University of Indiana Press.

Lipton, Eric. 1995. "On Day One, Virginians Hear a Call to Arms." *Washington Post*, July 4.

Lizotte, Alan J., David J. Bordua. 1980. "Firearms Ownership for Sport and Protection: Two Divergent Models." *American Sociological Review* 45:229–244.

Lizotte, Alan J., and David J. Bordua, and Carolyn S. White. 1981. "Firearms Ownership for Sport and Protection: Two Not So Divergent Models." *American Sociological Review* 46:499–503.

Loan, Kathy. 1995a. "Easier to Carry, Easier to Get." *Roanoke Times and World News*, June 18.

————. 1995b. "New Gun Laws Are in a Tangle." *Roanoke Times and World News*, July 31.

————. 1995c. "Virginians Are Fired Up to Carry Weapons." *Roanoke Times and World News*, July 6.

Loftus, Tom. 1994. *The Art of Legislative Politics*. Washington, DC: CQ Press.

Lowi, Theodore. 1988. "New Dimensions in Policy and Politics." In Raymond Tatalovich and Byron Daynes, eds., *Social Regulatory Policy*. Boulder: Westview Press.

Magleby, David B. 1984. *Direct Legislation: Voting on Ballot Propositions in the United States*. Baltimore, MD: Johns Hopkins University Press.

————. 1989. "Opinion Formation and Opinion Change in Ballot Proposition Campaigns." in M. Margolis and G. Mauser, eds., *Manipulating Public Opinion*. Pacific Grove, CA: Brooks/Cole.

Makinson, Larry, and Joshua Goldstein. 1996. *Open Secrets: The Encyclopedia of Congressional Money and Politics*. Washington, DC: CQ Press/Center for Responsive Politics.

Malcom, Joyce Lee. 1994. *To Keep and Bear Arms: The Origins of an Anglo American Right*. Cambridge, MA: Harvard University Press.

Marks, Alan, and C. Shannon Stokes. 1976. "Socialization, Firearms, and Suicide." *Social Problems* 23:622–629.

Mauro, Tony. 1991. "2d Amendment: A Right to Own Arms?" *USA Today*, November 20.

Mauser, Gary A., and David B. Kopel. 1992. "'Sorry, Wrong Number': Why Media Polls on Gun Control Are Often Unreliable." *Political Communication* 9:69–92.

"McClure/Volkmer: This Bill Endangers Police." 1986. *Police Chief* 53 (January).

McDonald, Katherine. 1989. "NRA a Wounded Giant." *California Journal* (August) 20:319- 321.

McDowall, David, and Colin Loftin. 1983. "Collective Security and the Demand for Legal Handguns." *American Journal of Sociology* 88:1146–1159.

McNair, Jean. 1996. "With State Blessing, They're Going for Their Guns." *Fairfax Journal*, March 20.

Meier, Kenneth J. 1993. *Politics and the Bureaucracy: Policymaking in the Fourth Branch of Government*. Monterey, CA: Brooks/Cole.

———. 1994. *The Politics of Sin: Drugs, Alcohol and Public Policy*. Armonk, NY: M. E. Sharpe.

Melville, M. Bigelow, ed. 1891. *Commentaries on the Constitution of the United States*. 5th ed. Boston: Little, Brown. Quoted in Glenn Harlan Reynolds, 1995. "A Critical Guide to the Second Amendment." *Tennessee Law Review* 62:461–512.

Metaksa, Tanya. 1996a. *NRA Institute, NETCOM Announce Internet Program for NRA Members*. Press release. April 18.

———. 1996b. "Victory Report from the States." *American Rifleman*. February:42–43.

Montgomery, Lori. 1994. "Increase in Number of Pistol-Packin' Mamas Exaggerated, New Survey Finds." *Fresno Bee*, December 2.

Mooney, Christopher Z., and Mei-Hsein Lee. 1995. "Legislating Morality in the American States: The Case of Pre-Roe Regulation Reform." *American Journal of Political Science* 39:599- 627.

Morain, Dan, and Max Vanzi. 1996. "Assembly OKs Concealed Gun Permits Bill." *Los Angeles Times*, February 1.

Morris, Vincent. 1996. "Keys, Coat, Handgun, and out the Front Door." *Fairfax Journal*, April 2.

Mundo, Philip A. 1992. *Interest Groups: Cases and Characteristics*. Chicago: Nelson-Hall.

National Opinion Research Center. *General Social Survey*. Chicago: NORC.

National Rifle Association. 1996a. "NRA Political Victory Fund: Voters Reelect Second Amendment Majority." Press release, November 6.

———. 1996b. "NRA Right to Carry Victory in South Carolina." Press release, June 14.

———. 1996c. *Factsheet: Semi-Automatic Firearms*. Fairfax, Virginia: NRA.

New York v. *United States*. 1992. 505 U.S. 144.

Nisbet, Lee., ed. 1990. *The Gun Control Debate*. Buffalo: Prometheus.

Noelle-Neumann, Elisabeth. 1993. *The Spiral of Silence: Public Opinion: Our Social Skin*. Chicago: University of Chicago Press.

O'Connor, James F., and Alan J. Lizotte. 1978. "The 'Southern Subculture of Violence' Thesis and Patterns of Gun Ownership." *Social Problems* 25:420–429.

O'Connor, Karen. 1980. *Women's Organizations' Use of the Courts*. Lexington, MA: Lexington Books.

Orasin, Charles J. 1981. "Handgun Control and the Politics of Fear." In Thomas Draper, ed., *The Issue of Gun Control*. New York: H. W. Wilson.

Owens, Thomas. 1995. Interview with author, May 19.

Paddock, Richard C. 1993. "Gun Control Push Begun at Law Firm." *Los Angeles Times,* July 7.

———. 1994. "Therapists to Trade Treatment for Guns." *Los Angeles Times,* October 4.

Plessy v. *Ferguson.* 1896. 163 U.S. 537.

"President's Message: House Vote Bans Assault Weapons." 1994. *Police Chief* 61 (June).

"President's Message: Law Enforcement Needs the Brady Bill." 1991. *Police Chief* 58 (April).

Presser v. *Illinois.* 1886. 116 U.S. 252.

Printz v. *United States.* 1997. No. 95–1478, dec'd June 27.

Quilici v. *Village of Morton Grove.* 1982. 965 F. 2d. 261.

Reynolds, Glenn Harlan. 1995. "A Critical Guide to the Second Amendment." *Tennessee Law Review* 62:461–512.

Riccardi, Nicholas. 1994. "LAPD Chief, Sheriff Back State Ban on Small Pistols." *Los Angeles Times,* October 21.

Riccardi, Nicholas, and Jeff Brazil. 1996. "Pasadena Shows Pitfalls of Anti-Gun Effort." *Los Angeles Times,* September 6.

"Richardson Seeks New Political Base; State Senator Mobilizing Fundamentalist Church Groups." 1985. *Los Angeles Times,* January 20.

Robin, Gerald D. 1991. *Violent Crime and Gun Control.* Cincinnati: Academy of Criminal Justice Sciences/Anderson.

"Roll Call." 1989. *California Journal* 20:6.

Ross, Michael J. 1996. *California: Its Government and Politics,* Fifth Edition. Belmont, CA: Wadsworth.

Rossiter, Clinton. ed. 1961. *Federalist Papers.* New York: Mentor.

Rourke, Francis E. 1984. *Bureaucracy, Politics and Public Policy.* Boston: Little, Brown.

"S. 49 Dispute Splits NRA and Law Enforcement." 1986. *Police Chief* 53 (April).

Sabatier, Paul A. 1977. "Regulatory Policy Making: Toward a Framework for Analysis." *Natural Resources Journal* 17:415–460.

Schattschneider, E. E. 1960. *The Semisovereign People.* Hillsdale, IL: Dryden.

Schmidt, Susan, and Amy Goldstein. 1988. "Maryland Assembly Enacts Strict Gun Controls." *Washington Post,* April 12.

Schneider, Howard. 1990. "Maryland Panel Approves More Guns for Sale: Law's Intent Frustrated." *Washington Post,* January 9.

Schuman, Howard, and Stanley Presser. 1981. *Questions and Answers in Attitude Surveys. Experiments on Question Form, Wording, and Context.* New York: Academic Press.

Scott, Steve. 1994. "Roberti Slays NRA Dragon." *California Journal* 25 (5):46–47.

Seligman, Katherine. 1994. "Women Taking Up Firearms: NRA Ad Campaign; Don't Be a Victim." *San Francisco Examiner,* February 8.

Sharkansky, Ira. 1968. "The Utility of Elazar's Political Culture: A Research Note." *Polity* 2:66–83.

Sheley, Joseph F., Charles J. Brody, James D. Wright, and Marjory A. Williams.

1994. "Women and Handguns: Evidence from National Surveys, 1973–1991." *Social Science Research* 23:219–235.

Siwik, Robert, and William Blount. 1984. "Law Enforcement Attitudes on Handgun Control." *Journal of Police Science and Administration* 12:157–163.

Slotkin, Richard. 1992. *Gunfighter Nation: The Myth of the Frontier in Twentieth Century America*. New York: Atheneum.

Smith, Douglas A., and Craig D. Uchida. 1988. "The Social Organization of Self-Help: A Study of Defensive Weapon Ownership." *American Sociological Review* 53:94–102.

Smith, Hedrick. 1988. *The Power Game*. New York: Random House.

Spitzer, Robert J. 1995. *The Politics of Gun Control*. Chatham, NJ: Chatham House.

Stange, Mary Zeiss. 1995. "Arms and the Woman: A Feminist Reappraisal." In David B. Kopel, ed., *Guns: Who Should Have Them?* Amherst, NY: Prometheus Books.

State of California. Assembly Office of Research. 1986. *Smoking Gun: The Case for Concealed Weapon Permit Reform*. June. Sacramento: Assembly Office of Research.

State of California. Department of Justice. 1996. *1995 California Firearms Laws*. Sacramento, CA: Office of the Attorney General.

State of California. Department of Justice. Division of Law Enforcement. 1996. *Dangerous Weapons Control Law 1996*. Pt. 4, Title 2, California Penal Code. Sacramento, CA: Bureau of Criminal Information and Analysis.

Stern, Phillip. 1992. *Still the Best Congress Money Can Buy*. Washington, DC: Regnery Gateway.

Stigler, George J. 1971. "The Theory of Economic Regulation." *Bell Journal of Economics and Management Science* 2:3–21.

Stone, Peter H. 1993. "Under the Gun." *National Journal* 25 (5 June):1334–1338.

Sugarawa, Sandra. 1982. "A Twist: Groups Fight to Keep Regulators." *Washington Post*, February 22.

Sugarmann, Josh. 1992. *National Rifle Association: Money, Firepower, and Fear*. Washington, DC: National Press Books.

Sweeney, James P. 1986. "Concealed Weapons Bill Passes Assembly." *San Diego Union-Tribune*, February 1.

"Taming the Gun Monster: Local Crusades." 1993. *Los Angeles Times*, December 3.

Tatalovich, Raymond, and Byron Daynes. 1988. "Introduction: What Is Social Regulatory Policy?" In Raymond Tatalovich and Byron Daynes, eds., *Social Regulatory Policy*. Boulder: Westview Press.

Tate, R. L. 1984. "Limitations of Centering for Interactive Models." *Sociological Methods and Research* 13:251–271.

Thomas, Pierre. 1992. "Report Criticizes U.S. Licensing of Gun Dealers." *Washington Post*, December 12.

———. 1993. "Texas Guns: Ask and You Shall Receive." *Washington Post*, March 9.

———. 1994. "Sheriffs Challenging Federal Authority." *Washington Post*, September 19.

Thornton, Mary. 1982a. "NRA Now Thinks BATF May Not Be That Bad." *Washington Post*, March 19.

———. 1982b. "BATF Furlough: 'It Would Blow Us Away.' " *Washington Post*, April 20.

Tonso, William R. 1990. "Social Problems and Sagecraft: Gun Control as a Case in Point." In Lee Nisbet, ed. *The Gun Control Debate: You Decide*. Buffalo, NY: Prometheus.

U.S. Senate. Subcommittee of the Committee on Appropriations. 1982. *Dissolution of BATF*. 97th Cong., 2d sess. February-March.

United States. 1995. *Budget of the United States, Fiscal Year 1995*. Washington, DC: U.S. Government Printing Office.

United States. 1996. *Appendix: Budget of the United States, Fiscal Year 1997*. Washington, DC: U.S. Government Printing Office.

United States v. *Cruickshank*. 1876. 92 U.S. 542.

United States v. *Lopez*. 1995. 93–1260 (slip opinion).

United States v. *Miller*. 1939. 307 U.S. 174.

Van Alstyne, William. 1994. "The Second Amendment and the Personal Right to Arms." *Duke Law Journal* 43:1225–1255.

Vellinga, Mary Lynne. 1996. "Gun Debate Packs Emotion." *Sacramento Bee*, February 12.

Vizzard, William J. 1997. *In the Crossfire: A Political History of the Bureau of Alcohol, Tobacco, and Firearms*. Boulder: Lynne Rienner.

Vobejda, Barbara. 1996. "NRA Is Said to Lay Off Dozens." *Washington Post*, September 23.

Vobejda, Barbara, and Kenneth J. Cooper. 1995. "ATF Agents Participated in 'Roundup.' " *Washington Post*, July 14.

Vose, Clement E. 1958. *Caucasians Only*. Berkeley: University of California Press.

Wald, Kenneth D., Dennis E. Owen, and Samuel S. Hill. 1988. "Churches as Political Communities." *American Political Science Review* 82:531–548.

Walters, Dan, ed. 1990. *California Political Almanac 1989–1990 Edition*. Santa Barbara, CA: Pacific Data Resources.

"West Hollywood May Ban Sales of 'Saturday Night Specials.' " 1995. *Sacramento Bee*, November 25.

Wilcox, Clyde. 1995. *The Latest American Revolution*. New York: St. Martin's.

———. 1996. *Onward Christian Soldiers: The Christian Right in American Politics*. Boulder: Westview Press.

Wills, Garry. 1987. *Reagan's America: Innocents at Home*. Garden City, NY: Doubleday.

Wilson, James Q. 1989. *Bureaucracy*. New York: Basic Books.

Wintemute, Garen J., Stephen P. Teret, and Jess F. Kraus. 1987. "The Epidemiology of Firearm Deaths Among Residents of California." *Western Journal of Medicine* 146 (March):374–377.

Winton, Richard, and Rick Holguin. 1995. "Pasadena Prepares to Enforce Ammunition Law." *Los Angeles Times*, March 2.

Wolfinger, Raymond E., Steven J. Rosenstone, and Richard A. McIntosh. 1981.

"Presidential and Congressional Voters Compared." *American Politics Quarterly* 9:245–256.

Wooten, Graham. 1985. *Interest Groups: Policy and Politics in America*. Englewood Cliffs, NJ: Prentice Hall.

Wright, Gerald C., Jr., Robert S. Erikson, and John P. McIver. 1985. "Measuring State Partisanship and Ideology with Survey Data." *Journal of Politics* 47:469–489.

Wright, James D. 1981. "Public Opinion and Gun Control: A Comparison of Results from Two Recent National Surveys." *Annals of the American Academy of Political and Social Science* 455 (May).

Wright, James D., and Linda Marston. 1975. "The Ownership of the Means of Destruction: Weapons in the United States." *Social Problems* 23:93–107.

Wright, James D., and Peter H. Rossi. 1994. *Armed and Considered Dangerous: A Survey of Felons and Their Firearms*, Exp. ed. Hawthorne, NY: Aldine De Gruyter.

Wright, James D., Peter H. Rossi, and Kathleen Daly. 1983. *Under the Gun: Weapons, Crime and Violence in America*. New York: Aldine.

Wright, John R. 1996. *Interest Groups & Congress*. Boston: Allyn and Bacon.

Young, John T., David Hemenway, Robert J. Blendon, and John M. Benson. 1997. "The Polls—Trends: Guns." *Public Opinion Quarterly* 60:634–649.

Young, Robert L. 1985. "Perceptions of Crime, Racial Attitudes, and Firearms Ownership." *Social Forces* 64:473–486.

———. 1986. "Gender, Region of Socialization, and Ownership of Protective Firearms." *Rural Sociology* 51:169–182.

Zimring, Franklin E. 1975. "Firearms and Federal Law: The Gun Control Act of 1968." *Journal of Legal Studies* 4:133–198.

———. 1991. "Firearms, Violence, and Public Policy." *Scientific American* 265:50

Index

261

About the Editors and Contributors

Graham Barron is a graduate student in the School of Public Affairs at American University.

John M. Bruce is an Assistant Professor of Political Science and Director of the Social Science Research Laboratory at the University of Mississippi.

Keith R. Eakins is a Ph.D. candidate in Political Science at Ohio State University.

James G. Gimpel is an Associate Professor of Government and Politics at the University of Maryland–College Park.

Marcia L. Godwin is a Ph.D. candidate in the Department of Politics and Policy at Claremont Graduate University.

David R. Harding Jr. is an Assistant Professor of Political Science and Public Administration at Arkansas State University.

Ted G. Jelen is a Professor and Chair of the Department of Political Science at the University of Nevada–Las Vegas.

Lael R. Keiser is an Assistant Professor of Political Science at the University of Missouri, Columbia.

Diana Lambert lives and works in Washington, D.C.

Wendy L. Martinek is a Ph.D. candidate in Political Science at Michigan State University.

Kenneth J. Meier is a Professor of Political Science at Texas A&M University.

Karen O'Connor is a Professor and Chair of the Department of Government at American University.

Samuel C. Patterson is a Professor of Political Science at Ohio State University.

Mark J. Rozell is an Associate Professor of Political Science at American University.

Jean Reith Schroedel is an Associate Professor in the Department of Politics and Policy at Claremont Graduate University.

Ronald G. Shaiko is an Associate Professor of Government and Academic Director of The Lobbying Institute at American University.

Marc A. Wallace is a Ph.D. candidate in Political Science at American University.

Clyde Wilcox is a Professor of Government at Georgetown University.

Harry L. Wilson is an Associate Professor of Political Science, Director of The Center for Community Research, and Chairperson of the Department of Public Affairs at Roanoke College.

Robin M. Wolpert is an Assistant Professor of Government and International Studies, University of South Carolina.